Snitching

Snitching

Criminal Informants and the
Erosion of American Justice

Alexandra Natapoff

NEW YORK UNIVERSITY PRESS
New York and London

NEW YORK UNIVERSITY PRESS
New York and London
www.nyupress.org

Library of Congress Cataloging-in-Publication Data
Natapoff, Alexandra.
Snitching : criminal informants and the erosion of
American justice / Alexandra Natapoff.
p. cm. Includes bibliographical references and index.
ISBN–13: 978–0–8147–5850–2 (cl : alk. paper)
ISBN–10: 0–8147–5850–9 (cl : alk. paper)
1. Informers—Legal status, laws, etc.—United States.
2. Criminal justice, Administration of—United States.
3. Informers—United States.   4. Law enforcement—
United States.   I. Title.
 KF9665.N38   2009
 363.25'2--dc22   2009017397

New York University Press books are printed on acid-free paper,
and their binding materials are chosen for strength and durability.
We strive to use environmentally responsible suppliers and materials
to the greatest extent possible in publishing our books.

Manufactured in the United States of America

10 9 8 7 6 5 4 3 2 1

For Raphael

Contents

Acknowledgments

SINCE I STARTED thinking about criminal snitching a decade ago, I have learned an immense amount from many people, including clients, neighbors, students, colleagues, and my family. My special thanks to Brie Clark, Kathy Frey-Balter, Debbie Gershenowitz, Lisa Griffin, Don Herzog, Dan Richman, Jonathan Simon, Andrew Taslitz, Bob Weisberg, Lauren Willis, and the ACLU Drug Law Reform Project. I am grateful for the institutional support I have received from Loyola Law School, including a grant from the Loyola Faculty Research Fellowship Program.

Portions of this book build on some of my previously published articles: "Snitching: The Institutional and Communal Consequences," 73 *U. Cincinnati L. Rev.* 645 (2004); "Beyond Unreliable: How Snitches Contribute to Wrongful Convictions," 37 *Golden Gate U. L. Rev.* 107 (2006); and "Deregulating Guilt: The Information Culture of the Criminal System," 30 *Cardozo L. Rev.* 965 (2009).

Introduction

A Tale of Three Snitches

Ninety-two-year-old Kathryn Johnston was dead, which meant big trouble for Officers Smith and Junier.

Three hours earlier, everything had looked so promising. Atlanta police had busted Fabian Sheats for the third time in four months, and the local drug dealer-turned-informant had tipped them off to a major stash at 933 Neal Street—an entire kilo of cocaine. Sheats wasn't one of their registered informants so they couldn't use him to get a warrant, but Smith and Junier applied for a warrant anyway by inventing an imaginary snitch. They called him a "reliable confidential informant" and told the magistrate judge that this nonexistent snitch had bought crack cocaine at the Neal Street address. The fabrication wouldn't matter in the end, after they got the warrant, busted in, and grabbed the kilo. It would be a major victory.

But nothing went the way it was supposed to. Sheats's tip was bad—there was no kilo at that address. Once inside the house, the officers opened fire. Now Mrs. Johnston was lying at their feet riddled with police bullets with no cocaine anywhere to be found. So Smith and Junier turned to one of their regular informants, yet another snitch named Alex White. They offered him $130 to say that he'd bought drugs at Mrs. Johnston's Neal Street home and to corroborate their false warrant application. It wouldn't bring Mrs. Johnston back, but at least no one would learn that they'd gambled everything on a weak lead from a bad snitch and that the informant in the warrant didn't exist.[1]

Although it rarely comes to light, criminal informant use is everywhere in the American legal system. From warrants to surveillance to arrests, police routinely rely on criminal suspects to get information and to shape investigations. From charging decisions all the way through sentencing, prosecutors negotiate with defendants for cooperation in exchange for dropped or reduced charges and lighter punishment. Especially in the expansive arena of drug enforcement, turning suspects into so-called snitches has become a central feature of the way America manages crime, while the secretive practice of trading lenience for information quietly shapes major aspects of our penal process.

This clandestine law enforcement tool has penetrated the popular consciousness, and the ensuing public debate embodies some of the deepest political and cultural tensions of life in high-crime urban neighborhoods. In 2006, the same year in which Atlanta police killed Mrs. Johnston, a group of well-known artists, Tats Cru, painted on an East Harlem building a mural of a cartoon rat with a noose around his neck and a sign that said "Stop Snitchin.'" Two years later, neighborhood leaders rallied to paint over what they considered to be the mural's antipolice message promoting a street code of silence. The Reverend Al Sharpton exhorted residents to reject the "stop snitching" message and to speak out against crime, while one city commissioner called the mural a "symbol of hate." Local teenagers took a somewhat different view of the mural's meaning. "It's not because it's not cool to snitch," explained a fourteen-year-old girl. "People are afraid they might get killed." Tats Cru, whose work has been featured by the Smithsonian, sued the city, arguing that the mural was designed to "get discussion going" over the state of police-community relations and that erasing it violated their First Amendment rights.[2]

The "snitching" phenomenon has political, cultural, and even personal dimensions, but it starts with the criminal system. Criminal informants are a potent and sometimes necessary crime-fighting tool. They can permit the infiltration of gangs, drug cartels, corporations, terrorist conspiracies, and other organizations otherwise impervious to law enforcement. Offering lenience to low-level offenders is sometimes the only way to get information about high-level criminals. From the challenges of international terrorism to those of gang-dominated city streets, criminal informants can be uniquely productive helpmates for the government.

The idea behind snitching is simple—a suspect provides incriminating information about someone else in exchange for a deal, maybe the chance to walk away, or a lesser charge or sentence. In practice, however, informant deals are as varied as the crimes they involve. Some are quick, informal, and routine. In the so-called buy, bust, flip technique, a police officer might release a drug addict or dealer in exchange for a tip. Other informant deals are complex, high-profile, and span many years. In 2006, corrupt lobbyist Jack Abramoff avoided decades in prison by agreeing to snitch on the politicians he bribed. Fifteen years before that, hit man "Sammy the Bull" Gravano testified against mafia boss John Gotti in exchange for drastically reduced punishment and witness protection. The power and flexibility of the informant deal has made it a ubiquitous weapon in the law enforcement arsenal.

At the same time, using criminal informants exacerbates some of the worst features of the U.S. justice system. The practice is clandestine and unregulated, inviting inaccuracy, crime, and sometimes corruption. It inflicts special harms on vulnerable individuals such as racial minorities, substance abusers, and poor defendants who lack robust legal representation. Because of its secretive and discretionary nature, it evades the traditional checks and balances of judicial and public scrutiny, even as it determines the outcomes of millions of investigations and cases. And finally, like the criminal system itself, it is rapidly expanding.

The most dangerous versions of snitching tend to occur when law enforcement deploys criminals to generate new cases. In the economically troubled town of Hearne, Texas, for example, 27-year-old criminal informant Derrick Megress wreaked havoc. In November 2000, a federally funded drug task force swept through the town arresting twenty-eight people, mostly African American residents of the Columbus Village public housing project. Megress, a suicidal former drug dealer on probation facing new burglary charges, had cut a deal with the local prosecutor. If he produced at least twenty arrests, Megress's new charges would be dropped. He'd also earn one hundred dollars for every person he helped bust. One of his innocent victims was waitress Regina Kelly, mother of four, who steadfastly refused to plead guilty and take a deal for probation even as she sat in jail for weeks. Another target, Detra Tindle, was actually in the hospital giving birth at the time when Megress alleged that she had sold him drugs. A lie detector test finally revealed that Megress had lied—mixing flour and baking soda with small amounts of cocaine to fabricate evidence of drug deals. Charges against the remaining Hearne suspects were dropped, although several had already pleaded guilty.[3]

While the Hearne case was unusual in that it garnered national attention and an ACLU lawsuit, the Texas task force's heavy reliance on its informant was par for the course. Federally funded drug task forces are large-scale consumers of snitches. A similar Massachusetts drug task force reported using over two thousand informants in fiscal years 2005 and 2006, who in turn conducted 45 percent of all the task force's drug transactions.[4] As a result, there is ongoing potential for Hearne-type disasters.

Unlike civilian witnesses, criminal informants represent a tense compromise with the core goals of the justice system—crime prevention and punishment. After all, informants trade information with the government in order to escape liability for their own crimes, and can even earn the ability to continue offending. Informants may work both ends of the deal, maintaining relationships with the police and turning in other offenders even as they continue to break the law. In this sense, using criminal informants by definition requires the toleration of crime. Indeed, the ability of cooperating drug dealers to remain at large has made snitching a well-recognized fact of life and a subject of heated debate in communities from Atlanta to East Harlem.

Moreover, unlike other investigative tactics, turning suspects into informants has implications that extend beyond the criminal process. The practice has political, cultural, even intimate dimensions, particularly when the government uses the informant deal to manipulate private relationships. For example, when police threatened first-time offender Amy Gepfert with a forty-year sentence for drug distribution, they offered to drop all charges if she engaged in oral sex with another suspect in exchange for money so that police could charge him with prostitution. She did; no charges were filed against her.[5]

Sometimes the creation of an informant disturbs an entire community. The orthodox Jewish community in Los Angeles was shaken

when a prominent member of the well-known Beth Jacob congrega-
tion turned state's evidence against a Hasidic rabbi in exchange for
lenience in his own fraud case. The betrayal was deemed all the more
traumatic because traditional Jewish law prohibits informing against
another Jew.[6]

Informant use disrupts vulnerable communities more than others.
Because police make disproportionately more drug arrests in black
neighborhoods,[7] the practice of "flipping" drug arrestees, i.e., turning
suspects into snitches, naturally creates more criminal informants in
those communities. This means that such neighborhoods must routinely bear the costs of snitching—including informant crime and
unreliability. One study, for example, found that innocent black and
Hispanic households in San Diego were disproportionately the target of bad search warrants, 80 percent of which relied on confidential
informants.[8] Such neighborhoods must also contend with significant
numbers of criminal offenders actively seeking information in order
to "work off" their own charges.

Because the criminal system occupies such a central place in our
social fabric, law enforcement tactics like snitching are not merely
penal policies: they are influential features of the way we govern. Not
only do criminal practices shape our social relationships; it is through
the penal system that we collectively distinguish between right and
wrong, punishing offenders and vindicating victims. The criminal system educates the public about the state of the law and about current
events. It can instill public confidence in government, or send fear
coursing through a neighborhood.

The penal system, moreover, is a multi-billion-dollar industry con-
trolling the lives of millions of offenders, employing millions of law
enforcement workers, and affecting the local economies of thousands
of communities. Over the decades, it has altered the shape of American government itself, investing it with increasingly vast powers to
investigate and punish.[9] Using criminal informants is an integral part
of this matrix, with many of these same weighty governance, educational, moral, and equitable dimensions.

Our penal system is also famously flawed. It is the most punitive system on the planet, incarcerating more people than any other

nation. It is expensive, pulling billions of dollars into prisons and away from social services and schools. It is secretive and sometimes sloppy, often unaccountable and inaccurate. And it is racially skewed, punishing African Americans and Latinos more often and more heavily than whites, and deforming the life trajectories of individuals and communities of color.[10] Snitching practices are intimately tied to many of these failings as well.

Understanding the U.S. criminal system in its complex entirety is one of the great challenges of modern legal and social studies; understanding criminal informant use is central to that challenge. This is because, paradoxically, informant use is both unique—with its own special subcultures and rules—and paradigmatic of the system as a whole. On the one hand, snitching cases comprise a special, albeit large, subclass: many nondrug criminal investigations and prosecutions do not involve trading guilt for information. In this sense, informant use creates a unique zone in the criminal system with its own rules, dynamics, and significance.

On the other hand, this zone exerts a strong influence on the rest of the system while revealing many of the system's core features. Snitching is paradigmatic of the American criminal process because it embodies three of its distinctive characteristics: secrecy, discretion, and the dominance of plea bargaining. Informant deals are mostly confidential; they are crafted at the sole discretion of police and prosecutors; and they resolve criminal liability through private negotiations largely without rules, trials, or judicial or public scrutiny. The increasing use of such deals has transformed key aspects of the adversarial process, including the roles of defense counsel, disclosure, plea bargaining, and trial. It also drives the entire system further underground. Unearthing the full story of criminal informant use is thus revelatory precisely because it uncovers significant features of the legal process that usually remain hidden. By understanding snitching, we can learn deep truths about how our entire penal system really functions.

The past five years have seen a spate of diverse reforms at the local, state, and federal levels as government officials struggle with the costs and benefits of using criminal informants. Illinois has instituted

"reliability hearings" for jailhouse snitches. Texas now imposes corroboration requirements on undercover operatives.[11] The next five
years will see more such legislation.

This growing interest in informant reform is fueled by several related developments. One is the "innocence movement": that collection of organizations, lawyers, students, professors, exonerees, and
families who over the past decade have uncovered hundreds of wrongful convictions.[12] Their advocacy, particularly in connection with improved access to DNA technology, has starkly revealed the unreliability of compensated witnesses who are promised lenience. According
to Northwestern University Law School's Center on Wrongful Convictions, 45.9 percent of documented wrongful capital convictions
have been traced to false informant testimony. This makes "snitches
the leading cause of wrongful convictions in U.S. capital cases."[13] As a
result of such revelations, several states, including California and New
York, have considered new legislation limiting the use of informant
testimony and demanding more accountability from prosecutors who
wish to reward their criminal witnesses.

Interest in reform has also been prompted by the steady stream of
news stories publicizing the violence, corruption, and injustice that
often accompany the use of criminal informants. In one widely noted
exposé, the *Dallas Morning News* revealed a "fake drug scandal" in
which paid informants set up innocent Mexican immigrants with fake
drugs (gypsum), while police falsified drug tests in order to inflate
their drug-bust statistics.[14] Such evidence of police-informant collu-
sion has galvanized numerous advocates and officials to reconsider
the unregulated use of criminal informants.

Popular culture has also zeroed in on snitching. In 2004, a homemade DVD entitled "Stop Snitching" circulated through the streets
of Baltimore, exhorting criminals to stop cooperating with police in
exchange for lenience deals. Because NBA basketball star Carmelo
Anthony appeared briefly in the video, it garnered national media
attention and concern over the antipolice connotations of the "stop
snitching" motto. A line of "stop snitching" t-shirts spread rapidly to
other cities. These shirts—popular among urban youth and hip hop
fans—were widely seen as promoting a street "code of silence" and

triggered a public backlash. Years later, the "stop snitching" motto remains a subject of deep contention. Resonating in cities such as East Harlem, Boston, and Pittsburgh, it has become part of the historic dialogue over the distrust between police and residents of high-crime minority communities.

Public reactions to criminal informant use have been passionate and diverse: from new rules of evidence to graffiti to community rallies. The astonishing breadth of response indicates how deep-seated and influential this clandestine law enforcement practice is, its importance to the overall integrity of the criminal process, and its relevance to fundamental questions about how we choose to police and govern ourselves. As this debate progresses, it cries out for more and better data.

Documenting criminal informant use, however, is easier said than done. The practice is secretive and informal, typically taking place off the record in unrecorded conversations between suspects and law enforcement. Because most criminal cases in the United States never go to trial, public records are sparse. Even when records do exist, court files involving informants may be sealed. Informing is also unregulated and uneven: practices vary from jurisdiction to jurisdiction, even from officer to officer. Importantly, while the benefits of informant use are often well recognized, its down sides and dangers typically remain invisible. As a result, the public has little information, and many misunderstandings, about this important arena of public policy.

This book is an effort to remedy that deficit of public information and understanding. It describes what we do know about the official use of criminal informants and the way it works. While it acknowledges the well-known strengths of the practice as a conventional crime-fighting tool, the bulk of the book is spent in the shadows, uncovering the hidden realities and troubling implications of informant use. The aim is not to present an unbalanced view, but to even out what has been a largely one-sided debate. By analyzing informants both as a law enforcement tool and as an engine of social influence and public governance, the book reveals the pervasive and often disturbing significance of this secretive law enforcement practice.

Importantly, this is *not* a book about everyone who gives information to the police. It does not address civilian witnesses, whistleblowers, undercover police officers, or even noncriminal paid informants, although these groups can be importantly affected by criminal informant policies. It is also not a book about "snitching" or loyalty in noncriminal arenas of society, such as schools, workplaces, or families. Rather, it addresses the very specific but widespread governmental practice of *rewarding informants who have broken the law*.

This book focuses heavily on street crime and drug enforcement because it is in those arenas that the human costs and social consequences of snitching are most profound. But the book also examines the wide range of other law enforcement arenas, such as white collar crime, in which informant use has become central. Chapter 1 gives an overview of the practice and its most important implications for individuals, communities, and the criminal system as a whole.

Chapter 2 lays out the contours of "informant law," namely, all the legal rules that govern criminal informants, from investigations to sentencing rewards to discovery rules to civil rights. While this chapter is written for anyone curious about how our legal system actually regulates the process of snitching, it is also designed to be useful to lawyers, judges, and legislators who professionally engage this body of law. Because there are so many facets of criminal informant use, the chapter covers a broad range of laws not usually associated with one another: it analyzes police and prosecutorial authority to create and reward informants as well as Fourth Amendment search and seizure law, defendants' rights when informants are used against them, as well as informants' civil rights against the government. Taken together, this collection of rules and practices comprises a body of law characterized almost uniformly by unfettered law enforcement discretion, pervasive informality, secrecy, and toleration of lawbreaking—characteristics of the American legal process that distinguish it from many other democratic nations.

Chapter 3 covers one of the best-known dangers of criminal informant use: its unreliability. It analyzes not only the data on wrongful informant testimony but also the way police and prosecutorial practices undermine the system's ability to check informant misinformation.

Chapter 4 explores a far less recognized consequence of informant use, which is its tendency to render the entire criminal process more secretive and less publicly accountable. Because informant practices tend to remain undocumented, investigations and cases involving informants recede from public view. On the theory that confidentiality is necessary to protect investigations and witnesses, courts and legislatures have been willing to tolerate high levels of executive secrecy. As a result, numerous disclosure rules involving discovery and public record keeping have been rolled back to accommodate informant confidentiality, with widespread impact on governmental transparency and accountability.

Of all the problematic aspects of informant use, the consequences of the practice for poor communities of color have been the least recognized, even though they pose serious obstacles to the viability and legitimacy of the practice. Chapter 5 examines the impact of pervasive informant use on high-crime, low-income urban communities, and in particular on the African American men who live there. This chapter estimates the extent of the snitching phenomenon and discusses its harmful effects on crime control, law enforcement, youth, families, and community stability.

Chapter 6 describes the "stop snitching" cultural phenomenon, and traces how a slogan on a homemade rap DVD and some knock-off t-shirts made its way into national consciousness. The chapter explores the problems of witness intimidation, police-community distrust, and the provocative political and cultural issues raised by the "stop snitching" theme.

Drug, street, and violent crime make up the bulk of the criminal system, and chapters 5 and 6 address informant use primarily in those contexts.[15] Particularly at the federal level, however, informants are used in the investigation and prosecution of all sorts of crimes, including fraud, embezzlement, antitrust, forgery, political corruption, bribery, and, of course, organized crime offenses such as racketeering and money laundering. Chapter 7 examines informant use in the prominent arenas of organized crime, political corruption, white collar crime, and terrorism. Each of these arenas has its own snitching histories, practices, and challenges; together they reveal the pervasive influence of criminal informant practices throughout the entire American system. The survey also reveals that while all forms of snitching retain some core problematic features, informant use can nevertheless operate more reliably, transparently, and fairly in more regulated law enforcement environments characterized by wealthier, better-represented defendants.

Because this book exposes the many harmful, sometime shocking consequences of snitching, it poses serious questions about the validity of the practice. Nevertheless, the book does not advocate eliminating informant use: this is for both pragmatic and principled reasons that are discussed throughout. Pragmatically, snitching flows from two dominant characteristics of our criminal system: plea bargaining, and a tolerance for a high level of law enforcement discretion. These structural features not only make snitching possible; to some extent they make it inevitable. As long as police and prosecutors have complete discretion over whom to target, useful suspects will evade arrest and prosecution. And as long as law enforcement can freely negotiate with suspects over what crimes to charge, some suspects will be able to trade cooperation for better treatment. In other words, banning snitching altogether would effectively require restructuring fundamental aspects of the American criminal process, a project that exceeds the scope of this book.

While some horse trading over guilt and information may be inevitable in a system like ours, however, the complete lack of regulation and oversight of the practice is not. Nor are the destructive and inegalitarian effects of the practice. Chapter 8 thus proposes a global approach to regulating and improving, not eliminating, informant use and describes the exciting array of reforms currently emerging at the federal, state, and local levels. These proposals promote increased accountability, reliability, and fairness within the existing frameworks of our criminal system.

The principled reason why this book does not advocate a ban on snitching is that our criminal system does not yet provide enough information about the practice to reveal its full implications—good and bad. This book itself represents the most comprehensive collection of publicly available information regarding informant use, and the most far-ranging analysis of its implications to date, and yet throughout it acknowledges that the lack of systemic data makes many of its conclusions provisional at best. Because the criminal process is primarily designed to conceal, not to evaluate, informant use, it prevents rigorous conclusions about, for example, when snitching practices become so unfair or destructive of law enforcement integrity that they should be eliminated, or, alternatively, when their crime-fighting benefits are worth important compromises. We do not know with any certainty how many neighborhoods have been devastated by snitches or how many innocent people have been convicted by false informant testimony, although we know that both things happen. Conversely, we do not know how many criminal organizations have been disabled or how many crimes have been prevented or solved by the practice, although we know that these things happen too. It is precisely this kind of information that is needed for an informed democratic debate over the phenomenon, one that can address the fundamental principles of justice at stake as well as the crime-fighting cost-benefit analysis.

Of all the proposed reforms in chapter 8, therefore, the most important is the most difficult: changing the culture of secrecy and deregulation that permits informants and officials alike to bend rules, evade accountability, and operate in secret. It is this culture that fosters snitching's worst dangers: wrongful convictions, unchecked criminal behavior, official corruption, public deception, and the weakened legitimacy of the criminal process in the eyes of its constituents. It is also the feature that prevents us from addressing the ultimate public policy questions with clarity. The system currently handles the problem by asking us to accept on faith that unregulated snitching is worth its risks, without either demonstrating its full benefits or revealing its true costs. For a public policy of this far-reaching importance, such faith is not enough.

The book concludes that criminal informant use is intimately connected to many of the greatest challenges facing our justice system. Because the practice touches nearly every aspect of the criminal process, from policing to plea bargaining to public perceptions of law enforcement, it provides a unique and yet revealing window into the deepest workings of the penal system. From the government's ability to pressure and deceive its constituents to the violence and social devastation that afflicts poor African American communities, the national dialogue over snitching implicates some of the hardest issues raised by modern-day policing. As we delegate ever greater authority to our overextended criminal process, grappling with this bedrock feature becomes more vital than ever.

CHAPTER 1

The Real Deal

Understanding Snitching

I want these new shoes, I want this or I want drugs to sell, or something like that . . . and the police asked me for information. I'm just gonna give it to them to get what I want, even if they gonna give me some drugs or give me some money, or whatever, whatever they gonna give me I'm still gaining. . . . I'm gaining to get something in my pocket. . . . And in another way, I could fucking well get caught with a gang of cocaine and I know the man they want, they'll tell me, "I'm gonna let you stay on the street a little bit longer if you tell me where he is." Sure I'm gonna tell him, he's right over there.

—interview with a street snitch[1]

The judicial process is tainted and justice cheapened when factual testimony is purchased, whether with leniency or money.

—*United States v. Singleton*[2]

THE CENTRAL, DEFINING characteristic of snitching is the deal between the government and a suspect. In that deal, the government ignores or reduces the suspect's potential criminal liability in exchange for information. From street corners to jailhouses to courtrooms around the country, thousands of suspects work off their guilt by cooperating with police or prosecutors. Their crimes may go lightly punished, or not punished at all. Indeed, if the deal takes place early enough, these crimes may never even be officially recorded.

This method of resolving criminal liability is a radical departure from the usual ways in which we handle questions of guilt. Typically, if the government suspects a person of wrongdoing, it will arrest and/ or charge him with a crime.[3] Such charges are a matter of public record and trigger numerous consequences, including the onset of the defendant's right to counsel. Likewise, a person charged with a crime must either go to trial to contest his guilt or publicly admit liability by pleading guilty. These processes of filing charges, going to trial, and pleading guilty are heavily regulated by procedural rules, many of which are grounded in the U.S. Constitution. The process is monitored by lawyers and judges and leaves a paper trail. While it is true that conventional plea bargaining involves significant horse trading over facts and guilt, and much of that bargaining process takes place in private, an interested member of the public can usually discern after the fact the basis on which a person was found guilty, and what his punishment was.[4]

Snitching is the clandestine, black-market version of this process. It resolves guilt mainly off the record, without rules, at the discretion of individual law enforcement officials. For example, instead of serving his sentence for running an identity-theft ring in San Francisco, Marvin Jeffery became an informant. While providing information to the police on the street, Jeffery continued to expand his illegal ring. Although he committed additional offenses, violated his probation, and incurred several arrest warrants, police permitted him to remain at large because of his cooperation. These numerous deals remained largely secret: even investigators on related cases were unaware of Jeffery's special status. Finally, after he sold an illegal AK-47 machine gun that was used to kill a police officer, he disappeared. Jeffery's long history of ongoing cooperation and wrongdoing came to light only because of the happenstance of his link to that lethal weapon.[5]

Informant practices such as these represent a fundamental alteration of the criminal system's response to wrongdoing. No longer simply the basis for arrest, prosecution, or punishment, criminal conduct becomes instead the starting point for negotiations that may never be publicly revealed, and in which police and prosecutors may tolerate ongoing crime. In deciding that an informant's usefulness outweighs his culpability, police often implicitly downplay the seriousness of the informant's crimes and the significance of holding such offenders accountable, while elevating the importance of future cases that the informant might help them make. Likewise, when prosecutors tailor charges not solely to the magnitude of the crime but to the cooperativeness of the criminal, they are making similar judgments.

Such practices represent a retreat from some core purposes of the criminal law, such as evaluating individual moral culpability and publicly condemning crime. Instead, they elevate very different values such as an offender's immediate investigative usefulness, law enforcement efficiency, or even mere convenience. Informant practices also alter some basic features of criminal procedure, from the ways in which investigations are conducted to the terms of plea bargains to the respective roles of defense counsel, judges, and juries. As law professor Graham Hughes once wrote, cooperation agreements are "sharply different from the general phenomenon of plea bargaining. They are exotic plants that can survive only in an environment from which some of the familiar features of the criminal procedure landscape have been expunged."[6]

Although all snitching requires a deal, informant arrangements vary widely, from Marvin Jeffery's informal understanding with his police handlers to elaborately written cooperation agreements worked out by counsel for both sides. The nature of the deal will be affected by the type of underlying crime, and the extent of involvement by police, prosecutors, or defense counsel. The resulting obligations imposed on informants—and their potential rewards—vary widely as well. What follows is thus a description of the general contours and variables of the informant bargain—in practice, each individual deal will look very different.

I. Anatomy of an Informant Deal

Police and prosecutors are the primary government officials who create and control informant deals, and they engage informants in distinct ways. Police are generally authorized to conduct investigations, make arrests, and sometimes, determine the nature of initial criminal charges. Prosecutors appear later in the process and file formal charges and handle plea bargaining, trials, sentencing, and other public aspects of the legal case. Police and prosecutors may also work together throughout a particular investigation or case, making decisions about informants' conduct and rewards.

A. Police

Sometimes referred to as "handlers," police officers and investigative agents are on the front lines of the informant phenomenon, with the most information about and influence over informants and their ongoing relationships with the government. Because police handle arrests, they typically make the first contact. Dennis Fitzgerald, retired DEA special agent and former Miami police sergeant, explains the process as follows:

> Offering an arrested individual the opportunity to cooperate and mitigate his situation is the technique most frequently used to recruit an informant. . . . [T]he incident should have taken place discretely [sic] and without fanfare. If not, word of his arrest will have spread quickly "on the street." Once booked into jail, his value to the agents as an informant may rapidly diminish.[7]

Police may also approach or arrest people expressly for the purpose of turning them into informants, even if there is insufficient evidence to prosecute them. According to Dr. Stephen Mallory, a 25-year veteran narcotics agent, former police trainer, narcotics bureau director, and member of DEA and FBI task forces, "[another] method that can be effective for recruiting informants is an 'informed bluff.' If the investigator . . . has failed to produce an indictable case, a bluff may be his only alternative. . . . When a potential informant believes that a case is pending on his activities, he/she may agree to cooperate."[8]

As Agent Fitzgerald acknowledges, the tactics used to recruit informants may themselves be illegal. Police, for example, may target a prospective informant and wait

> until he commits a crime or is suspected to be in possession of a controlled substance or other contraband. He is then "arrested"

following what is usually an illegal search and seizure. The subject, fearful of going to jail, may immediately agree to cooperate (flip) and be "unarrested." He will work as an informant laboring under the impression that charges will be filed unless he cooperates.[9]

Once the suspect agrees to cooperate, he will strike a deal with the officer. The deal may be verbal, with details to be worked out later, or it may involve a written agreement. As the street snitch quoted at the beginning of this chapter explains, sometimes the deal can be as simple as the officer's agreement not to arrest the suspect and to let him "stay on the street a little bit longer" in exchange for a tip. By contrast, the FBI requires its agents to write down all informant agreements.

Even if an informant is arrested and charged with a crime by a prosecutor, an active informant's most frequent contact will be with the police or investigative agent. The handler will control the informant's activities, tell him what to do, receive his information, and potentially act on it. The handler in turn will report to the prosecutor about the information obtained from the informant, about the informant's other activities—for example, if he has committed additional crimes—and about whether or not he has been cooperative. The police handler is thus the government official closest to the informant, with the most knowledge, control, and day-to-day contact with him.

The relationship between an active informant and his handler is complex, personal, and a two-way street. The more heavily police rely on snitches, the more important it becomes for them to work with, retain, and protect their informants. Agent Mallory describes the importance of maintaining an officer's personal reputation among criminals.

> The reputation of an investigator is paramount to informant re-
> cruitment. The criminal elements of a community know who the
> fair, productive, and professional investigators are in a police orga-
> nization. They know who to trust, whose word is good, and who
> will demonstrate persistence toward solving crimes. They also
> know who has influence with prosecutors, judges, and other law
> enforcement agencies. In other words, they know who to "weigh

in" with. . . . After a successful prosecution, my telephone would begin to ring. . . . These informants may be seeking help with their charges, calling out of fear of being charged, or just in need of money.[10]

Agent Mallory further describes handling informants as a form of employee management, dependent on "motivation, leadership style, and job satisfaction."

> Informants, like other productive people, must be motivated to reach their potential. . . . Once the investigator's positive reputation has become known in the community, informants will be more easily recruited and controlled by the investigator. He will be known as a police officer who understands and works with people.[11]

Views differ within the law enforcement community about how best to handle informants. For example, according to Agent Mallory, keeping informants motivated may involve delegating power to the informant to design investigations or select targets, in order to enhance his job satisfaction. "The investigator may use empowerment to motivate a potential informant. Although care must be used when allowing informants to exercise too much control or to have too much input into case planning, participat[ion] by the informant does seem to produce more cooperation."[12] By contrast, John Madinger, senior special agent with the Criminal Investigative Division of the IRS and former narcotics agent, believes that authority should never be delegated to informants, even though it may well produce good results.[13]

Police may work with an informant on more than one case, and in different ways. While a particular informant may be a key witness for one crime, he may merely provide corroboration or other information regarding another. Police may maintain their relationships with informants as a way of keeping feelers out in the community or tabs on a situation unconnected to any particular investigation. Agent Madinger describes one investigator in a small county who developed dozens of criminal informants, maintaining a set of cross-referenced three-ring binders in which he recorded all the information and crimes about which he learned. In the course of a single evening, this one agent might meet with six or seven individuals for debriefing.[14]

Investigative agents thus have immense power to decide the course of the criminal informant's relationship with the government. They are the most directly involved with the day-to-day instructions and management of investigations, including keeping tabs on the informant's ongoing criminal activities. They also heavily influence the eventual criminal charges that will be lodged against the informant, if any, because they have the discretion to decide whether to arrest him in the first place, what to charge him with initially, and what to tell the prosecutor.

B. Prosecutors

Prosecutors typically do not start working on a case until a police officer or investigative agent has made an arrest or produced some evidence of a crime. Once police have initiated a case, the prosecutor must evaluate the evidence and decide whether to file charges or to continue the investigation or both. Prosecutors may thus meet an informant for the first time after an investigative officer has already established a working relationship. Or, a suspect may be brought in for questioning and the prosecutor can decide to flip the suspect by offering a deal.

In the federal system, once a suspect has been formally charged, an informant deal will often come about as a result of a "proffer session." The defendant, his lawyer, the prosecutor, and, typically, the agent will all sit down in a room together. The parties will sign an agreement that nothing the defendant says in that room during that proffer session will be used as evidence against him. And then the defendant will talk.

In an effort to better understand the cooperation and proffer process, law professor Ellen Yaroshefsky interviewed numerous prosecutors and other attorneys in the Southern District of New York. The prosecutors explained that they spend a great deal of time and effort trying to discern the value and veracity of information obtained from informants, including extensive debriefings, investigation, and corroboration. They also described the dangers of the proffer process. "[C]ooperators are eager to please you," one prosecutor explained. "Telling them that you just want the truth is meaningless." According to another prosecutor, "Many of them come in believing that This is What They Want to Hear Time rather than This is What Happened Time." All the former U.S. attorneys reported that cooperators do not tell the truth in the first few sessions.[15]

Depending on what the defendant says, the prosecutor may decide that his information was not helpful and the defendant will get no benefit. Or he may get a sentencing break for being cooperative. Or he may embark upon a longer relationship with the government in which he agrees to testify before a grand jury, wear a wire, set up a meeting, arrange a deal, or engage in some further activity for which the government may, but is not required to, confer some benefit. If the defendant is released, the agent will typically take more control, acting as the handler for the informant and periodically reporting back to the prosecutor.

Prosecutors have a wide range of negotiating tools. They can delay an indictment or an existing case to give an informant a chance to testify before a grand jury, or to go back into the street and gather information, sometimes known as "working off a charge." They can drop charges, alter charges, or promise to make favorable recommendations to the judge at sentencing.

Prosecutors can also negotiate with respect to third parties by declining or dropping charges against the informant's family members if he cooperates, or threatening to proceed against them if he won't. For example, after the multi-billion-dollar collapse of the company Enron due to financial fraud, the government charged Enron's chief financial officer, Andrew Fastow, with numerous crimes. As part of its effort to get Fastow to cooperate against Enron CEO Kenneth Lay, the government also prosecuted Fastow's wife Lea. Only by cooperating could Fastow ensure that Lea would be able to negotiate a plea to a misdemeanor.[16] Alternatively, a defendant who has nothing to offer the government or who cannot cooperate himself may recruit a "brokered informant," a family member, friend, or associate whose cooperation will be credited to that defendant.[17]

Prosecutors and law enforcement agents do not always share the same attitude towards informants. A prosecutor may want to flip and reward a defendant that the police believe should be prosecuted to the fullest. Conversely, agents may not want to expose a valuable source, and therefore may not share all the information they have with the prosecutor. For example, police in Chicago and New York used to maintain "double file" systems in which police created two sets of investigative reports but gave only the public versions to prosecutors.[18] Furthermore, agents may not trust prosecutors with various aspects of informant management. Agent Fitzgerald voiced this concern when he asserted that "[m]any prosecutors are poorly prepared to deal with experienced criminals as they negotiate their fate as an informant."[19]

Law professor and former prosecutor Daniel Richman explains that agents and prosecutors have different relationships to the cultivation of informants and that "cultural difference can drive a powerful wedge between agents and prosecutors" in ways that lead to nondisclosure:

> Agents or even agencies seeking to justify their refusal to share information about sources and methods with prosecutors will assert a fear that such data will be misused when the prosecutor enters private practice. This tendency towards non-disclosure is bolstered by concerns that prosecutors have less "on the line" when it comes to investigative security. An agent's promise to an informant is bonded by his and his agency's professional reputation. The prosecutor who will soon move into another world is not so bound.[20]

The relationship between agent and prosecutor is thus an important wild card in the informant scenario.

C. Defense Counsel

Whether an informant has an attorney makes an immense difference in the nature and course of his cooperation. For a range of reasons, most informants do not have lawyers. As a matter of law, when a suspect is first stopped by police he does not yet have the right to counsel. If he is given Miranda warnings and decides to ask for a lawyer, he will be given counsel for the purposes of an interrogation, but the vast majority of suspects do not invoke their rights and therefore end up talking directly to police on their own.[21]

As a practical matter, police will often purposely approach suspects before they are represented precisely in order avoid involving defense counsel. As Agent Fitzgerald explains,

> The first attempt to recruit the individual occurs during the post-arrest interview, commonly referred to as interrogation. The interview occurs shortly after the arrest. The defendant is unnerved, confused, frightened, angry, or experiencing a combination of these emotions. Of greatest importance to the agent, however, is that the individual is probably not yet represented by counsel. This is the period when most defendant informants are recruited.[22]

A smaller percentage of informants negotiate cooperation deals with the help of a lawyer. Once a defendant is charged with a crime, he acquires the constitutional right to counsel, and prosecutors are ethically prohibited from contacting a represented defendant.[23] Whether suspects get lawyers in the first place, however, is a function of many factors, including their economic status, educational level, kind of crime they are suspected of, and their independent access to counsel. In white collar and political corruption cases, for example, defendants are more likely to have or retain counsel. In such cases, the government may even put a suspect on notice that he is a potential target of investigation and give him the opportunity to get a lawyer. For example, in 2008, federal prosecutors sent a "target letter" to Nicole Gestas, wife of personal trainer Greg Anderson. Anderson had refused to testify against his client, baseball star Barry Bonds, in connection with allegations that he provided Bonds with illegal performance-enhancing drugs. The letter informed Gestas that she might be charged with conspiracy and that she should contact the public defender's office if she could not afford counsel.[24]

As the use of cooperation has ballooned in the white collar context, so have the issues surrounding the role of counsel. For example, the U.S. Department of Justice formerly made a practice of pressuring corporate entities and employees to waive their rights to counsel and confidentiality as part of entering into cooperation deals. These controversial developments are discussed in more detail in chapter 7.

There are big differences between a counseled and uncounseled informant deal. To mention a few, counseled deals are typically written, determinate, and witnessed. There is a modicum of formality and scrutiny that is lacking in the informal street negotiation. At the most basic level, there is another witness to the deal. A defense attorney will know if the government is being unduly coercive, if improper pressure is being brought to bear, and what sort of cooperation the informant has provided.

An informant is also likely to get a better deal if he is represented. Professor Richman explains the "critical role of defense lawyers" as follows:

> Her legal knowledge and experience will help the defendant assess the likely outcome of a trial, the value of his information, the nature of both parties' obligations under a cooperation agreement, the likelihood and extent of a sentencing discount, and other such factors. Even more importantly, as a repeat player in the market where the government buys information, the defense lawyer helps guarantee that the government will meet its obligations in good faith.[25]

Unlike white collar and other wealthier defendants, street and drug snitches tend not to have counsel, a significant difference that permits many of the irregularities and dangers of the practice.[26]

D. The Crimes

What kinds of crimes does law enforcement investigate using informants? The short answer is "all of them," but different types of criminal investigations create and deploy informants in distinctive ways. The two dominant models come, respectively, from the worlds of organized crime and drug enforcement.

Many of the most famous instances of snitching involve long-term, high-level investigations of organized crime. This type of informant use tends to be internally regulated and documented. The U.S. Department of Justice has formal published guidelines governing the use of confidential informants by the FBI, DEA, and other federal agencies that require relatively extensive documentation and monitoring. High-level organized crime investigations also tend to demand communication, coordination, and access to high levels of decision making within governmental organizations. For example, the use of mafia hit man "Sammy the Bull" Gravano as an informant required coordination over several years among the FBI, federal prosecutors, local police, the court, and eventually the federal witness protection program, and left an extensive public paper trail.

By contrast, the practices surrounding drug informants are extremely varied and largely unregulated. This is in part because drug investigations are more common and diverse than high-profile mafia cases and take place at the state and local as well as federal level. In contrast to the Department of Justice's extensive guidelines, state and local police departments and prosecutor's offices may not have any written policies governing the use of informants at all. If they do, the guidelines are typically quite general and not publicly available. Where guidelines are lax or nonexistent, informant practices are left up to individual police and prosecutors to craft on a case-by-case basis. As a result, some drug snitches are street-corner addicts, while others are active dealers with control over large amounts of drugs. Some are family members or girlfriends; some may have already been charged with a crime, or are incarcerated or on probation, while others remain uncharged and at large at the discretion of their handlers. Recall Derrick Megress, the drug-using snitch in Hearne, Texas, who ran wild through the public housing project fabricating evidence against dozens of innocent residents.[27] If the high-level mafia informant is supervised, aimed at specific targets, and documented, drug informants are loosely controlled, widely targeted, and often leave no paper trail at all.

Between these two polar extremes, snitching is sprinkled throughout the system like salt, flavoring every kind of case from burglary to corporate fraud and political corruption, kidnapping, murder, and, increasingly, terrorism. The U.S. Department of Justice indicates that federal defendants have been rewarded for cooperation in connection with every single type of federal crime, including murder, sexual abuse, and child pornography. In sum, while law enforcement in different jurisdictions uses informants to varying degrees, and some kinds of investigations are more dependent on the practice than others, informing permeates all kinds of criminal cases.

E. The Rewards

This book focuses on the most common informant reward: lenience for crimes. Informants can obtain lenience in numerous forms, from avoiding arrest or the filing of charges in the first place, to reduced or dropped charges on a particular case or in other jurisdictions, to sentence reductions if the informant is eventually convicted. As noted above, informants can also earn lenience for friends and family.

Police and prosecutors often intervene personally in their informants' criminal matters. For example, as reported by the *Boston Globe*,

> Massachusetts State Trooper Mark Lemieux has spent most of the morning sitting on a hard wooden bench in Newton District Court, waiting for his confidential informant Patrick's case to be heard. . . . Lemieux must persuade the district attorney and judge to let Patrick back on the street quickly, despite today's charge of driving without a license, so the informant can act as a liaison with Fidel, a heroin trafficker. . . . Just as the case comes up, Lemieux whispers to the court officer, passes behind the dock, and confers with the assistant district attorney for less than a minute. Patrick's case is resolved: a fine of $450 and the continued suspension of his license. Lemieux walks out of the courtroom. "Everything is fluid," he says. "You gotta go with the flow." Outside, Patrick gets in his own car—already violating the new agreement with the court.[28]

Informants can also receive other sorts of benefits above and beyond lenience. Most famously, they get paid. In one year alone, the federal government paid nearly $100 million to its confidential informants, and forfeiture statutes authorize paying informants a percentage of the value of assets seized on the basis of their information.[29] DEA "super snitch" Andrew Chambers, for example, earned as much as $4 million over the course of his work for various federal agencies, notwithstanding a lengthy rap sheet of his own.[30]

Local police departments maintain informant funds that can range from hundreds to thousands of dollars.[31] Alex White, the snitch to whom Atlanta police turned after they killed Kathryn Johnston, typically received thirty dollars for each buy. Ironically, White subsequently sued the City of Atlanta for wrongful termination, arguing that by involving him in the scandal surrounding Mrs. Johnston's death, the police ruined his $30,000-a-year employment as a drug informant.[32]

Some informant reward arrangements are double edged and illegal. Police from New York to Los Angeles have been known to reward their informants with drugs. In 2006, Baltimore detectives William King and Antonio Murray were convicted of, among other things, "robb[ing] drug addicts in West Baltimore to reward their sources on the street."[33] The Los Angeles Rampart scandal revealed that officers not only gave drugs to informants but also stole drugs and money from them. Officers also used informants to frame suspects, fabricate cases, and cover up for police shootings. The ensuing federal consent decree required Los Angeles to restrict its police's ability to operate and pay informants; for several years Los Angeles banned the use of street-level informants by most police officers.[34]

Illicit reward arrangements can take place at the highest levels of governmental decision making. During the prosecution of the El Rukn gang in Chicago, the government was so heavily dependent on six cooperating gang leaders that federal prosecutors permitted those incarcerated defendants to buy and use drugs, have sex, and steal legal documents. As described by the court, "'benefits' included money, gifts, clothing, radios, beer, cigarettes, services and privileges, including the government providing means by which the witnesses' acquisition, possession and use of illegal drugs was facilitated." Informants were "observed snorting cocaine and /or heroin while in MCC [the Metropolitan Correctional Center] on a number of occasions." The government gave the informants telephone privileges, which one informant used to call his drug supplier to "complain[] about the poor quality of the cocaine he had recently received." Because the informants were allowed to move about freely within the U.S. Attorney's Office, they were able to steal a confidential "preindictment prosecution memorandum and other materials related to the case."[35]

The best-documented type of informant reward is the lower sentences afforded to cooperating defendants under the U.S. Sentencing Guidelines. As described in detail in chapter 2, federal law authorizes reduced sentences for defendants who provide "substantial assistance" to the government. Such reductions are particularly valuable in the context of federal mandatory minimum drug sentences, which can only be reduced if the defendant cooperates. In state courts that lack comparable guidelines, judges typically reward cooperating defendants with lower sentences as well.

For non–U.S. citizens, informing can also carry immigration benefits. The S-visa, sometimes referred to as the "snitch visa," may be available to deportable aliens who provide the government with information about a criminal or terrorist organization.[36]

Finally, a small number of cooperating defendants may be given witness protection benefits, which can involve relocation, payments, or even new jobs and identities. Such benefits are available mostly to federal defendants; state witness protection programs are relatively small or sometimes nonexistent.[37]

II. Implications of Informant Practices

The use of criminal informants has wide-ranging implications for the legal system. The following discussion charts the breadth of these implications: the remainder of the book explores them in depth.

A. Crime-Fighting Benefits

Good informant, good case. Bad informant, bad case.
No informant, no case.

—old law enforcement saying

Above all, informant deals are a powerful law enforcement tool. As one court put it, "our criminal justice system could not adequately function without information provided by informants. . . . Without informants, law enforcement authorities would be unable to penetrate and destroy organized crime syndicates, drug trafficking cartels, bank frauds, telephone solicitation scams, public corruption, terrorist gangs, money launderers, espionage rings, and the likes."[38]

Informants make it uniquely possible to penetrate group or organizational crimes. For example, Henry Hill was a mafia drug dealer with a 25-year career in organized crime whose life story was depicted in the popular movie *Goodfellas*. Arrested in 1980, Hill testified against many of his mafia colleagues in exchange for witness protection.[39] Similarly, it took the cooperation of Enron CFO Andrew Fastow to bring down Enron CEO Kenneth Lay.[40] Not only does the informant deal make possible such prosecutions of high-level operatives; informant use also destabilizes organized crime and group criminality because of the ever-present possibility that a member of the conspiracy may someday flip.

The informant deal also enables the government to go after politically powerful or otherwise insulated criminal actors. Jack Abramoff was a long-time lobbyist who used bribes, favors, and illegal influence to help his clients obtain favorable legislation and regulation. In 2006, he pled guilty to mail fraud, conspiracy, and tax evasion, and in exchange for a reduced sentence, agreed to cooperate with the government. His assistance to date has made possible the prosecution of at least one congressman and several high-level administration officials.[41] Without the cooperation of someone intimately connected to those arrangements, such wrongdoing would remain undetected.

Similarly, the 2008 federal investigation into illegal doping in track and field was based heavily on the testimony of Trevor Graham, a co-operating witness who provided prosecutors with names and documentation regarding numerous elite athletes. Graham agreed to cooperate in order to avoid being charged with drug trafficking and money laundering.[42]

Terrorism has generated new appreciation for the value of the informant deal. It was a convicted drug dealer who enabled law enforcement to intervene in a plot to blow up fuel tanks at New York's Kennedy International Airport.[43] As discussed further in chapter 7, informants are increasingly central to international efforts to stymie terrorist groups.

Informant deals are powerful in another way: they make law enforcement activities easier and cheaper. By using informants, investigators can often avoid the need for search warrants, wire taps, and other time-consuming procedures that require court authorization.[44] The secrecy that surrounds informant use can enable the government to avoid judicial scrutiny and to move more quickly and quietly against criminal activity.[45]

With respect to individual offenders, converting a defendant into an informant can be a quicker, easier way of resolving a case than going to trial or even negotiating a conventional plea. Unlike a plea bargain, an informant deal is temporary and partial: the government provisionally agrees to reduce or eliminate the suspect's criminal liability, while the suspect temporarily relinquishes his right to contest his guilt while promising to provide information about others. Instead of litigating the defendant's guilt or the precise terms of a plea agreement, the informant deal permits the government to come to an agreement while leaving the ultimate question of liability and punishment open ended. In our overloaded criminal system in which prosecutors lack the resources to pursue every case, the informant deal can be a time-saving, resource-efficient method of case management.

The informant deal thus offers many benefits to the government. At the same time, snitching is typically extremely beneficial for criminal offenders as well. It permits them to avoid liability, to escape punishment, and even sometimes to continue offending. These mutual benefits explain in part why the informant deal has become an increasingly popular way of managing criminal cases, for law enforcement and lawbreakers alike.

B. Compromising the Purposes of Law Enforcement

While using informants produces certain kinds of benefits, it also threatens some of the very purposes of the law enforcement endeavor. Two decades ago, sociologist Gary Marx worried that the government's increasing reliance on undercover tactics like informing was shifting public priorities away from fighting crime towards surveillance and social control as an end in itself.[46] His concerns turned out to be prescient: today's police give thousands of dollars worth of cash and drugs to addict snitches, purportedly in the name of conducting the "war on drugs." Just last year, Brooklyn police officers were caught paying informants with drugs taken from dealers who were arrested after the informants pointed them out. One officer bragged about the practice on tape, explaining that officers would seize drugs but report a lesser amount, keeping the unreported drugs to give to informants later on.[47]

More generally, the practice of letting known criminals walk away in exchange for information, and even facilitating their criminality to enhance their informational value, flips the law enforcement endeavor on its head. The U.S. Department of Justice's 2005 report indicates that 10 percent of the FBI's informant files contained evidence that the informant was committing unauthorized crimes about which the government knew.[48] Judicial cases and press accounts reveal handlers who turn a blind eye when their informants commit such crimes as extortion, fraud, money laundering, bribery, theft, tax evasion, prostitution, fencing stolen goods, illegal weapons possession, and even murder.[49]

Some informants commit new crimes under cover of their informant status. Tony Warren, for example, started working as a Secret Service informant in 2001 investigating a Nigerian check fraud scheme, after which he started his own check fraud scheme involving the theft of hundreds of thousands of dollars.[50] Armando Garcia, already convicted once for cocaine importation, was trying to earn some extra money by helping the FBI intercept twelve hundred kilograms of cocaine headed for Florida in a submarine. Garcia used his relationships with the FBI and DEA to cloak his own unauthorized 25-kilogram cocaine deal.[51]

Sometimes the lines blur between authorized and unauthorized informant crimes. In 2004, police told Troy Smith that he needed to produce six arrests in order to escape charges himself. In 2005, Smith sold methamphetamines to another informant. When Smith was charged as a dealer, he claimed that his handler had been pressuring him for a new arrest and that he was therefore authorized to sell the drugs in pursuit of his quota. The court did not permit Smith to call the police handler to the stand or to make the argument to the jury, and Smith was convicted and sentenced to thirteen years.[52] Similarly, when Ralph Abcasis was charged with importing heroin, he asserted that his New York drug enforcement agent handlers knew about and had implicitly authorized the scheme, while the agents asserted that Abcasis had been terminated as an informant prior to the heroin bust.[53] In such cases, whether new crimes have actually been authorized by the government is often a matter for debate and speculation.

Using informants alters other fundamental aspects of the criminal process, for example, the principle that the worse the crime, the worse the punishment. This foundational rule is routinely flouted in the world of snitching. For example, in the drug prosecution of Cedric Robertson—Crips gang member, drug dealer, and paraplegic—prosecutors also charged his girlfriend, Lakisha Murphy, as well as four active gang members. Although the judge recognized that Lakisha was not part of the gang or Cedric's drug business but was only marginally involved because she lived with and cared for her paraplegic partner, Lakisha received a mandatory ten-year sentence. Because the four active gang members cooperated against Cedric, they received lower sentences than Lakisha did, even though their crimes were far worse. Even the judge complained of the disparity, telling Lakisha that "it seems unfortunate in this case that you're doing more time than some of these guys did . . . and there's nothing I can do about it."[54]

Sometimes such disparities have racial dimensions. In 1999, mafia hit man John Martorano agreed to cooperate against his Boston mafia colleagues Whitey Bulger and Stephen Flemmi. In exchange, he received a twelve-year prison sentence for the twenty murders to which he admitted, in addition to extortion, money laundering, and racketeering charges. African American leaders complained that even as prosecutors cut the deal with cold-blooded killer Martorano, they were considering seeking the death penalty against young black local gang members accused of committing two murders. "It fosters distrust in our criminal justice system," asserted one Massachusetts state representative. "It mocks the fundamental principle that justice is blind and evenly applied."[55]

Such cases are species of the more general phenomenon that snitching skews the system's evaluation of guilt and innocence. As law professor William Stuntz put it,

> [D]efendants who have the most information to sell get the biggest discount. . . . Trading plea concessions for information means giving the biggest breaks to the worst actors. . . . [W]orse, . . . [i]n order to make their threats credible, prosecutors must punish defendants who fail to give them the information they want. . . . In a system (like ours) that rewards snitches generously, some defendants will be punished very harshly—nominally for their crimes, but actually for not having the kind of information one gets only by working at high levels of criminal organizations.[56]

This shell game of criminal liability weakens the force of the legislative process. When legislatures craft criminal laws, they define the conduct for which liability will attach and specify the range of punishment. The California robbery statute, for example, defines robbery specifically as "the felonious taking of personal property in the possession of another, from his person or immediate presence, and against his will, accomplished by means of force or fear," and sets specific sentences.[57] When legislatures define culpable conduct, and set the punishment for a particular crime at a higher level than for other offenses, this is a grave societal statement that we collectively consider this conduct to be worse.

The ability of informants to escape punishment for more serious behavior erodes the force of these highly specific legislative decisions. Instead, punishment turns on the amorphous and sometimes momentary decisions of police and prosecutors regarding the usefulness and convenience of an informant, even when he may have committed acts that the legislature has decided deserve substantial punishment.[58] In effect, snitching is the universal exception to every criminal law, as if each code provision read, "Here is the crime. Here is the punishment. Unless you cooperate."

C. Who's in Charge around Here?

"You're only as good as your informant," explained the police officers to the sociology professor.[59] "Informers are running today's drug investigations, not the agents," complained a twelve-year veteran of the DEA, "[and] agents have become so dependent on informers that the agents are at their mercy."[60] Even prosecutors worry: "These [drug] cases are not very well investigated. . . . [O]ur cases are developed through co-operators and their recitation of the facts. . . . Often, in DEA, you have little or no follow up so when a cooperator comes and begins to give you information outside of the particular incident, you have no clue if what he says is true." Another prosecutor revealed that "the biggest surprise is the amount of time you spend with criminals. You spend most of your time with cooperators. It's bizarre."[61]

Particularly in drug investigations, police and prosecutors rely heavily on informants to make basic decisions about cases: Who should be investigated? What should the charges be? Which accomplice should be the witness and which one should be the defendant? Because criminal informants are often key sources of information, their choices about what to reveal or conceal become crucial ingredients in the official decision-making process. As a result, government actors are all too often at the mercy of their own informants.

Heavy dependence on informants also displaces more independent decisional processes: according to one former DEA and customs agent, "reliance on informants has replaced good, solid police work like undercover operations and surveillance."[62] Prosecutors in Yaroshefsky's study described violent gang cases as "all based on cooperators . . . [and evidence] for which there is only one rat after another."[63]

Another consequence of this interdependence is to concentrate police attention on poor minority neighborhoods from which drug informants tend to come. Relying on informants naturally focuses attention on the people closest to those informants, since snitches are unlikely to know people outside their own socioeconomic group or community. The use of snitches thus becomes a kind of focusing mechanism on a community, guaranteeing that law enforcement will identify its new targets there.[64]

Finally, police and prosecutors often inadvertently validate the interests of their criminal informants. Law enforcement agents universally recognize the danger that informants may be cooperating in order to further their own aims: to eliminate competition, for example, or take revenge.[65] When this happens, it means that the state has effectively placed its power at the disposal of criminals. This is particularly problematic because the integrity of law enforcement discretion turns heavily on the way the system selects among a vast pool of potential culpable targets.[66] Indeed, because the majority of potential cases will never be pursued, it is the quintessential role of police and prosecutors to choose what crimes will be addressed in ways that validate broad public values of fairness and efficiency.[67] The more police and prosecutors rely on informants in selecting targets, the more the integrity of the system is compromised.

D. Mishandling and Corruption

According to the DEA, "Failure in the management of cooperating individuals constitutes, perhaps, the most obvious single cause of serious integrity problems in the DEA and other law enforcement agencies."[68] Agent Fitzgerald tells of one inexperienced agent who gave his informant free rein to commit new crimes, and who was so thoroughly at the informant's mercy that the agent actually served as a look-out during a burglary.[69]

The FBI's use of mafia informants during the 1970s, 1980s, and 1990s has been called "one of the greatest failures in the history of federal law enforcement" by the U.S. House of Representatives Committee on Government Reform. Over the course of those three decades, the FBI "made a decision to use murderers as informants. . . . Known killers were protected from the consequences of their crimes and purposefully kept on the streets."[70] Perhaps the most infamous incident of the era took place in the FBI's Boston office. For twenty years, Agent John Connolly and a handful of others managed a relationship with Irish mob hit men James "Whitey" Bulger and Stephen "The Rifleman" Flemmi, who provided the Boston FBI with valuable information about their rivals in the Italian mafia, La Cosa Nostra. As part of that relationship, Connolly protected Bulger and Flemmi from discovery and prosecution for their racketeering activities, extortion, and the murder of at least nineteen people. Connolly lied to prosecutors and other FBI agents in order to protect his sources, and is currently serving a ten-year prison sentence for racketeering. Bulger remains a wanted fugitive. During that period, in order to protect their informants, FBI agents also permitted four innocent men to be convicted of murder and to serve decades in prison, a violation of law for which, in 2007, the FBI was ordered to pay a judgment of $101 million.[71]

Informant-related misconduct also takes place on a small scale. Police officers in Columbus, Ohio, were having sexual relations with their informant Michelle Szuhay, and wanted to help her get a job as a stripper. So police took Ohio resident's Haley Dawson's identity—in the form of her driver's license and Social Security number—and gave it to Szuhay without Dawson's knowledge. An arbitrator ruled that the officers' actions in taking Dawson's identity and giving it to Szuhay were not illegal, although they constituted "a serious error in judgment."[72]

Finally, sometimes police use informants as a cheap and easy way to meet performance goals. Dallas police paid informants to plant fake drugs on immigrant workers, who were then arrested and sometimes deported before the scam was discovered. The busts were used to inflate the department's performance statistics.[73]

From the prosecutorial end, sometimes misconduct takes the form of misleading courts and defendants in order to obtain convictions. In prosecuting Blufford Hayes for murder, for example, a California prosecutor cut a deal with another criminal, Andrew James, to dismiss James's pending felony charges in exchange for his testimony against Hayes. James also received immunity against prosecution for his own possible involvement in the murder. The prosecutor then lied to the court, insisting that no deal had been made, and elicited James's perjured testimony in front of the jury.[74]

Similarly, in the effort to obtain a conviction in a gruesome double murder, another California district attorney cut a deal with Norman Thomas, one of the murder defendants who had admitted to dismembering one of the victims. In exchange for Thomas's testimony against his codefendant, the government dropped his murder charges and arranged that Thomas would avoid a psychiatric exam that might have undermined his reliability as a witness. The prosecution concealed this deal from the defense attorney and the court. Thomas's testimony was the sole evidence that the defendant personally committed the murder.[75]

Disturbing stories exist of law enforcement officials who deploy informants for their own personal gain, for example, when Boston police detective David Jordan teamed up with an informant to steal $81,000 worth of cocaine from a drug dealer.[76] But the far more common scenario is that of the agent or prosecutor who bends or breaks the rules on behalf of his source in pursuit of other criminals and cases. In these ways, otherwise well-meaning public officers end up breaking the law in their efforts to fight crime. Because using informants inherently demands the toleration of some levels of criminality, such official lawlessness is a predictable consequence of the practice.

E. Crime Victims

Although one of the central purposes of the criminal system is to provide relief and vindication to crime victims, using criminal informants requires constant compromises with that purpose. As one frustrated victim of Marvin Jeffery's identity-theft scheme put it, "I do everything legally. I vote. My credit is clean. I try to do all the right stuff, follow all the rules. Then there's this guy, driving around in a gold Escalade, laughing it up, cashing my checks."[77]

Releasing dangerous informants inherently poses the risk that they will commit new crimes. Darryl Moore, for example, was a known hit man, drug dealer, robber, rapist, and addict. His history of perjury was so extensive that his own mother indicated that she would not believe him under oath. Nevertheless, in exchange for his testimony in a murder case, Chicago prosecutors offered him a deal: weapons and drug charges against him would be dropped and he would be paid cash. Moore testified in the case, although he later stated that he fabricated his testimony. After his release and his return to his home neighborhood, he attacked an eleven-year-old girl with a gun and raped her.[78]

As trading liability for information becomes an increasingly common law enforcement practice, it desensitizes decision makers to the profound compromises that such practices entail. For example, it is a common drug enforcement practice to excuse property crime or violent offenders who provide drug-related information. Because property and violent crimes have victims, the practice conveys the message to those victims that their personal suffering or need for vindication is less significant than drug enforcement goals. As discussed at length in chapter 5, this problem has reached it zenith in poor, high-crime urban neighborhoods, in which the pervasive use of criminal informants may actually be exacerbating crime and insecurity.

F. Vulnerable Informants

Our penal system has little sympathy for criminal offenders. With the decline of the rehabilitative ideal and the punitive rhetoric of "tough on crime" politics, offenders whose rights are violated or who are physically or psychologically harmed during the criminal process are often perceived to be getting what they deserve for having broken the law in the first place. This hostility contributes to what legal scholar Jonathan Simon calls a "waste management" vision of corrections, in which a growing population of offenders is warehoused in increasingly harsh and dehumanizing conditions.[79]

In the context of informants, this unsympathetic posture has translated into a high tolerance for the risks and harms that often accompany cooperation with the government, even to the point of devaluing informant lives. As Judge Richard Posner of the Seventh Circuit Court of Appeals put it,

> confidential informants often agree to engage in risky undercover work in exchange for leniency, and we cannot think of any reason, especially any reason rooted in constitutional text or doctrine, for creating a categorical prohibition against the informant's incurring [costs such as] the usual risk of being beaten up or for that matter bumped off by a drug dealer with whom one is negotiating a purchase or sale of drugs in the hope of obtaining lenient treatment from the government.[80]

At the extreme, tolerating violence against snitches is dismissive, a way of writing them off. Less harshly, it reflects the assumption that informants and the government bargain on an equal footing and that the risks informants incur are their own responsibility. This assumption, however, overlooks the lopsided power dynamics of the way informants are often created in the first place. Informants can be the most defenseless players in the criminal justice drama—those without counsel or education, those with substance abuse problems, or those who are otherwise susceptible to official pressure. As one sociologist puts it, the creation of an informant "is not a paradigm of simple bargaining between equals but, rather, a complex interaction between personnel of the criminal justice system and vulnerable people."[81]

Indeed, part of the process of creating informants involves the purposeful manipulation of their vulnerability. As Agent Fitzgerald describes it, "The method selected for exerting the pressure [on the informant] varies and is limited only by the imagination, experience, and skill of the investigator."[82] Former narcotics agent Mallory is blunter:

> It is a widely accepted fact that individuals are most vulnerable to becoming cooperative immediately following arrest. . . . [I] learned to "strike" while the "iron is hot." Informants will often rethink their exposure and decide not to cooperate if given too much time to contemplate their decision. However, a night or two in jail can work for the investigator to help the informant decide to cooperate.[83]

As noted above, one of a suspect's most important resources is defense counsel, not only to advise him about how valuable cooperation might be but also to dispel the panic that many suspects feel when confronted with the possibility of prosecution or incarceration. Accordingly, well-represented, educated, well-resourced informants are in a better position to make rational judgments about whether and to what extent to cooperate, or whether to invoke the adversarial process and fight the charges against them. Vulnerable suspects such as addicts, juveniles, people with mental disabilities, or those for whom prison seems life-threatening, are more likely to agree to cooperate even if the benefits are uncertain or small, or the risks very high. They may also be more likely to provide false evidence under pressure to produce information.

Because police and prosecutors have wide leeway in negotiating informant deals, there are few limits to the concessions that can be extracted from cooperative informants. Amy Gepfert, for example, agreed to pose as a prostitute and engage in oral sex with another suspect in order to avoid cocaine charges. The police discouraged her from calling a lawyer and told her that she was facing a forty-year sentence, although in fact her maximum sentence would have been ten years.[84] Police from Portland, Oregon, to Fort Worth, Texas, have been fired for pressuring their drug informants into having sex with them.[85]

The problem of informant vulnerability recently received an unusual dose of public attention. In 2008, 23-year-old Rachel Hoffman, a graduate of Florida State University, was caught with a small amount of drugs, and she became an informant to avoid going to prison. Unbeknownst to her lawyer or family members, she agreed to engage in an undercover sting to buy a gun and a large amount of drugs from two other criminal targets. During the sting, she was killed by those targets.

Hoffman's death elicited public and media sympathy atypical for a criminal informant. ABC News devoted a segment of the show *20/20* to her death. Hoffman was described by friends as "naïve," "dainty," and "fragile," and experts opined that she should not have been used in such a dangerous operation. Commentators speculated that because she was female, educated, white, and attractive, she did not seem like the kind of criminal offender that people usually associate with drug dealing or other dangerous behavior.[86] Moreover, unlike the parents of many offenders, Mr. and Mrs. Hoffman had the personal wherewithal to publicly decry the government's treatment of their daughter, file a lawsuit, and lobby for new legislation to protect vulnerable informants like Rachel.[87] That legislative effort is discussed in more detail in chapter 8.

To be sure, not all criminal informants are vulnerable in these ways. Mafia hit men, international drug dealers, and high-level political operatives with well-paid defense attorneys have a wealth of resources at their disposal in negotiating with the government. Indeed, some of the worst debacles described in this book are the result of the government's inability to control such informants. But for the typical street offender or indigent suspect sitting in a jail cell, without counsel or other resources, all too often in the throes of substance abuse, the government can be a formidable opponent indeed. Such suspects may become informants out of fear, ignorance, and their perception that they have no choice.

G. Witness Intimidation and the Spread of Violence

"For real, little sis, you better not be snitching," Franklin M. Thompson told 14-year-old Jahkema Princess Hansen in Washington, D.C. A bystander said that Thompson made the remark after the teenager demanded to be paid in exchange for saying nothing about a killing she had witnessed five days earlier. Hours later, Hansen was shot dead.[88]

Witness intimidation is linked to informant use in a variety of ways. Criminal informants are routinely subject to threats or harm if they are perceived as snitches. To a lesser degree, civilian witnesses may also experience threats, or the fear of retaliation, when they agree to cooperate in a criminal case. While civilian witnesses and criminal informants inhabit very different worlds, the violence associated with criminal snitching has spilled over into the realm of civilian witnessing.

Witness intimidation is an increasingly public problem. Police and prosecutors in numerous cities have stated that it is difficult to get witnesses to serious crimes to come forward.[89] Many existing aspects of the criminal system are responses to this form of informant-related violence, from witness protection programs to solitary confinement provisions for cooperating inmates. The witness intimidation problem is discussed at length in chapter 6 in relation to the "stop snitching" phenomenon.

Witness intimidation, however, is just one of the ways in which using informants creates and spreads violence. The widespread culture of
snitching promotes violence against informants themselves; it tolerates
violence against victims of crimes perpetrated by informants; and it exacerbates violence against innocent bystanders who must live cheek-by-
jowl with the violent methods used by gangs to police themselves against
betrayal from the inside. For example, sixteen-year-old Martha Puebla
was killed by Los Angeles gang members because police misinformed
Jose Ledesma, a murder suspect, that Puebla had identified him and was
cooperating with the police. In fact, Puebla had told the police that she
had not seen Ledesma, but police forged Puebla's signature on a fake
photo array and showed it to Ledesma in order to pressure him to confess. Instead of confessing, Ledesma ordered Puebla's murder.[90]

Indeed, nearly every informant story contained in this book constitutes an example of informant-related violence, from snitch Darryl
Moore's attack on his eleven-year-old victim to the death of 92-year-
old Kathryn Johnston at the hands of Atlanta police operating on a
bad informant tip. One sociological study concludes that "snitching
is a pervasive element of inner-city street life that poses dangers for
street criminals and law-abiding residents alike."[91] Increases in violence are thus a particularly devastating cost of informant policies.

H. Systemic Integrity and Trust

The final set of implications associated with informant use has to do
with the perceived legitimacy of the criminal system itself. Law enforcement depends on the trust, acceptance, and cooperation of the
people and communities that it polices. Without that trust and acceptance, the entire system breaks down.[92]

Informant use erodes public trust in the criminal system in numerous ways that are explored throughout this book. For example, the
fact that more culpable offenders routinely receive lesser sentences
undermines the public sense of the system's fairness and evenhand-
edness. That violent and destructive offenders may be permitted to
remain at large is frightening to law-abiding citizens. The deterrent
effect of the law itself is eroded by the fact that, as one court put it,

"[n]ever has it been more true than it is now that a criminal charged with a serious crime understands that a fast and easy way out of trouble with the law is . . . to cut a deal at someone else's expense."[93]

The tragedy of Jahkema Princess Hansen's death reveals another kind of destructiveness: the fourteen-year-old's jaded understanding that justice is for sale, and that if she cooperated with criminals she would be paid, in precisely the same way that police pay criminals for their cooperation. More generally, that police appear to prize information over the immediate apprehension of criminal offenders can shake public faith in the police, a phenomenon discussed in chapters 5 and 6. Finally, the secrecy surrounding informant use exacerbates all these problems, obscuring the real costs as well as benefits of informant use, and driving a wedge between the law enforcement officials who use informants and the public who must live with the consequences.[94]

In all these ways, informant use inflicts significant wounds on the integrity of the criminal process, even as it contributes to the law enforcement project in unique and sometimes powerful ways. The remainder of this book explores this conundrum.

CHAPTER 2

To Catch a Thief

The Legal Rules of Snitching

> Courts have countenanced the use of informers from time immemorial;
> in cases of conspiracy, or in other cases when the crime consists of prepar-
> ing for another crime, it is usually necessary to rely on them or upon ac-
> complices because the criminals will almost certainly proceed covertly.
> —Judge Learned Hand[1]

FROM THE OUTSIDE, informant use often looks like a game without rules, in which everything is negotiable and no law is sacrosanct.
This state of affairs is a direct function of what I will call "informant
law": that body of laws and court doctrines that define the legal parameters of the relationship between informants and the government.
"Informant law" is centrally characterized by official discretion and
flexibility, the inapplicability of many traditional criminal procedure
constraints, and the overt toleration of criminal behavior and secrecy.
In other words, the official rules of the informant game are that the
usual rules do not apply.

The legal rules governing criminal informants fall roughly into
four categories. One set covers police and prosecutorial authority
to create and reward informants, to persuade offenders to become
informants, and to let them off the hook when they cooperate.
Another set governs the way informants may be deployed as investigative tools against third parties. A third set defines the procedural protections and information to which defendants are entitled when faced with evidence obtained from an informant. And
finally, a narrow group of rules sets limits, telling the government
what it cannot do in connection with or to its informants.

Each of these arenas has its own laws regarding record keeping and disclosure. Taken together, the informational rules regarding snitching have such a potent effect on the rest of the criminal system that chapter 4 is separately devoted to them.

I. Creating and Rewarding Criminal Informants

Police and prosecutors have vast discretion to create and reward informants. Central to this discretion is the authority to tolerate or authorize crimes committed by those informants. There are few legal limits on the extent to which government officials can reduce a criminal's potential liability or punishment in exchange for information, or, conversely, to increase liability when a defendant refuses to cooperate.

A. Police

As described in chapter 1, police, detectives, and investigative agents are the main officials who typically create and manage informants. It is initially up to them to decide whether to arrest or flip a suspect, to evaluate the potential usefulness of a source, and to convey information about the informant to the prosecutor. An informant and his law enforcement handler may maintain a relationship over many years, with the informant providing ongoing information in exchange for his handler's help in evading criminal liability.[2]

When an officer first confronts a potential informant, prior to an arrest or formal criminal charge, there are very few legal constraints. For example, a suspect's right to receive Miranda warnings is triggered only if he is in custody, so if the suspect has not yet been taken into custody or arrested, his unwarned statements to police can potentially be used against him.[3] Similarly, the Sixth Amendment right to counsel applies only once a suspect has been formally charged with a crime, so police can legally—and often do—negotiate directly with uncharged suspects without a lawyer.[4] As a result, police have wide latitude to confront, threaten, and negotiate with potential informants without the presence of defense counsel or other witnesses.

Police can legally reward informants in a variety of ways. They can refrain from arresting him in the first place, thereby permitting the informant to remain at liberty without creating an arrest or other record of the suspected offense. If they do arrest the informant, police can limit the initial description of the crimes or omit other information. For example, in *United States v. White*, the court described how Officer Mike Weaver manipulated the report writing process as part of his negotiations with a suspect:

> Weaver stated that if defendant cooperated with the questioning, Weaver would write the police report to reflect only a charge of possessing drug paraphernalia, a misdemeanor, and that if defendant did not cooperate, he would send the glass pipe [containing methamphetamines] to the crime lab and charge defendant with felony drug possession. These matters were entirely within Weaver's control, and in fact he fulfilled the promise: after defendant made the statements, Weaver wrote the police report to reflect only a misdemeanor charge.[5]

This discretionary police power translates into the practical ability to forgive informant crimes, simply by declining to arrest informants or by failing to record their conduct. This authority is rooted in constitutional law: the Supreme Court has held that no one can force police to arrest a criminal offender.[6]

Police also have the power to permit informants to commit new crimes, and police departments each handle this thorny question differently. Some agencies deny that active informants are permitted to commit crimes at all. For example, the police department in Eureka, California, along with several other California police departments, maintains a standard written policy stating that "criminal activity by informants shall not be condoned."[7] The Las Vegas Police Department informant guidelines state that "[c]riminal law shall not be violated in gathering of information," even though those same guidelines provide procedures for the purchase of "evidence" such as illegal drugs.[8]

By contrast, the U.S. Department of Justice has issued several sets of comprehensive guidelines governing the way the FBI and other federal investigative agencies handle informants. These guidelines designate "Tier 1" and "Tier 2 Otherwise Illegal Activity" that can be authorized by the handler. Tier 1 Otherwise Illegal Activity includes violent crimes committed by someone other than the informant, official corruption, theft, and the manufacture or distribution of drugs, including the provision of drugs with no expectation of recovering them. Tier 2 activity includes all other criminal offenses. The guidelines state that informants may never be authorized to participate in an act of violence except in self-defense, to obstruct justice, to commit illegal acts that would be unlawful if committed by a law enforcement official, such as breaking and entering, or to initiate a plan to commit a criminal offense. The guidelines also provide that illegal activity by confidential informants must be authorized in advance, in writing, and for a specific period of time, and that the authorizing agent must make a determination that "the benefits outweigh the risks."[9]

Police and investigative agents do not have the legal authority to bind prosecutors. This means that police cannot confer so-called immunity, i.e., they cannot promise informants that they will not be prosecuted for a crime they did or will commit.[10] But courts occasionally give weight to such promises anyway, on the theory that it is unfair to informants who reasonably believed that they would not be prosecuted for crimes they committed in order to provide the government with information. For example, in *United States v. Abcasis*, the defendants claimed that government agents authorized their heroin importation scheme. The court reasoned that

> [i]f a drug enforcement agent solicits a defendant to engage in otherwise criminal conduct as a confidential informant, or effectively communicates an assurance that the defendant is acting under authorization, and the defendant, relying thereon, commits forbidden acts in the mistaken but reasonable, good faith belief that he has in fact been authorized to do so as an aid to law enforcement, then estoppel bars conviction.[11]

The Federal Rules of Criminal Procedure even have a special provision governing cases where defendants allege that they committed their crimes with "public authority," meaning that the government authorized them to do it.[12]

If police do arrest an informant, file a complaint, or otherwise initiate criminal proceedings, then a prosecutor becomes in charge of that informant's case. At this stage, the defendant acquires the right to counsel, which means that police and prosecutor alike are not supposed to try to elicit further incriminating information without the lawyer's presence.[13] For this reason, charged defendants constitute an important subgroup of criminal informants because they are represented by counsel and therefore tend to cooperate in more formal, better-documented ways.

B. Prosecutors

Prosecutors have near-absolute discretion over charging decisions.[14] This means they can add, drop, or alter criminal charges in exchange for cooperation from a defendant.[15] Prosecutors can also confer formal or statutory immunity from prosecution pursuant to various immunity statutes, or confer informal immunity by entering into written agreements in which they promise not to pursue certain charges in exchange for a witness's testimony. Statutory immunity agreements are binding on prosecutors in other jurisdictions as well, although informal negotiated immunity grants may not be binding.[16] In practice, prosecutors are often willing to drop or reduce charges against someone who is cooperating with law enforcement in other jurisdictions, although this may depend on the seriousness of the new offense.

Prosecutors can also charge third parties, such as family members, in order to pressure a defendant to cooperate. This is sometimes referred to as a "wired plea" because the outcome of the family member's case is attached or "wired" to the defendant's cooperation.[17]

In deciding whether to turn a defendant into an informant, prosecutors may negotiate with defense counsel over a defendant's cooperation, potential charges, and sentencing concessions. They may also seek more information from the defendant before they decide.[18] Often the prosecutor and the defense will agree to postpone the case while the defendant tries to "work off" his charges by obtaining more information or generating new suspects.[19]

If a defendant does not want to cooperate, prosecutors can charge him with more serious offenses in order to induce a plea or cooperation. If the defendant remains uncooperative, the Supreme Court has held that the government can seek and a court can impose harsher punishment.[20]

In an example that became nationally infamous, Kemba Smith was charged with drug conspiracy in order to pressure her to testify against her boyfriend, a suspected drug dealer. Because she did not cooperate, she received a 24-year sentence even though she had no prior record and had never handled or sold any drugs herself. She served six years before her sentence was commuted by President William Clinton in 2000.[21]

Prosecutorial charging decisions are unreviewable by courts. The only exception is where there is clear evidence that a prosecutor has charged someone on an impermissible basis such as race, vindictiveness, or to punish the defendant for exercising his constitutional rights.[22] In the context of negotiating with informants, prosecutors have near-complete latitude.

C. Sentencing and the U.S. Sentencing Guidelines

Once a defendant has been convicted— typically as a result of pleading guilty—he can seek a lower sentence from the court for having cooperated with the government. The general theory is that a defendant who has been helpful to the government has mitigated his crime and shown some remorse, and therefore should be punished less harshly. Judges routinely impose lower sentences on defendants who have cooperated. In some jurisdictions, judges may do so however they see fit as a matter of sentencing discretion.[23] In other jurisdictions, notably in federal court, sentencing is governed by "guidelines" that tell judges what kinds of sentences they should impose. Such guidelines typically have special provisions authorizing judges to award lower sentences to cooperating defendants.[24] In Virginia, for example, the fact that a defendant "cooperated with authorities" is the reason most often given by courts in justifying the reduction of a sentence.[25]

Twenty years ago, Congress created special sentencing statutes and the U.S. Sentencing Guidelines, which have strongly influenced the law and culture of federal cooperation. First, as part of the war on drugs, Congress established high mandatory minimum sentences for drug crimes that can only be avoided through cooperation. It also created sentencing guidelines to guide all federal judges. The guidelines set presumptive sentences as well as a system of "departures" through which courts can impose higher or lower sentences than those contemplated by the guidelines. Because these provisions make cooperation central to a defendant's ability to get a lower sentence, they turned cooperation into a dominant feature of federal plea bargaining and sentencing, ensuring that a large percentage of federal defendants become informants of one kind or another.[26] More federal defendants receive departures, namely, reduced sentences, on the basis of their cooperation than for any other reason, and they do so in every category of federal offense, including child pornography and murder, although drug offenders constitute the largest class of cooperators, with one-quarter of all drug offenders receiving lower sentences.[27] Moreover, many more defendants cooperate and never receive public credit at all.[28]

The first way in which the federal system promotes cooperation is by permitting courts to impose sentences below the minimum sentence prescribed by statute if the government files a motion stating that a defendant has provided "substantial assistance." The statute reads,

> Upon motion of the Government, the court shall have the authority to impose a sentence below a level established by statute as a minimum sentence so as to reflect a defendant's substantial assistance in the investigation or prosecution of another person who has committed an offense.[29]

This provision is crucial because the statutory minimum sentences contained in the U.S. criminal code—especially for drug sentences—can be extremely high. For example, an offender charged with manufacturing five grams of crack cocaine (less than the weight of two sugar packets) faces a mandatory sentence of at least five years.[30] The only way such an offender can obtain a lower sentence for that offense is by providing the government with "substantial assistance."[31]

Separate and apart from these statutory requirements, the U.S. Sentencing Guidelines have a specific provision governing cooperation rewards. The provision is referred to as section 5K1.1 and it reads, "Upon motion of the government stating that the defendant has provided substantial assistance in the investigation or prosecution of another person who has committed an offense, the court may depart from the guidelines."[32] Typically, when the government is satisfied with a defendant's cooperation, the prosecutor will file a motion—often referred to as a "5K" motion—acknowledging the defendant's substantial assistance. The judge will then consider the motion in deciding whether to reduce a defendant's sentence below the range recommended by the guidelines.

Under old Supreme Court case law, courts had very little discretion to depart below the guidelines. Moreover, courts could not depart based on a defendant's cooperation unless the prosecution filed a motion.[33] This made cooperation one of the only ways in which a defendant could obtain a lower sentence. But the Court recently decided three cases that upended many aspects of guideline sentencing—*United States v. Booker, Gall v. United States,* and *Kimbrough v. United States.*[34] These cases held that courts may not increase sentences based on facts that have not been decided by a jury, a central feature of guideline sentencing. As a result, the U.S. Sentencing Guidelines were rendered merely advisory and no longer constrain federal judges as they used to. In particular, sentencing courts may consider a wide range of factors that they previously could not, such as a defendant's personal history or the proportionality of the punishment to the defendant's culpability. While sentencing courts must still calculate guideline sentences and use them as a "starting point and the initial benchmark," courts are free to impose sentences above or below the guidelines as long as they are adequately explained and justified.[35]

It is too early to tell what the full impact of these new cases will be on federal cooperation and sentencing. On the one hand, because courts can now impose lower sentences on any basis, cooperation is no longer the only realistic way in which a defendant can obtain a below-the-guidelines sentence. But cooperation remains powerful in many ways. First and foremost, sentencing departures are not the only benefits available to cooperators: their charges may be dropped or reduced before they ever get to sentencing. Federal defendants must also cooperate if they want a sentence below the statutory mandatory minimum. Moreover, even after *Gall* and *Kimbrough*, judges must still calculate the guidelines in setting sentences and so cooperation will remain a valuable commodity in persuading judges to impose lower sentences and in justifying those sentences. Interestingly, cooperating defendants can now circumvent the prosecution and bring evidence of their cooperation directly to the judge, even if the government does not file a 5K motion. As a result, courts are likely to play a greater role in evaluating and rewarding defendant cooperation.[36]

The Federal Rules of Criminal Procedure contain an additional provision that makes defendant cooperation even more valuable. Rule 35 is entitled "Correcting or Reducing a Sentence," and it permits courts to reduce sentences after they have been set, sometimes years after, as a reward for a defendant's further cooperation. Rule 35 reads in part,

(1) In General. Upon the government's motion made within one year of sentencing, the court may reduce a sentence if the defendant, after sentencing, provided substantial assistance in investigating or prosecuting another person.

(2) Later Motion. Upon the government's motion made more than one year after sentencing, the court may reduce a sentence if the defendant's substantial assistance involved:

(A) information not known to the defendant until one year or more after sentencing;

(B) information provided by the defendant to the government within one year of sentencing, but which did not become useful to the government until more than one year after sentencing; or

(C) information the usefulness of which could not reasonably have been anticipated by the defendant until more than one year after sentencing and which was promptly provided to the government after its usefulness was reasonably apparent to the defendant.

Rule 35 thus permits a sentenced defendant to continue to try to provide information to the government, even while he is incarcerated, in an effort to reduce his sentence. Some judges have publicly complained of the dangers inherent in this arrangement, pointing out that it encourages jailhouse snitches to fabricate information.[37]

In sum, the use of informants plays a powerful role during sentencing, and at least in the federal system, this is true by legislative design. Defendants, lawyers, and judges alike all recognize that the defendant's eventual sentence may depend heavily on whether he provides information to the government. This realization influences investigations, plea negotiations, legal strategies, disclosure rules, and all sorts of other decisions that shape sentencing and beyond.

D. Additional Benefits: Money and Drugs

Informants often work for money. The FBI and DEA have budgets of millions of dollars for paying informants—in 1993, federal agencies paid informants approximately $100 million.[38] Informants can also receive up to $500,000 or 25 percent of the take in a drug bust or seizures of other property or cash, whichever is less, though the rules of forfeiture.[39] For example, Rob Roy was facing up to eighty years' imprisonment for cocaine distribution in Philadelphia. Instead, as a result of his substantial cooperation with the FBI over four years, he eventually received a sentence of five years' probation, a $100,000 lump sum payment, and $84,424.77 to cover expenses.[40] Local police departments typically pay small-time informants through vouchers or in cash.[41]

Police also give drugs directly to informants, legally as well as illegally. The legal justification for doing so is to give informants the ability to set up deals. But some police admit that informants "skim" drugs from buys, or that police give small amounts of cash to addict-informants knowing that the money will be used for drugs. Sometimes police even give addict-informants drugs directly in exchange for information.[42]

II. Using Informants as Investigative Tools

The U.S. Constitution places significant limits on the government's ability to obtain and use incriminating information. Under the Fourth Amendment, for example, the government cannot engage in unreasonable searches and seizures, the government must get a warrant for certain kinds of searches, and the government needs a certain amount of evidence—"reasonable suspicion" or "probable cause"—before police can stop or arrest or otherwise deprive individuals of their liberty. The Fifth Amendment privilege against self-incrimination, famously embodied in Miranda warnings, protects suspects against being pressured to provide information. The Sixth Amendment right to counsel means that once a defendant has been charged with a crime, the government cannot question him or her without the presence of defense counsel.[43] Federal and state law further regulates the government's ability to obtain records or to deploy in private places bugs, wiretaps, video cameras, and other types of surveillance.[44]

These rules, particularly those in the Bill of Rights, famously protect individuals against official coercion and invasions of privacy. But the government's ability to use informants is a powerful and often easy way to circumvent many of these restrictions. Because these constitutional restraints generally apply only to official actors, a private individual acting as an informant can obtain information that the government could not easily obtain on its own. Criminal informants are thus potent investigative tools, not only because they can be effective information gatherers but also because they are exempt from many of the rules that otherwise constrain official investigative techniques.

In a seminal 1966 case, the Supreme Court decided that the governmental use of a compensated criminal informant is constitutionally permissible. That case—*Hoffa v. United States*—upheld the government's use of Edward Partin, a corrupt union official, to eavesdrop on Teamster president Jimmy Hoffa's conversations with his associates and attorney. The government had recruited Partin out of a Louisiana jail where he was facing state and federal charges of embezzlement and other crimes. Because Hoffa invited Partin into his private hotel room, unaware that he was working for the government, the Court held that Hoffa had assumed the risk that the informant would share the information he learned and therefore that Hoffa's right to privacy under the Fourth Amendment was not violated. As the Court put it, "The risk of being overheard by an eavesdropper or betrayed by an informer or deceived as to the identity of one with whom one deals is probably inherent in the conditions of human society. It is the kind of risk we necessarily assume whenever we speak."[45]

The Court also explained that the government's use of Partin to obtain Hoffa's incriminating statements did not trigger Hoffa's Fifth Amendment's protection again self-incrimination, because Hoffa was never officially compelled to speak. In *Illinois v. Perkins*, the Court went further, holding that an incarcerated defendant questioned by a jailhouse informant at the government's instigation did not have the right to be given Miranda warnings or to obtain counsel, even though he would have if the exact same questioning had been conducted openly by police. The Court reasoned that because the defendant did not know the snitch was acting as a government agent, he was not being coerced to confess in an impermissible way.[46]

After *Hoffa*, the Supreme Court further approved the extension of the government's use of informants through the use of technology. In *United States v. White*, the Court held that the warrantless use of a "wired" informant—i.e., an informant wearing a transmitter permitting police to hear the conversation—did not violate the defendant's Fourth Amendment privacy rights, even though one of the transmissions took place in his home. In dissent, Justice Douglas worried that the Court had missed the significance of the new technological advances. "Electronic surveillance," he wrote, "is the greatest leveler of human privacy ever known. . . . [M]ust everyone [now] live in fear that every word he speaks may be transmitted or recorded and later repeated to the entire world?" Also in dissent, Justice Harlan opined that "the practice of third-party bugging, must, I think, be considered such as to undermine that confidence and sense of security in dealing with one another that is characteristic of individual relationships between citizens in a free society."[47]

The convergence of informant use and new technologies has opened the door to even more intrusive and powerful forms of surveillance. Federal law imposes significant restrictions on official use of electronic surveillance, requiring police to obtain a court order before intercepting communications. A court may not approve a request for electronic surveillance unless it makes numerous findings, including a finding that that there is probable cause that a crime is being committed and that "normal investigative procedures have been tried and have failed or reasonably appear to be unlikely to succeed if tried or to be too dangerous."[48] But the federal electronic surveillance statute, typically referred to as "Title III," contains an exception for one-party consent, so that if an informant is party to the communication and consents to the recording, there is no need for court authorization. In other words, while the government must get a court order before it can wiretap a phone or place a camera in a private place such as a home or hotel room, it does not need a warrant to wire an informant to record communications or videotape in those same private spaces.[49] For example, in *United States v. Nerber*, the Ninth Circuit Court of Appeals held that the government could place a video camera in a hotel room with the consent of the informants who were inside, although once the informants left the room, it was no longer permissible to videotape the occupants absent a warrant.[50]

Thirty-two states follow Title III by authorizing one-party consent to electronic surveillance. A few states, however, have held that informant electronic surveillance in a person's home or other private places requires more regulation. The West Virginia Supreme Court has held that in contrast to federal constitutional and statutory law, the West Virginia Constitution prohibits wired informants from videotaping or recording transactions in an individual's home without a warrant.[51] Similarly, the supreme courts of Montana, Vermont, Massachusetts, Alaska, and Pennsylvania have all held that, under their respective state constitutions, wired informant surveillance in a suspect's home requires a warrant.[52]

III. Defendant Rights against Official Informant Use

For defendants who are charged with a crime based on evidence from a criminal informant, the central protections are informational and procedural. The government must turn over certain kinds of information about its informants, usually referred to as "discovery," and defendants can in turn use this information to challenge the veracity and credibility of informants in front of the jury or sometimes before a judge.

In *Brady v. Maryland*, the Supreme Court held that as a matter of fundamental due process, the government must provide the defendant with all "evidence favorable to an accused . . . where the evidence is material either to guilt or to punishment."[53] Evidence is considered "material" if it is reasonably likely to affect the outcome.[54] In *Giglio v. United States*, the Court held that evidence impeaching a government witness's credibility—i.e., evidence indicating that the witness might be lying—constitutes a form of *Brady* material and therefore must be disclosed as well.[55] The specific impeachment material at issue in *Giglio* was the government's undisclosed promise to its criminal informant witness not to prosecute him in return for his testimony.[56] Typical impeachment material also includes the informant's prior inconsistent statements, his criminal record, benefits conferred on the informant by the government in exchange for information in the instant case, and the informant's history of testimony and rewards in other cases.

More recently, the Court has restricted these informant disclosure requirements. In *United States v. Ruiz*, the Court held that the government need not produce *Giglio* material to a defendant before the entry of a guilty plea, but only if the defendant decides to proceed to trial.[57] This means that if a defendant goes to trial, he is entitled to information about informant witnesses, but if he pleads guilty—as do approximately 90–95 percent of all defendants[58]—he may never see that information. The implications of this increased secrecy are discussed in chapter 4.

State courts, as well as approximately one-third of federal districts, have specific rules governing *Brady* disclosures. Many states and districts simply track the constitutional requirements, but others impose deadlines and other additional procedures. Of the federal districts, Massachusetts has some of the most expansive discovery requirements: among other things it requires prosecutors to provide "a statement whether any promise, reward, or inducement has been given to any witness whom the government anticipates calling in its case-in-chief, identifying by name each such witness and each promise, reward, or inducement, and a copy of any promise, reward, or inducement reduced to writing."[59]

Sometimes the government will want to withhold the identity of an informant for protective or investigative reasons. During the investigative phase of a case, this so-called informers privilege is strong. For example, the police need not reveal the identity of an informer who provides them with information leading to an arrest or a warrant.[60] At trial, the privilege is more limited. The government may "withhold from disclosure the identity of persons who furnish information of violations of law to officers charged with enforcement of that law" only if the court decides that the government's need to withhold outweighs the defendant's right to a fair trial. "Where the disclosure of an informer's identity, or of the contents of his communication, is relevant and helpful to the defense of an accused, or is essential to a fair determination of a cause, the privilege must give way."[61] In deciding whether the government may withhold that information, the court must "balance[e] the public interest in protecting the flow of information against the individual's right to prepare his defense." If the government refuses to disclose information necessary to a fair trial, the court may dismiss the case.[62] In addition, the Confrontation Clause of the Sixth Amendment guarantees defendants the right to cross-examine witnesses and therefore limits the government's ability to use evidence from confidential informants at trial without actually producing the informant in person.[63]

Congress has restricted the federal government's obligation to disclose an additional form of informant-related material: prior witness statements. Under the Jencks Act, federal prosecutors need not produce a witness's prior statements until after the witness has testified on direct examination.[64] Such prior statements might include inconsistent statements, admissions of perjury or recantations of prior assertions, admissions of the falsity of other statements, or statements regarding the defendant.

Because of growing concerns regarding informant unreliability, a few states have imposed additional discovery and disclosure obligations on the government when it wants to use a criminal informant as a witness. For example, Illinois passed a law that requires additional discovery and a "reliability hearing" whenever the government seeks to use an in-custody informant, or "jailhouse snitch," as a witness in any capital case.[65] Texas law requires that informant testimony be corroborated.[66] In 2007, the California Commission on the Fair Administration of Justice proposed a law that would have required corroboration of the testimony of all in-custody informants. The legislature enacted the bill twice, but it was vetoed both times by Governor Arnold Schwarzenegger.[67] Over the past few years, the American Bar Association, numerous public interest organizations, and innocence projects have advocated heightened scrutiny of informant testimony, and an increasing number of states have considered imposing new rules.[68] These reforms are discussed in chapter 8.

IV. Legal Limits: What the Government Can't Do

As this survey reveals, there are few legal limits on the government's authority to create, reward, and use informants. Police and prosecutors have broad discretion to forgive informant crime, to offer lenience and other rewards, to deploy informants to obtain information against others, and to keep information about the process out of the hands of defendants and off the public record.

One federal appellate court briefly considered limiting prosecutorial authority. In 1998, in *United States v. Singleton*, the government promised Napoleon Douglas reduced charges and other sentencing benefits as a reward for his testimony against Sonya Singleton. A panel of the Tenth Circuit held that this reward essentially constituted a bribe, and that prosecutors could not pay witnesses in this way without violating the federal antigratuity act, which prohibits providing "anything of value" to a testifying witness. The full Tenth

Circuit court reversed, holding that this provision against bribery did not apply to prosecutors.[69]

There are, however, some things the government may not do. For example, if a police officer lies in a warrant application about an informant's tip, it may invalidate the warrant. If a prosecutor knowingly uses a lying informant to obtain a conviction or permits an informant to lie about his reward for testifying, the case may be dismissed.[70] Because proving such falsehoods after the fact is extremely difficult, however, such rules provide few practical controls.[71]

In addition, the government may not use an informant in a way that constitutes "outrageous government conduct."[72] Courts rarely consider the official use of informants to be outrageous, but it occasionally happens in extreme cases. For example, in *United States v. Twigg*, the court reversed a conviction for drug manufacture because the government, through its informant, had so thoroughly set up the defendant. The informant had provided the defendant with key ingredients for the drug, a place to manufacture it, and chemical expertise, all of which was paid for by the government. The court considered this level of government promotion of crime fundamentally unfair to the defendant, who, as the court said, was "lawfully and peacefully minding his own affairs" before the informant came along.[73]

In a related doctrine, law enforcement cannot use an informant to entrap a defendant into committing a crime, as long as that defendant is not predisposed to commit the crime in the first place. More typically, however, courts find that the government can use informants to promote, support, assist, and encourage people to commit crimes, and still prosecute those people later.[74] For example, the FBI used Helen Miller—a prostitute, heroin addict, and fugitive from Canadian drug charges—as an informant to investigate Darrel Simpson. Over the course of five months, Miller had sex with Simpson and pretended to be his girlfriend in order to obtain evidence against him. The court held that neither the use of deceptive sexual intimacy as against Simpson nor the manipulation of Miller into having sex in order to escape criminal charges herself nor Miller's continued illegal drug and prostitution activities while serving as an informant constituted outrageous government conduct.[75]

When the government uses an informant in a way that violates a defendant's rights, the typical remedy is to overturn the conviction. Whether the government can also be sued civilly—either by defendants or others—is a separate question that depends on the nature of the violation and whether the government actor is immune from suit.

Sometimes an informant will hurt people in the course of cooperating with the government. While courts have been reluctant to characterize informants as government employees,[76] where informants act with the knowledge and acquiescence of their government handlers, they may qualify as government agents subject to the same constitutional restrictions as other official actors, thus rendering the government liable for their actions.[77] Private parties cannot, however, force the government to prosecute its bad informants, or sue the government for failing to do so.[78]

Some individuals harmed by informants have sued the federal government under the Federal Tort Claims Act, with varying results. In *Ostera v. United States*, the court found no governmental liability for the FBI's decision to release an informant with known violent tendencies. By contrast, in *Luizzo v. United States*, the court found that the government was potentially liable for authorizing an informant to participate in an operation that led to the death of another.[79]

What if police harm an informant or otherwise violate his or her rights? Police have qualified immunity from suit, which means that they are not liable if "their conduct does not violate clearly established statutory or constitutional rights of which a reasonable person would have known."[80] For example, police lied to Amy Gepfert about her potential sentence in order to pressure her to perform oral sex on another suspect. She complied in order to avoid drug charges, but later sued the police for having coerced her into having sex in this way. Even though the court found that the police might have violated Gepfert's rights by using threats and fraud to get her to have sex, it found that the police were immune from suit because the right was not clearly established at the time in a way that a reasonable police officer would have known.[81] The court was also careful to note that not all threats or frauds will render such arrangements illegal, and that in general there is no rule against police obtaining sex-related or other dangerous or distasteful cooperation from a suspect who wants to avoid criminal charges.[82] Similarly, in *Shuler v. United States*, the court held that an informant who was shot in the back because the FBI blew his cover, and then failed to protect him as promised, nevertheless could not recover damages from the government under the Federal Tort Claims Act.[83]

Prosecutors are absolutely immune from suit—and therefore cannot be sued civilly at all—for decisions or conduct that is "intimately associated with the judicial phase of the criminal process," such as initiating a case and deciding what charges to file, what evidence and which witnesses to use, and what arguments to make. This includes knowingly using false evidence or lying criminal informants in a particular case, even when such use leads to a wrongful conviction.[84]

However, prosecutors do more than merely charge and litigate existing cases. They may initiate or direct investigations, select potential targets, and otherwise work hand in hand with law enforcement agents. Courts have found that when prosecutors act administratively or like investigative agents, they relinquish their absolutely immunity from civil suit, and may be sued for things they do while "advising the police during the investigative phase of a criminal case" or performing investigative acts generally considered functions of the police.[85]

In sum, while governmental liability for informant misconduct is limited, there remain a number of legal theories under which the government might be held responsible for the informants it deploys.

V. Informant Use in Comparative Perspective

The United States permits law enforcement to use criminal informants more freely subject to less regulation than do many other countries. These differences highlight some fundamental policy choices adopted by American law enforcement and courts. One is the tolerance of high levels of informant unreliability. Another is the notion—central to the practice of plea bargaining—that it is permissible to trade away criminal liability for information. Another is reflected in the governmental acceptance of, and even engagement in, ongoing criminal activity. These are controversial precepts that many other nations have resisted or declined to accept altogether.[86] As law professor Jacqueline Ross explains with respect to Europe in particular, "The United States and European nations conceptualize, legitimate, and control undercover policing in substantially dissimilar ways."[87]

For some countries, the unreliability associated with informants has made them a highly disfavored tool. In 1997, for example, the government of Ontario, Canada, appointed a commission to review the wrongful murder conviction of Guy Paul Morin. After hearings that lasted over five months and called 120 witnesses, the Kaufman Commission concluded that Morin's wrongful conviction was due in large part to the testimony of two jailhouse informants who fabricated evidence that Morin had confessed to the murder. The commission also found that "the systemic evidence emanating from Canada, Great Britain, Australia and the United States demonstrated that the dangers associated with jailhouse informants were not unique to the Morin case. Indeed, a number of miscarriages of justice throughout the world are likely explained, at least in part, by the false self-serving evidence given by such informants." The commission issued dozens of recommendations for reform, including limiting the use and reward of informants, increased disclosure, and improved police and prosecutorial training.[88] As a result of the commission's recommendations, the Canadian attorney general established new policies limiting jailhouse informant use.[89]

For other countries, the covert practices associated with informant use are considered legally or even morally problematic. Methods such as the "bust-and-buy" sting and informant lenience deals, while standard in the United States and United Kingdom,[90] have been resisted by other European countries, often on the principle that the government should neither engage in criminal conduct nor tolerate it. Well into the 1970s, "[t]hroughout most of continental Europe, . . . virtually all these [undercover] techniques were viewed, even by police officials, as unnecessary, unacceptable, and often illegal." Today, many European countries engage in some form of these tactics, but to a lesser degree than does American law enforcement.[91]

In the Netherlands, for example, the Dutch began adopting American-style undercover tactics in the 1970s. In the 1990s, the government was rocked by scandal when it was revealed that police and highly paid criminal informants were actively running drug operations, importing tons of drugs into the country, some of which were released onto the streets. The resulting Parliamentary Inquiry from 1995 to 1996 led to significant restrictions on law enforcement authority to use criminal informants and to engage in U.S.-style undercover operations.[92]

Central to the Dutch public debate over informant use has been the contrast with American practices. According to Police Commissioner René Karstens, Dutch and American law enforcement take fundamentally different approaches to questions of informant legality and the need for regulation: "the philosophies on infiltration [by informants] were rather divergent. Where we [Dutch] feel that certain limitations are needed on infiltration as a method, the Americans are inclined to let the end justify the means. With them anything goes."[93]

In Italy, criminal informant use is broadly constrained by the "concern that undercover operations might corrode the rule of law by enabling police to engage in 'crime.'" If they have not obtained explicit authorization, Italian law enforcement officials may be prosecuted for crimes they commit or permit in pursuit of criminal targets and investigations. In order to permit some undercover investigations, Italian law thus contains a series of narrow exceptions that relieve police of criminal liability for specific acts such as the simulated drug buy, or postponing arrests and seizures for investigative purposes—acts that would otherwise be deemed illegal police conduct.[94] Under U.S. law, by contrast, such decisions are committed to law enforcement discretion without threat of criminal liability.

Similarly, the legal culture in Germany includes a prohibition against the official toleration of lawbreaking. In 1992, under pressure to permit greater use of undercover tactics, Germany passed reforms designed to legitimize a limited form of undercover policing. Those reforms permit the use of undercover informants only in connection with serious crimes and only when it is extremely difficult for police to obtain evidence by other means. The reforms were accompanied by great controversy: as one German official commented, "undercover investigations should always be considered a tactic of last resort."[95]

Such social and legal distaste for informant use stands in stark contrast to the former Soviet Union, where the use of informants was considered not so much a "necessary evil" as a "fundamental means of pursuing both ordinary criminals and individuals who might prove a political threat to the regime." There, a lack of legal safeguards and the official premium placed on the state's interest made informant recruitment and use widespread.[96]

The ongoing evolution of informant use around the world reflects broader developments in international law enforcement. Collaborative international drug enforcement efforts, for example, have had a significant impact on the law and practices of European nations. Drug policy expert Ethan Nadelmann describes the "Americanization of European drug enforcement" as the gradual adoption of DEA-style methods of drug investigation by countries such as Germany, the Netherlands, Austria, Belgium, France, Spain, and Italy.[97] Such methods have introduced more reliance on undercover criminal informants, more trading of liability, and more tolerance of ongoing crime than European criminal systems have historically accepted.

In the antiterrorism arena in particular, there have been calls for the harmonization of legal standards to permit more international collaboration. Professor Ross has pointed out the significant challenges that such cooperation entails:

> Nations would need to renegotiate the tense political compromises legitimating undercover operations (which are everywhere controversial, but for different reasons). And they would need to revise the practices and procedures not just of undercover investigations, but of their domestic policing regime, including in areas that at first glance appear unrelated. Champions of closer cooperation who call on countries to overcome insularity in the interest of collective struggles against international crime and terrorism do not appear to appreciate the scale and depth of the requisite transformation of domestic policing regimes or the difficulty of reshaping the political compromises currently legitimating undercover operations.[98]

VI. American Informant Law

The laws of informant use embody a nation's stance towards weighty issues: How much should the government tolerate crime? What are the appropriate limits on police authority? How much protection should be afforded to individual privacy? Each nation's "informant law" reflects the confluence of legislative, judicial, and executive authority, as well as public values. The United States is notable for the ways in which the legislative and judicial branches have ceded authority on this issue to executive law enforcement. As Professor Marx pointed out years ago, "Unlike some Western European countries or Japan, legislatures in the United States have indirectly supported undercover practices by their consistent failure to set standards and goals for police performance. Legislatures, like the courts, generally prefer to leave such matters to police, thus enacting a kind of legitimacy by default."[99] The U.S. philosophy of informant law thus stands at the far end of the international spectrum, privileging law enforcement authority and discretion over the dangers and intrusions posed by criminal informant use.

The overall picture of American informant law presented in this chapter is one of tremendous official authority and discretion to use and reward criminal informants with few legal limits. The constraints that do exist tend to focus on the government's informational obligations rather than substantive limits on the way the government can use criminal informants, and even those informational obligations are tied to litigation and trials that occur infrequently. The end result of this laissez-faire, unregulated approach is that the American practice of using criminal informants is centrally shaped by individual decisions of police and prosecutors, with few external controls and little judicial oversight or legislative or public scrutiny.[100]

CHAPTER 3

Beyond Unreliable

In the 25 years I have been in this business, I have worked with hundreds of informants. I believe that exactly one of them was completely truthful, and there is no way to be 100% sure about him.

—John Madinger, senior special IRS agent
and former narcotics agent[1]

[Informants'] willingness to do anything includes not only truthfully spilling the beans on friends and relatives, but also lying, committing perjury, manufacturing evidence, soliciting others to corroborate their lies with more lies, and double-crossing anyone with whom they come into contact, including—and especially—the prosecutor. A drug addict can sell out his mother to get a deal, and burglars, robbers, murderers and thieves are not far behind.

—Judge Stephen S. Trott, U.S. Court of
Appeals for the Ninth Circuit[2]

ALL TOO OFTEN, the U.S. criminal system convicts the innocent. The now-steady stream of exonerations is stark evidence that even in the most serious cases, innocent defendants may still plead guilty or be convicted at trial despite the existence of some of the most elaborate procedural protections in the world.[3] The sources of this disaster are complex: an overwhelmed public defender system, long sentences, high trial conviction rates, and systemic pressures that steer defendants into guilty pleas are just some of the reasons why innocent defendants may dread their day in court.

Criminal informants are an important piece of the wrongful conviction puzzle. This is not merely because they often lie. After all, any witness is potentially unreliable. It is rather because informants have such predictable and powerful inducements to lie, because law enforcement relies heavily on their information, and because the system is not well designed to check that information. As a result, unreliable informant information permeates the process in ways that predictably lead to bad results such as wrongful arrests, bad search warrants, and fabricated evidence, as well as the ultimate failure of the wrongful conviction.

I. Lying Informants

> It is difficult to imagine a greater motivation to lie than the inducement of a reduced sentence.
> —*United States v. Cervantes-Pacheco*[4]

In their ground-breaking book *Actual Innocence,* Jim Dwyer, Peter Neufeld, and Barry Scheck estimated in 2000 that 21 percent of wrongful capital convictions are influenced by criminal informant testimony.[5] Four years later, a study by Northwestern University Law School's Center on Wrongful Convictions traced 45.9 percent of documented wrongful capital convictions to false informant testimony, making "snitches the leading cause of wrongful convictions in U.S. capital cases."[6] Another report estimated that 20 percent of all California wrongful convictions, capital or otherwise, resulted from false snitch testimony.[7] The Illinois Commission on Capital Punishment, in reviewing that state's wrongfully convicted capital defendants, identified "a number of cases where it appeared that the prosecution relied unduly on the uncorroborated testimony of a witness with something to gain. In some cases, this was an accomplice, while in other cases it was an in-custody informant."[8] Law professor Samuel Gross's study on exonerations likewise reports that nearly 50 percent of wrongful murder convictions involved perjury by someone such as a "jailhouse snitch or another witness who stood to gain from the false testimony."[9]

Because snitching has become so pervasive, the threat of perjured testimony goes beyond the problem of the individual bad witness. In

2006, for example, a federal jury wrongfully convicted Ann Colomb and her three sons for allegedly running one of the largest crack cocaine operations in Louisiana. The Colomb family served four months in prison awaiting sentencing before all charges were dismissed. Their wrongful convictions were based on fabricated testimony obtained from a ring of jailhouse informants who bought and sold information about the Colomb family inside the local federal prison. The ring worked by selling inmates files of documents and photographs that would permit them to fabricate testimony in order to reduce their own sentences. The government planned to use thirty-one such informants against the Colombs.

The scheme was revealed when a disgruntled inmate, Quinn Alex, gave twenty-two hundred dollars to another inmate in order to get a file. When the file never came through, Alex wrote an angry letter to the prosecutor demanding that the other inmate be charged with theft. The presiding judge, U.S. District Judge Tucker Melancon, told a journalist afterwards, "It was like revolving-door inmate testimony. The allegation was that there was in the federal justice system a network of folks trying to get relief from long sentences by ginning up information on folks being tried in drug cases. I'd heard about it before. But it all culminated in the Colomb trial." Judge Melancon ordered the U.S. Department of Justice to investigate.[10]

While all compensated criminal informants pose the risk of fabrication, jailhouse snitches are particularly pernicious. In an infamous 1989 interview with *60 Minutes*, jailhouse snitch and admitted perjurer Leslie Vernon White described how he was able to obtain information about other inmates and fabricate their confessions, even while in prison, and trade those fabrications for reduced sentences. The White scandal led to a grand jury investigation into the use of jailhouse snitches in Los Angeles, which concluded not only that jailhouse snitches routinely lied but that police and prosecutors knowingly relied on and exploited unreliable informants.[11] For example, the grand jury found evidence that police and prosecutors would purposely place a suspect inmate in the "informant tank" at the jail, surrounded by snitches working with the government, "in the hope that one or more of the informants would 'come up with information' to strengthen the case against the inmate."[12] As the grand jury recognized, the practice of using informants to elicit incriminating information from charged suspects violates those suspects' constitutional rights.[13]

The jailhouse snitch problem is a concentrated version of a more general danger associated with criminal informant use, and that is the threat to innocent suspects who happen to be incarcerated, who have criminal records, or who are otherwise associated with a criminal milieu such as drug use. Innocent people with criminal associations are more susceptible to informant targeting and conviction because law enforcement and jurors alike are predisposed to believe in their guilt. Incarcerated or recidivist suspects are thus particularly vulnerable to wrongful conviction based on unreliable snitch information because it is harder for them to defend against informant lies.[14]

Of course, sometimes informants tell the truth, even unreliable ones. Cooperation from long-time mafia assassin Aladena "Jimmy" Fratianno, aka "Jimmy the Weasel," helped convict at least two dozen mob members during the late 1970s.[15] In Pennsylvania alone, drug informants have been credited for victories such as the breakup of "one of the largest cocaine distribution rings in Western Pennsylvania" and for "wip[ing] out the two competing drug rings responsible for 75 to 80 percent of the heroin sales in the Scranton/Wilkes Barre area."[16]

In other words, the problem is not that criminal informants always lie. Rather, it can be extremely hard to tell when they do and when they don't. And unlike other kinds of witnesses, informants are deeply self-interested in their false stories. Their ability to convince the government that their information is true and valuable may mean the difference between their freedom and incarceration, or even life and death. As law professor George Harris put it, "A witness whose future depends on currying the government's favor will formulate a consistent and credible story calculated to procure an agreement with the government, and will adhere religiously at trial to her prior statements."[17]

II. Law Enforcement Dependence on Informants

Despite their known unreliability, law enforcement relies on informants, sometimes heavily. This is not only because police and prosecutors need information to make cases but also because law enforcement success is often measured in terms of numbers of arrests and prosecutions, thereby putting pressure on police and prosecutors to use the cheapest and fastest methods rather than the most reliable. This is particularly true in drug enforcement, where the government has become profoundly reliant on informants in conducting investigations, selecting targets, making arrests, and obtaining convictions.[18]

Because law enforcement officials need to create cases, they have incentives to believe informants when they offer information that seems valuable. These incentives grow stronger once informants become trusted, cases are initiated, and the official becomes dependent on the informant for the success of the case.

This dependence can become so great that it creates a sort of perverse romance: "falling in love with your rat." A prosecutor explains the phenomenon:

> You are not supposed to, of course. . . . But you spend time with this guy, you get to know him and his family. You like him. . . . [T]he reality is that the cooperator's information often becomes your mind set. . . . It's a phenomenon and the danger is that because you feel all warm and fuzzy about your cooperator, you come to believe that you do not have to spend much time or energy investigating the case and you don't. Once you become chummy with your cooperator, there is a real danger that you lose your objectivity.[19]

Another prosecutor describes how reliance on a cooperator affects numerous crucial decisions down the line. Once the government believes an informant,

> it is a certainty that the information obtained from the cooperator will become part of the base of information utilized to evaluate future would-be cooperators. Moreover, the information will

affect future questioning of witnesses and defendants; it will alter how investigators view the significance of witnesses and particular pieces of evidence; and it may taint the way the case is perceived by the prosecutors and agents. In other words, false information skews the ongoing investigation. The false information may prove critical to issues that have far greater import than whether to accept as true the proffer of another would-be cooperator. Rather, it might impact decisions regarding charges to be filed against other defendants, it might affect decisions related to an appropriate plea for a given defendant, and it might even influence whether the government decides to seek the death penalty.[20]

Studies show that police and prosecutors, like everyone else, tend to interpret information in ways that support their previous decisions, and resist interpretations that suggest that they got it wrong the first time around. In other words, once law enforcement officials accept informant information, it becomes important for the government to preserve the credibility of that information and that informant, even when other evidence suggests that they may be unreliable.[21]

This psychological dynamic has troubling legal implications. The Due Process Clause of the U.S. Constitution requires prosecutors to discover and disclose to defendants impeachment material about government witnesses, namely, evidence suggesting that the witness might be lying.[22] The adversarial process depends on this disclosure to ensure that defendants can meaningfully ferret out informant lies. But police and prosecutors lack incentives to seek out such material, not only because it could literally destroy their cases but also because they have vested interests in believing their informants. Moreover, police in possession of impeachment material may be reluctant to share it with prosecutors, knowing that it will have to be disclosed to the defense. This means that the usual protections against unreliable witnesses—prosecutorial ethics and discovery—may be unavailable precisely because prosecutors themselves have limited means and incentives to discover the truth.

Sometimes police and prosecutors are taken in by their own informants. For example, prosecutors believed Marion Albert Pruett's

1982 testimony against a prisoner accused of killing Pruett's cellmate, and put Pruett into the federal witness protection program. Pruett subsequently committed a string of bank robberies and murdered two convenience store clerks, and eventually confessed that he had killed his cellmate himself.[23]

Sometimes government officials lack information about the risks that their source is lying. The Baltimore prosecutor in Tony Williams's 2003 murder trial, for example, was unaware that the state's key witness, a jailhouse snitch, was also on the Baltimore police payroll as an informant.[24]

Sometimes this ignorance is intentional. Tom Goldstein was wrongfully convicted of murder in 1980, spending twenty-four years in prison on the basis of testimony from jailhouse snitch Edward Fink. Although he lied about it at trial, Fink had received lenience for numerous offenses by working as an informant for the local police department for many years. However, because the Los Angeles County prosecutors' office lacked procedures to keep track of informants and their deals, the prosecutor on Goldstein's case did not know Fink's history in that office and therefore never disclosed the information to the defense.[25] In its 1990 investigation of informant abuses, the Los Angeles grand jury concluded that the Los Angeles District Attorney's Office had intentionally decided not to keep track of its informants and their unreliability. The reasons for this decision were twofold: because "the defense might discover information" if it were documented, and because "the Sheriff's Department might be deemed to be violating defendants' rights to counsel" if full information about informant practices was revealed.[26] In other words, the prosecutors' office purposely refrained from learning about and documenting its use of unreliable snitches under pressure to make cases and to shield law enforcement from scrutiny.

In other situations, officials may ignore or even affirmatively encourage informant mendacity, concealing informant lies from the defense as well as the court in order to obtain convictions. For example, prosecutors lied for twenty years about their key informant witness, from Delma Bank's 1980 murder trial through his appeal and state habeas petition. Informant Robert Farr had set Banks up in

exchange for cash and lenience, a fact that the government continu-
ously denied.[27] Similarly, James Walker spent nineteen years in prison
for a 1971 murder he did not commit, on the basis of allegations of
a drug-addict criminal informant, John Snider. Although they had
proof that Snider was lying, police and prosecutors covered up his
lies and withheld evidence regarding Snider from the court and from
the defense.[28]

These examples of official wrongdoing are not meant to impugn
the vast majority of police and prosecutors who do not engage in
such conduct. But they do illustrate the dangers and temptations with
which all police and prosecutors must contend. Informant witnesses
represent a kind of perfect storm: deeply unreliable sources managed
by officials with strong incentives to accept and defend their information. In these ways, the interdependence of law enforcement and its
informant witnesses can threaten the entire fact-finding process.

III. Juries

Although only about 5 percent of felony cases actually go to trial, the
jury remains one of the American system's most important checks on
informant reliability. The threat of a trial in which a snitch might have
to testify in open court is an incentive for law enforcement to ensure
that its informants are accurate. Once at trial, the informant must
convince a jury that he is telling the truth, subject to cross-examination by the defense. The jury will typically learn that the informant
is receiving a benefit for his testimony, and may hear about previous
instances in which the informant testified in exchange for lenience.
In some jurisdictions, the court will also instruct the jury that the
informant's testimony should be carefully scrutinized for potential
unreliability.

In 1966, the Supreme Court upheld the constitutionality of using
criminal informants in large part because it believed that the jury trial
provides an adequate check against compensated criminal witnesses
with strong incentives to lie. The Court relied on what it called "[t]he
established safeguards of the Anglo-American legal system [which]

leave the veracity of a witness to be tested by cross-examination, and the credibility of his testimony to be determined by a properly instructed jury."[29]

Jurors can indeed sometimes be an effective check against lying informants. Judge Trott concludes that "[o]rdinary decent people are predisposed to dislike, distrust, and frequently despise criminals who 'sell out' and become prosecution witnesses. Jurors suspect their motives from the moment they hear about them in a case, and they frequently disregard their testimony altogether as highly untrustworthy and unreliable, openly expressing disgust with the prosecution for making deals with such 'scum.'"[30]

Juror distrust, for example, cost the government its massive 1981 racketeering case against the Hell's Angel's motorcycle gang. In that case, jurors felt that the government's key witnesses—former Hell's Angel's members, one of whom was paid $30,000—were "despicable and beneath contempt."[31] That same kind of distrust led to Todd Ruffin's acquittal by a Stamford, Connecticut, jury for the charge of selling drugs to an informant. "They just didn't believe a word [the informant] said," said the prosecutor, who spoke with jurors after the trial. "He has a terrible record, so they felt he was inherently untruthful."[32]

On the other hand, jurors—and the jury system—are far from fully effective protection against informant unreliability. The first reason is structural: because 95 percent of felony cases are resolved by plea and do not go to trial, informants in those cases will never have to testify, the defense may never see impeachment material regarding those witnesses, and jurors will never get to evaluate their credibility.

Even when defendants do go to trial, numerous exonerations reveal just how often juries believe lying criminal informants, even when juries know that the informant is being compensated and has the incentive to lie. A report by the Center on Wrongful Convictions at Northwestern University School of Law describes fifty-one wrongful capital convictions, each one involving perjured informant testimony accepted by jurors as true. For example, jurors believed Paula Grey, an accomplice to a double murder in the infamous 1985 "Ford Height Four" case. Her testimony led to the wrongful conviction of three men before the actual killer confessed ten years later. Likewise, jurors at Randy Steidl's 1986 murder trial believed informant Debra Reinboldt, even though later evidence revealed that Reinboldt could not possibly have witnessed the murder about which she testified because she had been at work at the time.[33]

Such cases indicate that the "established safeguards of the Anglo-American system" such as cross-examination, discovery, and jury instructions do not successfully prevent juries from convicting innocent defendants on the basis of lying informant witnesses. One reason for this may be psychological. Recent studies indicate that jurors may simply ignore the fact that informants are compensated and that they have strong incentives to lie, preferring instead to accept the testimony at face value. In one study, mock jurors were divided into two groups. The test group was told that the witness was being given a lenience deal in exchange for his testimony, while the control group was not told this fact. The test group convicted at approximately the same rate as the control group. In other words, knowing the informant's incentives to lie did not undermine the jurors' belief in his testimony.[34]

Our system relies heavily on information sharing and disclosure as a check on wrongful convictions. But false informant testimony is more powerful than this model acknowledges. Exoneration data and psychological studies show that even a well-informed, properly instructed jury may still accept a lying informant's testimony and convict an innocent defendant. The problem, moreover, is not limited to jurors but extends to all the players who might rely on the informant's information, including police, prosecutors, and even judges.

IV. When the Innocent Plead Guilty

Most American defendants plead guilty and never see a jury. For this vast majority, a lying informant can alter the calculus about whether to go to trial, making it more likely that the defendant will take a plea rather than risk the higher sentences that flow from losing at trial.

In 2008, for example, fourteen men in Cleveland, Ohio, were found by a federal judge to have pled guilty to false charges levied by a DEA informant. The first defendant in the case, a mother of three, insisted on her innocence, went to trial, and was convicted. She received a sentence of ten years. The remaining fourteen men then pled guilty in exchange for lower sentences.[35]

This kind of tragic calculus occurs throughout the penal system, although the nature of plea bargaining and the appellate process make it impossible to know just how often it happens. Innocent defendants plead guilty for a number of reasons. They may think that they will lose at trial and that their punishment will be heavier than the one offered in a plea. The federal sentencing guidelines expressly encourage this sort of calculation by imposing longer sentences, the so-called trial penalty, on defendants who do not take a plea.[36] Defendants may also plead guilty because they are being held without bail and a plea provides the immediate freedom of probation or a sentence of time served. Or they may plead guilty because their lawyers tell them to, or because they are ignorant of their rights and other options. They may even plead guilty because they think they are guilty of an offense when they are not.

Professors Samuel Gross and Barbara O'Brien conclude that it is almost impossible to determine how many innocent defendants actually plead guilty because false convictions are "invisible at their inception." Because most defendants who plead guilty do not appeal, and because even if they do, it is relatively difficult to overturn a guilty plea, "[t]he exonerations that we know about are overwhelmingly for convictions at trial." But Gross and O'Brien offer ways of thinking about the probabilities. For example, they note that

> it's entirely possible that most wrongful convictions—like 90% or more of all criminal convictions—are based on negotiated guilty pleas to comparatively light charges, and that the innocent defendants in those cases received little or no time in custody. If so, it may well be that a major cause of these comparatively low-level miscarriages of justice is the prospect of prolonged pretrial detention by innocent defendants who are unable to post bail.[37]

Sometimes, however, wrongful pleas do make it to the public record. Gross and O'Brien describe some infamous examples:

We do know about a substantial number of exonerations of innocent defendants who pled guilty and received comparatively light
sentences—in one particularly disturbing factual context. In the
past decade, several systemic programs of police perjury have been
uncovered, which ultimately led to exonerations of at least 135 innocent defendants who had been framed for illegal possession of
drugs or guns in Los Angeles, in Dallas, and in Tulia, Texas. . . .
Most of these innocent drug and gun defendants pled guilty, and
had been released by the time they were exonerated two to four
years later.[38]

Each of these examples involved criminal informants and/or undercover narcotics agents operating in the mode of an informant. In the
Los Angeles Rampart scandal, officers used informants to set up innocent targets. In Dallas, police used informants to plant fake drugs
on suspects. In Tulia, Texas, a single undercover narcotics officer fabricated drug evidence against dozens of African American targets.

In sum, while we do not know how many innocent defendants
plead guilty, we know that it happens, probably on a regular basis,
and that informants are a dangerous aspect of the problem. When a
criminal informant fingers an innocent person, the pressures of the
criminal system may drive that person to plead guilty rather than face
worse consequences. This is especially true for defendants with prior
criminal records or associations, who are less likely to be presumed innocent by law enforcement officials and jurors. It is also especially true
for defendants with overworked, underpaid public defense counsel
who lack the resources to fully investigate and litigate the case.[39] Moreover, in order to avoid trial and protect the identity of the informant,
prosecutors may offer reduced charges, probation, or low sentences
to persuade a defendant not to contest the case. The tragedy remains
invisible because the informant's misinformation is never tested or revealed. Because the vast majority of cases are resolved through guilty
pleas rather than trials, the possibilities for this sort of miscarriage of
justice are both widespread and nearly impossible to discover after the
fact.

V. The Important but Limited Role of Procedural Protections

Legislators in a number of jurisdictions have recognized the unreliability of criminal informants and the inadequacy of existing procedural protections. These jurisdictions have considered a variety of reforms aimed at reducing the likelihood of wrongful convictions. These reforms are discussed in depth in chapter 8; they include such things as corroboration requirements, reliability hearings, and stronger discovery and disclosure requirements for the government when it seeks to use informants as witnesses.

Better procedural protections improve the chances that the defense will be able to uncover an informant's lies, and as such they are important tools in protecting against wrongful convictions. But such procedures are inherently limited because they do not address the underlying phenomena that drive the use of unreliable informants. First, and foremost, such procedures are typically applicable only at trial, and therefore do not directly affect plea bargains, namely, the vast majority of criminal cases. They also do not affect the process of using informants in investigations or to obtain warrants, techniques that lead to thousands of bad searches and arrests every year. Such procedures also do not reduce informants' underlying incentives to lie in the first place. Finally, they leave untouched police and prosecutorial reliance on unreliable informants in shaping investigations, arrests, and charging decisions. For all these reasons, trial procedure reforms are only one aspect, albeit an important one, of the larger challenges posed by unreliable informants.

CHAPTER 4

Secret Justice

Every thing secret degenerates, even the administration of justice;
nothing is safe that does not show it can bear discussion and publicity.
—Lord Acton[1]

Publicity is justly commended as a remedy for social and industrial
diseases. Sunlight is said to be the best of disinfectants; electric light
the most efficient policeman.

—Justice Louis Brandeis[2]

INFORMANT PRACTICES ARE inherently secretive: snitches often
need their identities to be protected for safety, while the effectiveness
of informant-driven investigations turns on their clandestine nature.
But the secretive effects of using informants go far beyond protecting
ongoing investigations or concealing particular informants' identities.
Snitching has altered the ways in which investigations are conducted
and recorded; it affects public record keeping by police and prosecutors, discovery practices, and what gets written down during plea negotiations. It has also shaped the informational rules prescribed by
Supreme Court doctrine, internal judicial branch information policies, and even information-sharing between the Department of Justice and Congress. In other words, the pressure to conceal informant
practices broadly affects the criminal system's culture of record keeping, adversarial information sharing, public policy, and disclosure,
making the entire process less transparent and accountable.

Sometimes informant practices make it harder for the public to access documents and processes that have traditionally been publicly

available. For example, in 2007, driven by concerns over informant confidentiality, federal courts for both the Eastern District of Pennsylvania and the Southern District of Florida adopted new protocols that eliminate public website access to docket entries and to all plea agreements in all criminal cases. The purpose of the new protocols is to make it impossible to discern without physically coming to the courthouse whether a defendant is cooperating. They also prevent the public from seeing whether court documents are sealed—considered a red flag that suggests cooperation.[3]

Similarly, a 2006 investigation by the Associated Press revealed the existence of widespread sealing and "secret dockets" in the federal court system for Washington, D.C. Nearly five thousand criminal cases remained sealed long after the case was over, and for hundreds of those cases, the system falsely indicated that there was "no such case" if the case number was entered into the system. Most of the cases involved cooperating government witnesses.[4]

These are a few ways in which using informants pressures the system to curtail public access to information about how we adjudicate guilt and impose punishment. The loss is significant because we rely on such information to monitor whether the criminal system is effective and fair—in individual cases as well as more broadly. Taking such information off the public record thus bolsters law enforcement authority while reducing the ability of legislatures, the press, and the public to evaluate executive actors and hold them accountable. This is a powerful and often troubling hallmark of informant culture, and one of its dynamics that tends to go unremarked precisely because it takes place beneath the public radar. This chapter traces the depublicizing influence of informant use through the main areas of the criminal process: investigation, plea bargaining, discovery, and global public access to information about the penal system.

I. Investigation

As a general matter, the process of investigating crime is one of the least regulated, least public aspects of the legal system.[5] Police decisions such as whether to investigate a crime or make an arrest are for the most part not subject to legal challenge or judicial review.[6] They are accordingly subject to few documentation requirements.[7] Police reports—which record such decisions and the information gathered during investigations—are notoriously partial and provide only a limited window of information, if they provide any information at all.[8] Houston police, for example, are not required to write any report if they do not believe that a rape complaint constitutes a crime.[9] Sometimes police reporting is purposefully opaque: Chicago and New York police departments long maintained a system of "double files" in which publicly accessible police reports, including those given to prosecutors, contained only a partial version of the facts, while the department's internal "street files" contained fuller information.[10]

This tradition of undocumented investigative decision making has been challenged in a variety of ways, including decades-long demands for civilian review boards.[11] More recently, there have been numerous attempts to require police to collect data on racial profiling practices.[12] The bitter struggles over these kinds of reforms reflect deep-seated traditions of discretionary policing, in which collecting public policing data is a foreign and often difficult innovation.

The use of criminal informants is a paradigmatic example of this kind of discretionary, undocumented decision making; it is also a powerful engine of its expansion. In practice, police can flip a suspect, obtain information, and maintain an ongoing relationship with an informant without ever publicly revealing the transactions. Police reports will often omit mention of informant sources, while search warrant applications typically do not reveal informant identities. If police so choose, the crimes committed by cooperating informants may never be recorded. Informant-based investigations thus slip easily beneath the radar of the criminal system's documentation processes.

The unregulated character of informant investigations is no accident. Starting with its decision in *Hoffa v. United States*, the Supreme Court has methodically exempted informant creation and deployment from the kinds of constitutional regulations that cover other investigative techniques, including Fourth Amendment rules on searches,

seizures, and warrants, the Fifth Amendment requirement that suspects be given Miranda warnings and counsel, and Sixth Amendment
right-to-counsel rules.[13] In turn, because police are less constrained
when using informants, this naturally makes informant-based investigations easier, cheaper, and more inviting. If the police can persuade
an informant to cooperate in order to obtain information about a target, that decision is hard for others to challenge, and if it turns up no
evidence, it need never be revealed. Likewise, a wired informant can
collect information whenever the police want him to, off the record.
By contrast, if the police apply for a warrant or a wiretap, they must
justify their requests to a court, their requests could be denied, and
their justifications can be challenged later by defense counsel.

For example, instead of getting a warrant, Virginia police used convicted burglars as informants to break into a suspect's home to look
for marijuana. According to one of the informants, Renaldo Turnbull,
police assured them that they would be protected if they burglarized
the suspect's home: "The [police] dude said he was going to look out
for us, so let's go do it," he said. Turnbull also explained the general
instructions that he received from his police handler: "He told me
what to look for. He said, if you know of any burglaries or anything,
let [him] know. He said no evidence, no pay. He said if you know
where it is, go get it."[14]

When police do decide to seek a warrant, the process becomes
more regulated and requires more documentation. To get a warrant,
an officer must submit to a judicial officer a sworn affidavit containing information sufficient to find "probable cause," namely, enough
evidence from which the judicial officer could conclude that there is
a fair probability of criminal activity. When a police officer proffers an
informant tip in order to obtain a warrant, she needs to provide the
judge with enough information about that informant and that tip so
that the judge can independently determine whether the informant is
sufficiently reliable and therefore whether probable cause exists. This
process is designed to ensure that warrants issue in conformity with
the Fourth Amendment, which states that "no warrant shall issue but
upon probable cause supported by oath or affirmation."[15]

Even in this more regulated, documented arena, using informants erodes public transparency. In his study of narcotics warrants issued in San Diego in 1998, law professor Lawrence Benner discovered that informant-based warrant applications involve more secrecy and demand less rigor than warrant doctrine contemplates. For example, 64 percent of all warrant applications studied relied on a confidential informant, or "CI," and 95 percent of those warrant applications withheld the identity of the informant from the magistrate. They justified doing so on the basis of the following generic boilerplate language contained in each warrant application:

> I desire to keep said informant anonymous because CI has requested me to do so, and because it is my experience that informants suffer physical, social and emotional retribution when their identities are revealed, because it is my experience that to reveal the identity of such informants seriously impairs their utility to law enforcement, and because it is my experience that revealing such informants' identities prevents other citizens from disclosing confidential information about criminal activities to law enforcement officers.[16]

As Benner points out, the use of such boilerplate language provides no factual or case-specific support for the proposition that the particular informant's identity needs to be withheld from the court, which violates the rules as well as the spirit of the warrant process.

> A public entity is granted a privilege to refuse to disclose the identity of an informant only if the public interest requires it because the "necessity for preserving the confidentiality of [the informant's identity] outweighs the necessity for disclosure in the interests of justice." . . . The use of boilerplate in the manner described above, however, bypasses this entire process and indeed denies judges the very information they would be required to have in order to make a determination that the CI's identity should not be revealed.[17]

The same study also revealed the practice of using "phantom affidavits," in which the officer seeking the warrant does not know the confidential informant on whom she is relying for the information, but rather swears under oath that another officer told her that the informant provided that other officer with the incriminating information. This practice means that the officer applying for the warrant does not know the identity of her source for probable cause, and that, more generally, no officer ever has to swear under oath to the existence of the informant at all.[18]

Such practices do not necessarily mean that police are fabricating informants or that informants are lying. But they do weaken established provisions for judicial oversight of search warrants and obscure from public view the means by which police obtain their evidence. Because informants can so easily be kept secret—even from the very police officer seeking the warrant—they become a cheap, unregulated means for police to obtain the weighty investigative authority of a warrant.

Because investigative constraints tend not to apply to informant practices, this has generated a culture of secrecy that goes beyond the lack of documentation. Using snitches has become a method of concealing investigative techniques, a practice in which the usual disclosure rules do not apply, and in which cutting corners and breaking rules can easily be hidden. By way of example, the Brooklyn police officers who traded drugs for information from their addict-snitches were responding to systemic incentives: to use illegal informant deals to get quick and easy drug busts. They could do so because their investigatory relationship with those addict-snitches was discretionary, undocumented, and likely never to come to light. The same dynamic fueled the tragic death of Mrs. Kathryn Johnston described at the beginning of this book, in which Atlanta police used an unreliable tip from a drug dealer to get a warrant, fabricated an informant in the warrant application, and then pressured another snitch to lie to cover up their misrepresentations. They could behave this way precisely because they knew that their use of snitches—real and fabricated—would likely never be revealed, that they had tools at their disposal to prevent their misconduct from being exposed, and that if they did in fact produce drugs or a conviction, the ends would justify the means.[19]

In sum, the discretion and secrecy associated with using criminal informants promotes a clandestine culture that extends beyond individual cases. From constitutional rules that do not apply to police misconduct that will never be discovered, informant-based investigations ensure that much of the criminal process will remain under wraps, inaccessible to public or judicial scrutiny.

II. Plea Bargaining

Approximately 95 percent of all felony cases in the United States are resolved by plea.[20] This means that trials and litigation are rare, while negotiated deals are overwhelmingly the norm. This fact has implications for the transparency of the criminal system. While trials and hearings are public, plea bargaining is private. While litigated facts become part of the public record, negotiated facts remain off the record, known only to the bargaining parties. The trend towards plea bargaining has thus been accompanied by a trend towards the depublicization of the criminal system. Information gathered by the government—and the investigative methods used to get it—are increasingly difficult for the public to learn about. Public information about the kinds of crimes that are actually committed and by whom is likewise disappearing, replaced by information about the deals struck between the government and defendants. As criminal liability is increasingly resolved privately through deals, the public loses sight of the way the system really works. As legal scholar Stephanos Bibas puts it, while inside players such as prosecutors, defense attorneys, and judges have quite a bit of information about the way the system operates, the public experiences the criminal process as "opaque, tangled, insulated, and impervious to outside scrutiny and change."[21]

Informant deals are extreme versions of plea bargains. An informant deal resembles a plea in that it resolves the informant's potential criminal liability, at least temporarily, in exchange for information. It is also like a plea bargain in that the resolution of liability is negotiated, and takes place in private between the law enforcement official and the defendant, or perhaps the defense attorney.

But informant deals are more secretive than plea bargains for a number of reasons. Unlike a plea, the deal may never come to light at all. A typical informal agreement between a police officer and a street dealer—in which the dealer avoids arrest and the police obtains information—may never be written down or revealed to anyone else. Whatever crimes the dealer committed will remain unknown to the public, to prosecutors, and even to other members of the police department.

Even if the informant is arrested, his potential liability may be handled in ways that evade documentation or scrutiny. For example, in *United States v. White*, police officer Mike Weaver searched Shawn White's car and found a glass pipe containing what appeared to be methamphetamines. Weaver offered White a deal. Before reading White his Miranda rights,

> Weaver stated that he wanted to ask defendant some questions and see how cooperative he would be that night. . . . Weaver explained that if he sent the glass pipe to the crime lab and the lab found methamphetamine residue, he could charge defendant with a felony of possessing methamphetamine. Weaver said that the "deal" was that he could write the police report to reflect a charge of possessing drug paraphernalia, a misdemeanor, or possessing methamphetamine, a felony. Weaver advised that depending on defendant's level of cooperation, defendant could decide to "take the whole 100 yards, or deal with the small stuff." Weaver told defendant that he could help in a lot of ways, or he could "sit there like a lump on a log," which was not in his best interest. Weaver told defendant that if he did not cooperate, Weaver would simply list charge after charge and take defendant to the county jail.[22]

White cooperated, and as promised, Officer Weaver wrote the report to reflect only the possession of paraphernalia. The writing of the police report in effect constituted a plea bargain, in which White's actual criminal conduct was never fully recorded.

Prosecutors also alter criminal cases and charges to reflect a defendant's cooperation. A prosecutor may decline to indict on the understanding that the informant will start "working off" his charges. Charges may be dropped or reduced, and facts pertaining to charges and sentencing—for example the amount of drugs at stake—may be negotiated between the parties so that the record will reflect the agreement. In other words, the court and the public will eventually see only what the parties decide to reveal.

To be sure, informant deals vary immensely and take place along a spectrum of secrecy. At the most transparent end, a represented defendant will sit down with his attorney and negotiate a written agreement with the government, with relatively precise terms of cooperation in exchange for known benefits. Such deals are typical of white collar and political corruption cases.[23] The plea agreements entered into by lobbyist Jack Abramoff and Enron CFO Andrew Fastow are a matter of public record, as is the extent of each man's cooperation, making it possible for the public to figure out what benefits were exchanged.[24] By contrast, at the most secretive end of the spectrum, no one but the police officer and offender may ever know what crimes were committed and what information was obtained. Because the bulk of informant use takes place in drug- and street-crime enforcement, where investigations and deals tend towards the informal, informant use as a whole tends towards the secretive.

In these ways, pervasive informant use exacerbates the trend toward the secret adjudication of crime. The greater the reliance on informant deals rather than traditional plea bargains and trials, the less the public learns about the crimes being committed and about how the criminal system resolves liability.

III. Discovery

Once a case is filed, the defendant is entitled to certain kinds of information from the government. Discovery is the primary formal mechanism through which the government's evidence and investigative methods are revealed, and therefore is important not only to individual defendants but also to the public interested in learning how the government does the work of criminal justice. While there are other mechanisms by which the public can sometimes obtain government records, for example the Freedom of Information Act,[25] defendants' ability to obtain government-generated information and place it on the public record is a crucial source of public access. Because the governmental use of informants tends to truncate defendants' access to discovery, it simultaneously restricts public access to that information as well.

As explained in chapter 2, the Supreme Court has held that impeachment material regarding the credibility of government witnesses must be disclosed to the defense.[26] Typical impeachment material includes any promises made to the informant, his criminal record, the benefits conferred on the informant by the government in exchange for information in the instant case, and the informant's history of testimony and rewards in other cases.[27] If the government wishes to withhold the identity of its informant at trial, it must justify nondisclosure against the defendant's weighty right to a fair trial, as well as his right to confront the witnesses against him.[28]

In 2002, in *United States v. Ruiz*, the Supreme Court sharply reduced defendant entitlements to discovery regarding informants. Angela Ruiz was charged with possessing thirty kilograms of marijuana. Prosecutors offered her a so-called fast track plea bargain in which, in exchange for a recommendation of a downward departure under the U.S. Sentencing Guidelines, she would "'waive the right' to receive 'impeachment information relating to any informants or other witnesses.'"[29] Ruiz rejected the offer and eventually pled guilty without a deal. On appeal, she argued that she should not have been required to waive her rights to exculpatory impeachment material to which she had a constitutional right.

The Ninth Circuit Court of Appeals reversed Ruiz's conviction, deciding that the government could not constitutionally withhold that impeachment information and that therefore it could not pressure Ruiz to bargain away her right to it. It reasoned that defendants must be entitled to receive from the government the same exculpatory evidence before pleading guilty as they are before trial because "guilty pleas cannot be deemed intelligent and voluntary if entered without knowledge of material information withheld by the prosecution."[30]

The U.S. Supreme Court disagreed. It ruled that although defendants are entitled to such information if they proceed to trial, "the Constitution does not require the Government to disclose material impeachment evidence prior to entering a plea agreement with a criminal defendant."[31] The Court worried in particular about restricting the government's use of informants, noting that disclosure "could 'disrupt ongoing investigations' and expose prospective witnesses to serious harm."[32]

Accordingly, after *Ruiz*, the government need not produce *Giglio* impeachment material before a guilty plea, and must do so only if the defendant decides to proceed to trial. Because approximately 95 percent of all criminal cases are resolved by plea, the effect of *Ruiz* is to declare a vast amount of information about informant use exempt from discovery. In practice, some prosecutors' officers provide this information to defendants anyway, even though constitutionally speaking they do not have to. But as *Ruiz* demonstrates, the government's preference will often be to withhold it so as to strengthen its bargaining position. This means that a great deal of information about the government's use of criminal informants will never come to light, either for defendants or for the public.

Ironically, the very existence of discovery rules can drive police and prosecutors to act in more clandestine ways. As policing scholar Jerome Skolnick described decades ago, police truncate their written, discoverable reports to hide the existence of their informants.

> [P]olice will not say in an arrest report that they cajoled, or, in rare instances, threatened a suspect to get information. More importantly, they will not, if possible, reveal that an informant was utilized at all. Indeed, this concealment is a major task of police. [I]t almost never happens that an informant is not used somewhere along the line in crimes involving "vice." . . . Nevertheless, of the five hundred and eight cases in the narcotics file of the Westville [California] police during [a two-year period], less than nine percent mentioned the use of an informant.[33]

More recent studies confirm that police often avoid revealing informant information in warrant applications or to prosecutors. Police may also decline to arrest informants in the first place in order to avoid a paper trail.[34] Prosecutors likewise avoid making overt promises to informants in order to escape *Brady* disclosure requirements.[35] In other words, both prior to discovery and during the discovery process itself, using informants tends to cloak the workings of the criminal process.

IV. Public Transparency and Executive Accountability

The secrecy that attends informant use is in tension with some fundamental aspects of American criminal justice. Our penal system promises transparency and public access to information in ways that are important not only to the adjudication of specific cases but to the democratic process itself. From the Sixth Amendment right to a public trial to the First Amendment right of free speech and press, many aspects of our criminal system demand that cases and processes be made public so that voters, legislators, and the media can view the workings of the executive branch.

The Supreme Court explains this commitment to transparency as a form of governmental accountability. The idea that criminal processes, records, and results should be public, or what the Court has referred to as the "right to gather information,"[36] is part of a larger democratic commitment to public accountability and responsiveness. In discussing "the therapeutic value of open justice," the Court quoted the philosopher Jeremy Bentham:

> Without publicity, all other checks are insufficient: in comparison of publicity, all other checks are of small account. Recordation, appeal, whatever other institutions might present themselves in the character of checks, would be found to operate rather as cloaks than checks; as cloaks in reality, as checks only in appearance.[37]

Information access is also connected to political and intellectual freedom. In establishing the public's right to observe criminal proceedings, the Court has said, "The First Amendment goes beyond protection of the press and the self-expression of individuals to prohibit government from limiting the stock of information from which members of the public may draw."[38]

Because transparency and public access to information are so important, they cannot be dispensed with lightly. If the government wants to keep information secret, it must justify that secrecy against a presumption of openness and the value of maintaining a public and open justice system. As the Supreme Court has written, "The presumption of openness may be overcome only by an overriding interest based on findings that closure is essential to preserve higher values and is narrowly tailored to serve that interest."[39]

For example, in a 1985 decision, then-Judge now Justice Anthony Kennedy unsealed an informant's file because the government and the informant had failed to justify the need for secrecy.[40] In that case, informant William Hetrick had pled guilty to drug and tax evasion charges. The media sought access to Hetrick's request for a sentence reduction in connection with his testimony against celebrity automobile executive John DeLorean. At the request of both Hetrick and the government, the district court sealed the proceedings. The court of appeals ordered that they be unsealed. Kennedy explained as follows:

> We begin with the presumption that the public and the press have a right of access to criminal proceedings and documents filed therein. . . . The primary justifications for access to criminal proceedings [have been] first that criminal trials historically have been open to the press and to the public, and, second, that access to criminal trials plays a significant role in the functioning of the judicial process and the governmental system. . . . The interest which overrides the presumption of open procedures must be specified with particularity, and there must be findings that the closure remedy is narrowly confined to protect that interest. . . . The penal structure is the least visible, least understood, least effective part

of the justice system; and each such failure is consequent from the others. Public examination, study, and comment is essential if the corrections process is to improve.[41]

The meaning of such reasoning is that the need for informant secrecy should not be assumed; rather, it must be evaluated each time on the specific facts of each case. Even though "information relating to cooperating witnesses and criminal investigations should be kept confidential in some cases,"[42] the countervailing importance of public access must be accounted for every time. When in doubt, transparency is supposed to win. Blanket acceptance of informant anonymity, undocumented deals, or sealed case files contradicts this fundamental idea.

Another important feature of the Supreme Court's publicity jurisprudence is the critical role of the defendant in producing public information. Even as the Court recognizes the public's need to understand the way the system works, it assumes that the adversarial process produces enough information to satisfy that need.[43] As the Court puts it, "In an adversary system of criminal justice, the public interest in the administration of justice is protected by the participants in the litigation."[44] Essentially, the public only gets to watch trials that the parties actually decide to conduct. By permitting public access to record information produced by actual cases, the Court's idea is that the public will obtain a sufficiently full and accurate picture of the way the criminal system works to satisfy underlying First Amendment free-speech and information-gathering values. In this sense, defendants function as proxies for the broader public interest in access to government information.

When it comes to informant use, however, this model breaks down because snitching practices undermine the Court's assumption that parties to criminal litigation will produce a robust public record. As plea bargaining and informant use curtail defendant access to information about law enforcement practices, so too is public information reduced. To put it another way, one of the reasons why the public lacks access to and understanding of the criminal process is that defendants who plead guilty—i.e., most defendants—lack tools to access information held by the government about their own cases. As cases like *Ruiz* further handicap defendants' ability to obtain informant-related discovery, in conjunction with police and prosecutorial informant practices that evade documentation and review, the entire criminal process becomes less public.

The move towards informant secrecy affects not only public access to information but other branches of government. When defendants lack access to informant-related data, courts are also deprived of the ability to review that information. The culture of nondisclosure affects legislative access as well. For example, in the 2004 congressional report entitled "Everything Secret Degenerates: The FBI's Use of Murderers as Informants," the U.S. House of Representatives Committee on Government Reform documented its inquiry into the FBI's mishandling of its mafia informants throughout the 1970s and 1980s. During that investigation, the FBI and the U.S. Department of Justice used numerous mechanisms to withhold information from the committee, to cover up wrongdoing by government officials and their informants, and generally to stonewall the investigative process. "Throughout the committee's investigation, it encountered an institutional reluctance to accept oversight. Executive privilege was claimed over certain documents, redactions were used in such a way that it was difficult to understand the significance of information, and some categories of documents that should have been turned over to Congress were withheld."[45] The committee concluded that one of the central harms associated with FBI informant practices was the agency's resistance to public transparency and legislative oversight.

V. Informants and the Internet

Modern information technology and the internet raise new and dramatic challenges. Courts are increasingly moving towards digitized dockets and public records made accessible over the internet. While such records were always technically available to the public, the ability to access them easily, remotely, and for free raises new issues about confidentiality and safety.[46]

The controversy over the website Whosarat.com has brought these challenges into sharp relief. Created in 2004, the website collects and posts some public court records and information about individuals who are cooperating with the government. Such information can be used by defendants who want to discredit informants who are testifying against them. It can be used by defense as well as prosecution investigators who want information about potential witnesses. It can be used by researchers to learn about the scope and nature of informant use. It can also be used by defendants or others who want to intimidate or threaten informants.

Whosarat.com triggered heated debate over the problem of witness intimidation as well as the competing need for public transparency. The *New York Times* ran an editorial on the dilemma:

> We believe that transparency is essential to a fair judicial system and it would be a mistake to overreact to one odious Web site by pulling down plea agreements from the Internet wholesale. But whosarat.com should serve notice that a different level of caution may be necessary in the wired age. In selective cases, where the life of the witness may be in jeopardy, courts should consider not putting the documents online.[47]

The court system's reaction to the potential threat has been more draconian. In November 2006, the U.S. Judicial Conference sent a memorandum to the entire federal bench, recommending "that judges consider sealing documents or hearing transcripts . . . in cases that involve sensitive information or in cases in which incorrect inferences may be made."[48] In its report on public access to electronic case files, the Judicial Conference recommended against making criminal court records electronically available to the public primarily because of the risk of exposing informants. Specifically, the conference reasoned as follows:

> Routine public remote electronic access to documents in criminal case files would allow defendants and others easy access to information regarding the cooperation and other activities of defendants.

Specifically, an individual could access documents filed in conjunction with a motion by the government for downward departure for
substantial assistance and learn details of a defendant's involvement
in the government's case. Such information could then be very easily used to intimidate, harass and possibly harm victims, defendants
and their families.[49]

Several judicial districts responded to the potential threat by restricting public access to such records, and by promoting increased
sealing.

Today's informant culture thus goes beyond the inquiry in any
specific case about whether it might be dangerous to reveal the name
of an informant or whether a particular investigation might be compromised by such revelations. Rather, the system is moving towards
wholesale policies of keeping cases, dockets, and practices secret. This
trend stands in stark contrast with Justice Kennedy's constitutional
analysis, in which he explained that the presumption of openness
must be outweighed by specific reasons for closure on a case-by-case
basis. Today, the potential threat to some witnesses is seen by courts
as a reason to overcome the presumption of openness for all criminal
records.

In these ways, the practice of using informants undermines public
transparency throughout the criminal system. By resolving liability
in secret, it insulates investigative and prosecutorial techniques from
judicial and legislative scrutiny. This reduced public access affects numerous other constituencies as well, making it more difficult for the
press, crime victims, families, and policy analysts to obtain information about the workings of the justice system or about specific criminal cases. Informant use has thus become a powerful and destructive
informational policy in its own right, reducing public transparency
and obscuring the real impact of criminal practices on individuals,
communities, and other institutions.

CHAPTER 5

Snitching in the 'Hood

No single tactic of law enforcement has contributed more to violence in the inner city than the practice of seeding the streets with informers and offering deals to "snitches." . . . [R]elying on informers threatens and eventually cripples much more than criminal enterprise. It erodes whatever social bonds exist in families, in the community, or on the streets—loyalties which, in past years, kept violence within bounds.

—Dr. Jerome Miller[1]

Ostensibly color blind, the war on drugs has been waged disproportionately against black Americans.

— Human Rights Watch[2]

ONE OF THE most infamous aspects of the U.S. criminal system is its impact on poor, black, urban communities. Largely in connection with the war on drugs, criminal law enforcement has become a pervasive presence in the nation's inner cities, especially for the young African American men who live there. Street sweeps and arrests are more prevalent in these neighborhoods; police tactics are more intrusive; and the penal process treats young black male offenders especially harshly.

Statistics offer a glimpse of the scale of the phenomenon. Approximately one in three African American males between the ages of twenty and twenty-nine are under criminal justice supervision at any given time. In some cities such as Washington, D.C., and Baltimore, the rate is as high as 50 percent, and in some neighborhoods it is higher still. One in twenty black men over the age of eighteen is in state or federal prison, compared to one in 180 white men. The chance of a black man born in 1991 spending time in prison at some point in his life hovers around one-third—higher than his chances of attending college, getting married, or joining the military.[3]

These statistics result in large part from the disparate treatment of black drug offenders. Although blacks and whites use drugs at approximately the same rates—9.7 percent for African Americans and 8.1 percent for whites—African American men are arrested and incarcerated for drug offenses at vastly higher rates than white male offenders. Nearly sixty percent of all incarcerated drug offenders are black, even though they comprise only 13 percent of the population. For every one hundred thousand black Americans, 359 are imprisoned on drug charges; for whites, the analogous number is twenty-eight. In at least fifteen states, black drug offenders are incarcerated at twenty to fifty-seven times the rate of whites. Race also affects sentencing: even where black and white defendants commit the same offenses and have the same criminal histories, black defendants routinely receive harsher punishments.[4]

While data on Latinos are not as readily available, the trends are disturbingly similar, with Latinos comprising an ever greater proportion of the criminal system's population and receiving harsher punishments than white defendants. Together, African Americans and Hispanics comprise nearly 75 percent of drug offenders in state prisons.[5] Because drug offenses make up approximately one-third of all convictions—the largest single category of offense—the racial skew in drug enforcement distorts the entire system.[6]

In the poorest urban communities, crime statistics flow from a bleak social context. African Americans endure the highest rates of crime and victimization, with homicide victimization rates nearly eight times that of whites.[7] And crime is just one piece of the puzzle. Poor inner-city neighborhoods suffer from pervasive joblessness, substandard housing, and racially segregated schools of poor quality.[8] Drug dealing and other grey-market economic activities are inextricably intertwined with the legal economy and with everyday experiences. As sociologist Sudhir Venkatesh puts it, "figuring out exactly what is and isn't 'criminal' can be very hard in the ghetto, because it is difficult to find much in people's day-to-day lives that does not involve the underground economy."[9] High levels of criminal offending and victimization thus take place within a larger framework of poverty and social insecurity.[10]

For these socially fragile, heavily policed communities, law-enforcement policies have special significance. In many ways, criminal enforcement is the most palpable form of governance to make itself felt in these neighborhoods. Not only do criminal policies affect individuals and their families who are touched by crime, but routine experiences with police, prosecutors, probation officers, and courts affect the way residents perceive the entire governmental apparatus. In communities where the penal system plays such a large role, law enforcement practices color people's more general perceptions of the legitimacy, effectiveness, and fairness of the government, above and beyond its narrow crime-fighting function.[11]

Informant use is one such practice. Drug enforcement has focused its resources in these neighborhoods, resulting in the heaviest concentrations of drug-related arrestees and convicted offenders in the country.[12] Central to this pervasive drug enforcement presence is the creation and maintenance of criminal informants. These already vulnerable communities thus experience the consequences of snitching to a higher and more extreme degree. This confluence has several important implications.

First, there are more criminal informants in these communities than elsewhere, in some neighborhoods many more. This fact alone has significance for extended families and social networks. Second, pervasive snitching exacerbates certain kinds of crime, worsening the very neighborhood conditions that law enforcement is trying to remedy. And third, the widespread use of criminal informants alters the role of the police—their interactions with suspects as well as their relationships with residents.

I. More Snitches

How many criminal informants are there in poor, urban neighborhoods? This is a difficult question because no one, not even the officials who use them, knows with any certainty how many informants exist in the entire system. Because there is no direct data, we therefore need to extrapolate.

The federal system provides the most information. The U.S. Department of Justice reports that in 2007, 14 percent of all federal defendants received a sentencing departure for cooperation, and 25 percent of drug defendants did.[13] An earlier report by Sentencing Commission researchers estimates that as many as two-thirds of all federal defendants actually cooperate in some way, although less than half of all cooperating defendants receive a recorded sentencing benefit.[14] If only half of all cooperating defendants get sentencing credit, this would suggest that about 30 percent of all federal offenders—and half of all drug offenders—cooperate in some way even if their sentences do not publicly reflect it.

While important, these federal statistics are of limited value in assessing the national state of affairs. First, the federal system is small, comprising only about one-tenth of the U.S. criminal system. Furthermore, as described above, the federal sentencing guidelines and U.S. criminal code are expressly designed to promote cooperation through the mechanics of mandatory minimum sentences and constraints on judicial discretion. State criminal systems treat these issues differently. Accordingly, while the federal picture of pervasive cooperation is relatively clear, it is only a piece of a larger puzzle.

At the state and local level, we have less direct information. Unlike the federal system, most states lack systemic record keeping to track defendants who benefit at sentencing from having cooperated. Likewise, there is little or no data on suspects who provide information and receive benefits at earlier stages in a case. Nevertheless, while state and local law enforcement does not directly reveal how often it uses or rewards informants, we can still deduce the probable impact of informant use on urban black communities.

First of all, we know that drug arrests and prosecutions are concentrated in black neighborhoods: African Americans account for 32 percent of national drug possession arrests, 47 percent of drug sale arrests, and an even higher percentage of convictions.[15] In certain states and urban areas, rates are even higher.[16] Criminal informants are staple features of such investigations and cases. All by itself, therefore, the scale of drug enforcement in black communities indicates that the scale of criminal informant use will be similarly and disproportionately large.

We also know that a staggering proportion of young African American men are under criminal supervision at any given time. As of 1995, 32 percent of all black men nationally between the ages of twenty and twenty-nine were either incarcerated or on probation or parole at any given time. But this average hides the fact that the phenomenon varies widely from community to community. Some predominantly black neighborhoods have low to nonexistent arrest rates, and some economically and educationally advantaged African American men have a much lower chance of being touched by the criminal system. Conversely, some black neighborhoods have massive arrest and incarceration rates far exceeding 32 percent, and black men with low education levels from economically depressed communities have a much higher chance of criminal involvement.

For example, studies estimate that approximately half of the black male populations of Washington D.C., and Baltimore are under criminal justice supervision.[17] Within such cities, the impact of the criminal system is further concentrated. Fourteen percent of all offenders released from Maryland prisons in 2001, nearly 40 percent of whom were drug offenders, returned to a mere six Baltimore neighborhoods.[18] Similarly, half of all released prisoners in Illinois returned to Chicago, and 34 percent of those returned to just six neighborhoods.[19] In other words, criminal-system involvement is often highly localized in specific neighborhoods in ways that national statistics and averages obscure.

How much of this localized involvement in the criminal system implicates snitching? One way of approximating an answer is to ask how much of this criminal involvement involves drug offenses, addiction, or other crimes that law enforcement typically handles by creating or using informants. The answer is, probably about half. Approximately 34 percent of all state felony convictions are drug offenses, 46 percent of which involve African American defendants.[20] In turn, approximately 40 percent of African American convictions involve drug offenses, the sort of crime in which defendants are often heavily pressured to provide information.[21]

Drug convictions are not the only high-snitch arenas. Burglary, for example, is an arena in which police traditionally rely on informants, and it comprises a little over 8 percent of all state felony convictions.[22]

Widespread substance abuse among the criminal justice population also plays a crucial role. Many offenders commit addiction-related crimes such as burglary, theft, and other property crimes in order to feed their habits. For example, in 1996, 16 percent of all jailed offenders in the United States committed their offenses in order to get money for drugs, and one-quarter of property and drug offenders did.[23] More broadly, approximately one-third of criminal offenders are under the influence of drugs at the time of their offenses, while as many as 80 percent of inmates have a history of substance abuse.[24] A large percentage of property crimes and other offenses are thus "drug-related," in the sense that the defendant commits the crime because of his chemical dependency. Because such defendants have knowledge of and connections to the drug world, they are prime candidates to become informants. The pervasiveness of addiction in the criminal justice population—and the law enforcement predilection for turning addicts into snitches—therefore suggests that pressure to inform is being brought to bear in a wide range of cases.

Taken together, this means that close to half of the entire U.S. criminal justice population is either a drug offender and/or chemically dependent. More than half of the African American criminal justice population will fall into this category because they make up a higher proportion of drug cases. The system naturally puts pressure on this half of the population to become informants by virtue of the nature of their offenses, their potential addiction problems, and the increasingly heavy sentences that drug and recidivist offenders face.

But pressure is one thing and snitching is quite another. How many suspects actually bend to the pressure and provide information? Again, we need to extrapolate. Federal statistics suggest a general cooperation rate of 30 percent, and 50 percent for drug offenders, but that will not hold true for all state or local jurisdictions. The pressure to cooperate is probably higher for federal drug crimes than it is in jurisdictions that lack high minimum sentences, lack mandatory sentencing guidelines, or generally sentence at a lower threshold. On the other hand, the federal system deals less with the kinds of petty drug offenses that are ripe for snitching, and the kinds of informal street deals described above are more likely to occur between local addicts and beat cops than with the FBI.

For the sake of argument, let us assume that state and local drug offenders snitch at half the rate of federal drug offenders. In other words, let us assume that one-quarter of this high-risk group actually cooperates with law enforcement, providing information about accomplices, acquaintances, friends, neighbors, or family.

The implications of this estimate are potentially dramatic. In those localized high-crime neighborhoods in which approximately half of the black men between the ages of twenty and twenty-nine are under criminal supervision, half of *those* fall into the high-risk snitching group. If as many as one quarter of *those* individuals are actually snitching, that would mean that in some of these small neighborhoods, one in sixteen black men in this age group—or about 6 percent—may actually be giving the government information at any given time.

Six percent would be a lot. It would implicate many extended families, apartment complexes, neighborhood events, and church congregations. It would make it likely that someone—maybe more than one someone—in that group or institution or network would have already given information, or might actively be trying to find incriminating information about others, and would have the police's ear when he does.

To be sure, this estimate may be too high. In some districts, police and prosecutors indicate that they do not routinely rely on criminal informants, even in drug cases. Alternatively, this estimate may be too low. Many observers of the criminal system, from judges to sociologists, conclude that drug cases almost always involve snitches, that street criminals routinely cooperate with the police, and that informing is pervasive.

In sum, we simply do not know directly or with any certainty how many people are actually working criminal informants, or how many young African American men are under pressure to inform. And the most serious manifestation of the phenomenon will be limited to those neighborhoods with the highest concentrations of crime, police presence, and social vulnerability. But we do know that the structure of the penal system, and its deep penetration into poor black communities, together with the habits of law enforcement, make it likely that in our most economically distressed neighborhoods a significant proportion of the young black male population is under heavy governmental pressure to provide information about others in order to avoid incarceration.

Answering the empirical question of how many snitches there are does not, of course, answer the normative question—what's wrong with a lot of snitching? After all, residents of high-crime communities have the deepest interest in crime control, not least because high crime rates mean high victimization rates. Such communities need ways to get information to the police and to prevent and solve crimes. Using criminal informants is one way that police can get such information.

Numbers alone also cannot explain what is problematic about living with snitches. It is sometimes said that only the guilty should fear informants, because only the guilty have something to hide. If the practice successfully disrupts criminal activity, law-abiding citizens benefit.

There is some truth in both these propositions. It is indisputable that high-crime communities need better crime control, better cooperation between police and residents, and more safety and security. The tricky question is whether those goals are promoted by creating criminal informants in the ways that we currently do. And although the criminal process resists disclosure on this subject, the limited evidence suggests that snitching practices may be counterproductive in precisely this regard. Not only can informants exacerbate crime, violence, and other destructive phenomena, but even for the innocent, the pervasive presence of criminals trying to work off their charges can create fear, distrust, and social dysfunction. These problems are explored below.

II. More Crime

Criminal informants commit crimes. This is true both by definition and in practice. First, by definition, an informant provides information in order to escape the consequences of having already committed a crime. That means that every snitch deal inherently involves a governmental decision not to pursue and punish that informant's previous crimes. Active criminal informants also typically commit new crimes or help others do so while they are cooperating with the government.

For example, as part of its investigation into a fencing ring in Portland, Oregon, the FBI permitted and promoted the ongoing theft of retail merchandise from local stores in order to collect evidence against the illegal second-hand sellers. As part of this effort the FBI enlisted the help of two criminals—Lorie Brewster and David Pankratz. According to the court,

> Brewster . . . drove boosters [drug-addict shoplifters] to retail outlets to shoplift merchandise. In exchange for her cooperation as an informant, the FBI granted her transactional immunity and allowed her to keep approximately $130,000 she later received from the boosters as payment for her services as a driver. . . . Pankratz [was] a wholesale purchaser and an online reseller of "specialized" stolen merchandise, such as office products, inkjet cartridges, and computer software and accessories. The FBI induced Pankratz to continue his activities and act as an informant. In exchange, Pankratz also received transactional immunity and was allowed to keep more than a million dollars worth of the proceeds from his on-line resale activities.[25]

Above and beyond such authorized crimes, however, informants also routinely commit unauthorized crimes. In other words, once a criminal agrees to provide information to the government, he may continue to commit new offenses on his own initiative to which police and prosecutors may or may not turn a blind eye. The fact that law enforcement tolerates some unchecked criminality by its informants constitutes one of the practice's major dangers and poses a special threat to high-crime communities in which this unchecked criminality takes place. For example, from the *Pittsburgh Tribune*:

> Brenda DelBene was stocking blueberry Pop-Tarts when a masked man stuck an AK-47 in her face. "Look away, look down and get on the ground," said the gunman. . . . Robert E. Harper—the man charged with the robbery—was no ordinary criminal. Harper should have been in jail to await sentencing for [six] other armed robberies. But he was on the streets because he bought his freedom with information in a grand jury probe of drug dealing at the . . . jail. Twice he was granted house arrest with electronic monitoring at the request of jail officials and [the] District Attorney. . . . [W]hile on house arrest Harper committed 16 armed robberies and shot two people.[26]

In Tampa, Florida, police handlers permitted their informant to use his government-issued cell phone to "scheme[] to steal property and beat up his friends. While his police handlers listened in and looked the other way, he even threatened to beat the mother of his child so badly 'that her brain will seep from her ears.'"[27]

In his classic study of police practices in a typical midsized American city, Professor Jerome Skolnick concluded that as a general matter, "burglary detectives permit informants to commit narcotics offenses, while narcotics detectives allow informants to steal."[28] More generally, sociological studies find that police assume and know that their informants commit unauthorized crimes. One study described a St. Louis street snitch who "stayed out of sight for several days after giving information to the police" since snitching had permitted him to escape his "third weapons charge" and "he reasoned [that his] quick appearance almost certainly would indicate that he had snitched in exchange for his freedom."[29]

Finally, every time police reward an addict with cash for drugs or even drugs themselves, they enable that informant's continued illegal drug use. As one officer put it,

Payment to addict-informants puts the officer in something of a moral quandary. We can be reasonably certain that monies given to an addicted person are going to be used to support that addiction. Because the addiction can only be maintained by violating the law, this places the officer in the position of tolerating or at least knowing of ongoing criminal activity—something we are paid to stop.[30]

Of course not all informants commit new crimes, authorized or unauthorized. Some simply provide information about past crimes and hope for reduced punishment for what they've already done. But active informants populate a gray world of continuing criminal activity, in which some crime is openly encouraged by the government, some crime is tolerated or ignored, and some is never discovered. These new crimes typically occur in the communities in which informants live, forcing friends, families, residents, and businesses to contend with higher incidents of drug use and dealing, thefts, weapons, violence, and the myriad other offenses that informants commit while working for the government.

III. More Violence

In the quotation at the beginning of this chapter, Dr. Jerome Miller explained in 1996 how using criminal informants exacerbates violence in inner-city communities. Not only do snitches commit crimes themselves, but they erode social mechanisms for keeping the peace by creating distrust and inviting retaliation.

Ten years later, sociologists confirmed this observation. Richard Rosenfeld, Bruce Jacobs, and Richard Wright write that police snitching tactics "contribute to the violence in already dangerous communities." Their street-level studies of police and informant behavior reveal that because criminals cannot trust each other, "dependence on firearms is likely to rise; without accomplices, guns become the backup." More generally, "[t]he practice undermines trust and breaks apart communities. It erodes faith in official authorities. It foments retaliation, which ignites the street-level microstructure in potentially deadly conflict spirals." They conclude that "snitching is a pervasive element of inner-city street life that poses dangers for street criminals and law-abiding residents alike."[31]

Gangs and other criminal organizations famously use violence to deter snitching. Researchers in organizational science have long recognized that deploying informants in any organization can be expected to lead to violence, as the organization responds by trying to police itself more firmly.[32] Government studies found that the spike in witness intimidation in the mid-1990s was directly linked to increased gang activity, and was most prevalent in connection with violent crime.[33] Even more specifically, studies of violence in the drug trade identify the "elimination of informers" as a structural source of ongoing violence.[34]

The death of sixteen-year-old Martha Puebla exemplifies the violent side effects of snitching policies. In an effort to obtain a confession, Los Angeles police lied to a gang member and told him that Puebla was informing on him. This misrepresentation led not to a confession but to Puebla's murder.[35] Likewise, when police in Brea, California, turned seventeen-year-old Chad MacDonald into an informant, it led not only to MacDonald's death but also to the rape and shooting of his sixteen-year-old girlfriend by gang members against whom MacDonald was informing.[36] In other words, when government officials turn to criminal informants as a law enforcement tool, particularly in connection with drug gangs, they should expect to provoke more violence in the communities most affected by those tactics. Because fear and violence constitute some of the most devastating aspects of impoverished inner-city life, this particular effect of snitching policies is one of the most costly and disturbing.

IV. Racial Focusing

Another collateral consequence of informant use is that it focuses law enforcement attention on the communities in which informants live.

After all, snitches tend to snitch on the people with whom they live and interact. When police rely heavily on informants to direct new investigations, police resources will naturally be channeled back into the communities from which the informants come.

This phenomenon has special significance for high-crime urban communities to which drug enforcement resources are already overly devoted. It suggests that the use of informants is part of the reason why minority communities are overrepresented in drug enforcement efforts. For example, the San Diego Search Warrant Project concluded that search warrants were issued disproportionately against black and Hispanic residences in predominantly minority neighborhoods. Although blacks and Hispanics comprise less than one-third of the San Diego population, over 80 percent of all warrants—and 98 percent of all warrants seeking cocaine—targeted black and Hispanic households. The majority of those warrants turned up no evidence, while two-thirds of warrants directed at white homes produced contraband. One reason for this disparity is that 80 percent of warrants were based on confidential informants. Because informants tend to give information about individuals in their own racial groups, the study hypothesized that disproportionate arrests of African Americans and Hispanics would lead to disproportionate—and inaccurate—targeting of black and Hispanic homes.[37]

The racial focusing phenomenon also means that urban communities and their minority residents are overexposed to the unreliability associated with informants. False accusations, mistaken warrants, erroneous raids, and wrongful convictions associated with snitches will be more frequent in communities in which the practice is prevalent. The fact that many of the wrongful convictions described throughout this book involve African Americans is not a coincidence. Rather, it is the natural consequence of the deployment of criminal informants in poor black neighborhoods and against black defendants.[38]

V. More Tension between Police and Community

A long-standing legacy of distrust exists between African American communities and the police. As law professor Randall Kennedy writes,

> For a long time, criminal law—not simply the biased administration of law but the law itself—was the enemy of African-Americans. In many places, for several generations, it was a crime for blacks to learn to read, to flee enslavement, or to defend themselves, their families, or their friends from physical abuse. . . . More recently, during the civil rights era, African-Americans violated criminal laws . . . to uproot the Jim Crow system. . . . That is . . . why James Baldwin wrote in 1966 that "to respect the law in the context in which the Negro finds himself is simply to surrender . . . self-respect." [39]

The distrust is also socioeconomic and personal, flowing from urban economic and policing policies as well as the individual experiences of many African Americans. As sociologist Robert Sampson puts it, "inner city contexts of racial segregation and concentrated disadvantage, where inability to influence the structures of power that constrain lives is greatest, also breed cynicism and perceptions of legal injustice." The fact that "low income and minority-group populations are most likely to perceive injustice . . . and to express cynicism about the legitimacy of laws and the ability of the police to do their job in an effective and nondiscriminatory manner [is] contextual in origin and not reducible to differences in crime rates." [40] Personal experiences with racial profiling, violence, and victimization make African American relationships with police all the more tense.[41]

The official deployment of criminal informants is one more ingredient in this already-volatile matrix. As discussed at greater length in the next chapter, criminal informants can affect community trust in and reliance on police. Some press accounts suggest that people associate snitching with police failure. One reporter's interviews revealed young people who thought that "police gave too much power to informants" and that "[w]hoever gives them (police) a story, they believe." The interviewed youth concluded that "police should rely less on informants" and that "snitching should stop."[42]

Others like David Kennedy, director of the Center for Crime Prevention and Control at the John Jay College of Criminal Justice in New York, attribute the breakdown of trust between community and police directly to the war on drugs: "This is the reward we have reaped for 20 years of profligate drug enforcement in these communities." When law-abiding residents resist cooperating with police, Kennedy thinks their silence "doesn't come from fear, but from anger," an anger that flows in part from the drug enforcement tactic of manipulating criminal cooperation.[43]

The loss of trust fuels a vicious cycle because the legitimacy and efficacy of law enforcement practices depend heavily on public perception. Psychologist Tom Tyler has studied the importance of the perception of legitimacy, arguing that when people feel that law enforcement is fair, evenhanded, and effective, they are more likely to obey the law and cooperate with police. Conversely, when people perceive law enforcement as racially biased, unfair, or unprincipled, they are less likely to cede legitimacy and authority to the police.[44]

The widespread use of informants affects public perceptions of police legitimacy in numerous ways. It erodes the appearance of fairness because it represents the open toleration of crime by the very people charged with enforcing it. Residents who see police tolerating open drug dealing, or failing to arrest other kinds of perpetrators, or letting arrestees go immediately are likely to lose faith in the enforcement process. Particularly when residents have personal connections to individuals who commit crimes but are not punished for them, their sense of law enforcement commitment and efficacy is bound to suffer.

Snitching also teaches a destructive lesson in civics: that the law is for sale. Criminals who escape punishment by informing have in effect bought their freedom. The government's willingness to trade away liability even for violent and destructive crimes sends the public message that the law can be broken under the right circumstances, and that people can get away with murder if they know how to play the game. When police tolerate further criminality from their informants, the message is even worse. It says that the government prizes its informers over law and order itself.

Finally, criminal informants make the legal process secret and unpredictable, governed by personal relationships between police and criminals rather than by public rules. Crime and punishment can be negotiated off the record, under the table, subject to the law of the urban jungle. For communities in which the criminal system is often the most visible manifestation of the government itself, this kind of governance is a powerful reminder that power, not law, is the name of the game.

It is also terribly ironic, for it is the residents of these very same communities who suffer the most from criminal law's harshness: intrusive policing, long sentences, and the many devastating collateral consequences of criminal convictions, such as disenfranchisement and the deprivation of public benefits. In other words, the very same people who are punished most harshly for breaking the law are also taught by snitching that the law is contingent, erratic, a matter of power and luck, and sometimes not enforced at all. It should thus come as no surprise that these communities are often pervaded by distrust of the law and of police, and by the belief that the criminal system does not deliver justice.

VI. More Distrust

> What bothers me the most is that the law puts these young men in a position to snitch on each other. And they'll make them say things, put such fear in them and make them say things, you know, cause them to snitch on people that have been friends and family. That's, I guess, the most profound thing is that family members are telling lies on family members in order to save themselves.
>
> —Pastor Elaine Alford, Mobile, Alabama[45]

The final sort of toll that informant policies can exact from high-crime communities is social in nature. What is it like to live in a community in which as many as 6 percent of the young male population might be criminal informants? What is it like to know that people around you may be committing crimes and working with the police at the same time? Recall that these are not just any communities but primarily high-crime, economically unstable, socially vulnerable neighborhoods in which many families are dependent on governmental services, many individuals are already on probation or parole, and social networks are already fragile.

Pervasive informing can distort the most intimate of relationships. When Paulyn Miller was arrested on forgery charges, she volunteered to police that she had information implicating her son in a four-year-old murder case. She agreed to wear a wire and testify against him, in exchange for which she received a sentence of probation.[46] By contrast, Lula May Smith served seven years in federal prison because she refused to testify against her son Darren. The prosecutor on her case admitted that Lula May was only prosecuted in order to get to her son, that he "kept hoping [and] pray[ing]" that she would be acquitted, and that even at the time of her trial he believed that she should not have gone to jail.[47]

The caustic effects of such arrangements are not limited to individuals or even families. Interpersonal trust is a crucial ingredient for community survival, and studies show that poor urban neighborhoods are particularly dependent on social trust networks. Because such communities typically lack strong economic and public institutions, people rely on family and informal networks for jobs, income, shelter, child care, and other vital resources.[48] Social networks also play a vital role in preventing crime in the first place. According to Professor Sampson's research, crime and disorder directly correlate with a neighborhood's ability to maintain cohesive social networks. Strong networks facilitate order; weak ties permit disorder.[49]

Poor urban neighborhoods are especially vulnerable to criminal informants because social networks are more disorganized and people's lives and spaces are less private. As Professor Michael Tonry writes,

> For a variety of reasons, it is easier to make arrests in socially disorganized neighborhoods. . . . [Specifically,] it is easier for undercover narcotics officers to penetrate networks of friends

and acquaintances in poor urban minority neighborhoods than in more stable and closely knit working-class and middle-class neighborhoods.[50]

This means that personal relationships in poor, high-crime communities are more fragile and vulnerable, making intrusive law enforcement tactics such as snitching both more potent and more devastating.

VII. Snitching as a Costly Social Policy

The potential implications of informant use for socially disadvantaged, crime-ridden communities are formidable: more snitches, more crime, more violence, more police-community dysfunction, and more distrust. Taken together, they tell us that informant use is not merely a law enforcement tactic but rather an important social policy in its own right, affecting families, social networks, and public perceptions of the legal system itself.

To be sure, the dramatic impact of snitching will be limited to a small number of neighborhoods. For most U.S. communities and institutions, snitching is not a quality-of-life issue. There are simply not enough informants to impact the everyday experiences of residents, and those informants who do exist remain invisible. Not so for our poorest, high-crime, inner-city neighborhoods. In these concentrated areas, there are likely to be many informants, enough so that residents live with the knowledge of their presence as well as the threats of informant-related crime and violence. In neighborhoods where police relations are already tenuous, informant policies can further erode residents' sense of personal security and social trust, and undermine public faith in the police. Although these communities may be few in number, they constitute the most troubling subjects of the penal system, both because they are home to so many people enmeshed in the criminal process and because they pay the highest price when our justice policies go awry. An official practice that threatens them with special harms thus deserves our closest scrutiny.

The special circumstances of urban poverty also alter the cost-benefit analysis of informant use. First and foremost, the harms of the policy are greater in these neighborhoods. But second, the benefits may also be smaller due to the flexible nature of the drug economy and the fungibility of individual players. Analysts from across the political spectrum have concluded that twenty years of harsh law enforcement tactics have been largely ineffective against the illegal drug economy: the United States maintains record rates of drug use, and illegal drugs are cheaper than they were two decades ago.[51] This means that using informants as part of an overall drug enforcement strategy does not produce the kinds of long-term benefits that it may in other arenas. For example, the FBI's use of mafia informants over the years helped to capture numerous high-level bosses and to destabilize the organizational strength of the mob.[52] By contrast, when police use criminal snitches to bust a midlevel drug dealer or shut down a crack house, new dealers and houses spring up to take their places. This means that even as the harms associated with that informant persist, the benefits of his deployment may quickly dissipate. The tragedy is that in the high-crime neighborhoods most in need of better law enforcement, pervasive criminal snitching could be making things worse.

CHAPTER 6

"Stop Snitching"

People using drugs, selling guns and posted on the corner. Snitches.
—seventh-grader's description of her Hartford,
Connecticut, neighborhood[1]

Guys doin' all this crime and not doin' no time because they're telling
on the next man.
—Rayco Saunders's explanation for why he wore a
"Stop Snitching" t-shirt to court[2]

IN 1998, I taught an after-school law class in inner-city Baltimore. The class attracted a variety of kids, ranging from elementary-school to high-school age. Some were interested, some were just hanging around the community center with nothing else to do, and some had parents, coaches, or probation officers who pressured them into attending. I was trying to explain several complex constitutional principles, and the students were losing interest. Finally, a bright-eyed boy who looked to be about twelve years old raised his hand.

"I got a question," he said, leaning forward intently. "Police let dealers stay on the corner 'cuz they snitchin'. Is that legal? I mean, can the police do that?"

The question took me off guard. I had to think for a minute, and then explained that the police did indeed have discretion to let offenders remain free. The boy's face sagged with disgust. "That ain't right," he huffed, and a number of other young people chimed in. "They ain't doing their jobs!" exclaimed one. "So all you gotta do is snitch," another concluded, "and you can keep on dealing."

Six years later, the now-infamous "Stop Snitching" DVD circulated the streets of Baltimore, making national headlines and introducing much of the country to the concept of snitching. A local rapper named "Skinny Suge" (born Ronny Thomas) walked the streets
of West Baltimore with a camera, talking to local residents. Hanging
out in cars and on street corners, many of the interviewees identified
as being dealers or "in the game," as they referred to it. They "talked
trash" about themselves and each other, told stories, and complained
about corrupt police officers (two of whom were later convicted as
a result). They laughed, they rapped, and they told jokes. They also
talked about snitching. They said that people "in the game" shouldn't
snitch in order to escape punishment. They made threatening statements, suggesting that snitches might "get a hole in their head." One
man identified another person as a potential snitch: "He's dead," he
rapped, "because I don't believe he's from the 'hood."[3] Two interviewees displayed guns.

Few would have paid attention this low-budget, off-beat home
movie except for two things. The first was the brief appearance in one
sequence of basketball star Carmelo Anthony, forward for the Den-
ver Nuggets and Baltimore native, who happened to be home for a
visit. While 'Melo did not make any threats against cooperating witnesses, he stood by and laughed while two neighborhood acquaintances talked trash and suggested that snitches would come to harm.
Anthony later denied knowing the substance of the video and repu-
diated the "stop snitching" idea, saying that he was "not that type of
person."[4] As a result of Anthony's presence in the video, however, it
was widely picked up by national media outlets.

The second thing was that the video spawned a new rash of "stop
snitching" t-shirts—usually the word "SNITCH" circled in red
and crossed out like a no-smoking sign, or sometimes just "STOP
SNITCHING" emblazoned in large letters. The t-shirts had been
spotted in other cities, but after the DVD a large number appeared
in Baltimore as well as Boston, Pittsburgh, and Milwaukee, and the
media took notice. In turn, several high-profile events made the "stop
snitching" t-shirt a cultural icon in its own right. In 2005 in Pittsburgh, Pennsylvania, an assault victim named Rayco Saunders wore

a t-shirt to the trial of his alleged assaulters. Fearing that the shirt would disrupt the trial, the prosecutor had Saunders removed from the courthouse. Eventually the cases against the three defendants were dismissed for the lack of Saunders's cooperation.[5] Saunders's explanation for why he interfered with the prosecution of his own attackers is quoted at the beginning of this chapter.

That same year in Boston, Mayor Thomas Menino tried to ban the shirts, arguing that they were impeding law enforcement and intimidating witnesses. "We're going into every retail store that sells the shirts and removing them," Mayor Menino declared. Although the city backed off the ban after the ACLU objected, several stores took the shirts off the shelves.[6]

The "stop snitching" phenomenon gained additional traction when several rap artists publicly refused to talk to police about crimes they had witnessed. In 2005, rap artist Lil' Kim was sentenced to a year in prison for lying to a federal grand jury about a shooting. BET ran a story on the period leading up to her incarceration, entitled "Countdown to Lockdown," in which it portrayed Lil' Kim as going to prison with her "mouth shut and head held high."[7] The next year, rapper Busta Rhymes refused to speak to police about the shooting death of his bodyguard, Israel Ramirez. Police allege that Rhymes was standing next to Ramirez when he was shot.[8]

In 2007, "stop snitching" hit prime time when CNN anchor Anderson Cooper hosted a series of shows on the phenomenon. The first, which ran on *60 Minutes*, focused on the links between the music industry and the "stop snitching" motto. Playing snippets of songs in which rappers exhort listeners to "stop snitching," the segment suggested that the music industry was actively exploiting antipolice sentiment. In an interview with rap artist Cam'ron, Cooper asked him why he did not talk to the police after he was shot in both arms. Cam'ron responded, "Because of the type of business I'm in, it would definitely hurt my business, and the way that I was raised, I just don't do that. I was raised differently, not to tell." Cooper also asked the rapper whether he would call the police if he knew that a serial killer lived next door to him. Cam'ron answered, "No, I wouldn't—I wouldn't call and tell anybody on them, but I'd probably move. But

I'm not going to call and be like, you know, 'The serial killer's in 4E.'"[9] Cam'ron later apologized for the remark.

Commentators' reactions have varied widely. In 2007, journalist Ethan Brown, who writes extensively about hip hop in relation to "stop snitching," described the furor over Rhymes, Cam'ron, and the t-shirts generally as "overheated rhetoric with no effort by pundits or politicians to explore and examine the complex tangle of legal and cultural issues that helped create the phenomenon."[10] Others such as CNN's Cooper blame the music industry for a marketing world that glorifies crime, violence, and antipolice sentiment for profit.

Finally, the "stop snitching" motto has melded with the long-standing problem of witness intimidation, and the related reluctance of civilian witnesses to come forward when they observe violent crime. In 2007, in Trenton, New Jersey, seven-year-old Tajahnique Lee was shot in the face by a stray bullet from a gang fight in front of at least twenty people. No one came forward to identify the shooters. One woman who was standing ten feet away said she was too distracted to see. The girl's grandmother refused to talk to police, expressing fear that she would "have to move out of the country."[11] In the minds of many, this kind of reticence has become associated with the motto.

Such events have elevated the public profile of the "stop snitching" phenomenon, which turns out to be complex, deep-seated, and long-standing. It did not begin with a DVD or a rap song, nor will it end when the t-shirts go out of style. It is simultaneously a criminal code of the street, a reflection of widespread communal distrust of police, as well as, more recently, a tool of intimidation against civilian witnesses. While the phenomenon was born in the penal system, it has spread beyond its criminal roots, a product of the multifaceted challenges of urban crime, gang violence, race, drugs, and policing through criminal informants.

I. "In the Game"

The 2004 Baltimore "Stop Snitching" DVD was a self-proclaimed product of the drug economy. Part of an ongoing conversation among individuals who work in or around the underground world of drug dealing, it advocated a particular code of the street: those who choose to make their living by breaking the law should not be permitted to escape the costs of that choice by turning in their criminal associates.

As the DVD's producer Rodney Bethea made clear, "Stop Snitching" was not directed at civilian witnesses, senior citizens watching out their windows, or innocent bystanders calling 911. Bethea explained as follows: "When we refer to snitches, we are referring to a person engaging and profiting from illegal activities. And when they get arrested, to save themselves, they tell on everyone else they know." Bethea said that in the DVD, the "snitch" label did not refer to "the little old lady on the block" who calls the police. "She is not considered a snitch. She's a civilian doing what she's supposed to do."[12]

Most commentators agree that the original meaning of "stop snitching"—and thus much of its continuing significance—flows from the world of criminal offenders and does not refer to civilian witnesses at all. As Harlem social activist Geoffrey Canada put it in an interview on CNN, "this issue of snitching has come straight from the penitentiary."[13] Hip hop executive and producer Damon Dash agrees that it's not snitching "if you're someone who hasn't committed to the game."[14]

After rapper Cam'ron's interview on *60 Minutes*, veteran gangsta rapper and actor Ice-T, who plays a police officer on the television show *Law and Order SVU*, weighed in:

> A snitch is someone who commits a crime with a partner and gets caught. Instead of keeping his mouth shut and taking responsibility for his criminal activity, he cuts a deal with the police for lighter sentencing in exchange for ratting out his partner. The "Stop Snitching" code is one shared among those in the underworld and has nothing to do with someone who is uninvolved in being a witness to a crime.[15]

The fact that the "stop snitching" idea originated as a criminal code of conduct has not prevented it from taking on a complex life of its own;

it now has a wider variety of meanings in the law-abiding world. But the criminal roots of the idea remain important because they demonstrate how criminal policies can impact civil society far beyond their intended law enforcement goals. The twenty-year official practice of relying heavily on criminal informants in high-crime communities turned out to be an influential social policy. It changed not only the ways in which offenders perceive the system but also the ways in which law-abiding residents perceive law enforcement. Under governmental pressure to flip, criminal offenders ratcheted up existing taboos against snitching. That response spilled over into the broader culture, coloring the ways in which children, families, and community members understand the act of talking to police.

II. Distrust of the Police

The fact that criminal snitching weakens civil perceptions of law enforcement raises a thorny question: Why does this particular criminal policy resonate so strongly with a noncriminal audience? After all, most law enforcement tactics do not inspire movies or fashionable apparel. In other words, why does "stop snitching" make sense to anyone who isn't "in the game"?

At the heart of the broader "stop snitching" phenomenon lies distrust of the police, a long-standing problem in poor and minority communities. The history of policing in African American neighborhoods has been famously fraught with official violence and racism, and the tolerance of black-on-black crime.[16] Some of the most famous riots in urban American history, including those in Los Angeles and Miami, have been triggered by police brutality against black men.[17] Racial profiling remains a nationwide problem. High-profile cases in New York City such as the torture of Abner Louima and the fatal police shootings of unarmed Amadou Diallo and Sean Bell are constant reminders that too many police view too many black males as threats and fair targets.[18]

Public opinion reflects this distrust: in current polls black respondents typically express less faith in police and the justice system than their white or Hispanic counterparts.[19] One-third of black respondents expressed "very little" confidence in the police, compared to 60 percent of whites who expressed a "great deal" of confidence.[20] As former U.S. attorney general Janet Reno put it, "the perception of too many Americans is that police officers cannot be trusted. . . . Especially in minority communities residents believe the police have used excessive force, that law enforcement is too aggressive, that law enforcement is biased, disrespectful and unfair."[21] While there have been vast improvements since 1944 when sociologist Gunnar Myrdal wrote that "the police officer stands not only for civic order but also for White Supremacy," tension between police and African Americans remains substantial.

This distrust is not only historical and communal but personal. After NBA star Carmelo Anthony was lambasted in the press for appearing in the "Stop Snitching" DVD, he apologized and distanced himself from the "stop snitching" idea. But months later, in a more intimate interview with *ESPN Magazine*, he described in greater detail his own conflicted relationship to the police growing up in Baltimore. Police, for example, beat him up. "Nothing major," he said. "They'd just choke me, drag me around." By contrast, "drug dealers funded our programs. Drug dealers bought our uniforms." They didn't ask Anthony for anything in return, he said. "They just wanted to see you do good."

Despite his previous repudiation, Anthony appeared to accept the "stop snitching" ethos. "I would never snitch," he said to ESPN. "I would never testify on anything. That's just the street code. If you snitch, you're talking about someone's life."[22]

Jeremy Travis, president of the John Jay College of Criminal Justice, considers the distrustful "stop snitching" phenomenon to be a function of the failed policies of the war on drugs. "We have every reason to suspect," he says, "that our criminal justice policies are undermining respect for the law, as we witness the growth of a 'stop snitching' culture in communities of color that punishes young people who cooperate with the police."[23] Journalist Ethan Brown is even more specific, arguing that the phenomenon is "often propelled not by a reflexive anti–law enforcement mentality but a real sense that the federal system is out of whack and that people are being put away for the rest of their lives based on [testimony from] informants."[24]

Inner-city America has been living with drug informants for the duration of the war on drugs—over twenty years. That represents two decades of twelve-year-olds like my Baltimore student watching the "police let dealers stay on the corner 'cuz they snitchin.'" It represents two decades of criminals remaining on the street, or receiving reduced sentences in exchange for turning in others, and two decades of the kinds of unreliability and violence that we now know to be associated with informant use. For residents of those communities, it has also been two decades of watching addicts, girlfriends and boyfriends, family members, and other vulnerable acquaintances succumb to police pressure to provide information under threat of increasingly severe mandatory drug sentences. "Stop snitching" is thus not merely a reflection of historic distrust: the public policy of using informants itself contributes to the sense that today's law enforcement is all too often unreliable or unfair.

For law-abiding citizens committed to working with police, distrust remains a live issue. In 2008, New York writer Touré summed up many of the competing questions in short essay entitled "A Snitch like Me." Poised to buy a home, he realized that the house across the street was a crack house. He decided to call the police. But, as he put it, "that option was fraught with psychological problems."

> As a black male New Yorker, I've long regarded the boys in blue as the opposition. I know if the dice had fallen differently, I could have been Amadou Diallo or Abner Louima or Sean Bell. And I come from the hip-hop generation, in which snitching against a black person is treason.
>
> But would it really be snitching? The term truly refers to criminals ratting on other criminals, not taxpaying citizens reporting what they've seen criminals do. And should I protect poisoners of people and the neighborhood just because they're black? [25]

Psychologist Tom Tyler has written extensively on issues of public trust and police cooperation.[26] In one recent study, he examines the question, why do people cooperate with the police? He concludes that although people help police fight crime in part because they think it is in their self-interest to do so, a much more powerful motivation is that they consider the police to be legitimate, deserving of deference and cooperation. This legitimacy depends on the procedures that police use. Tyler writes,

> For the police to be successful in combating crime and maintaining social order they must have public cooperation. To some degree cooperation occurs when the public views the police as effective . . . . In addition, [however,] the public cooperates with the police when they view them as legitimate authorities who are entitled to be obeyed. Such legitimacy judgments, in turn, are shaped by public views about procedural justice—the fairness of the processes the police use when dealing with members of the public.[27]

By "procedural justice," Tyler means all the ways in which police handle residents and decision making, regardless of the outcome. "It includes judgments about the quality of decision-making, which includes neutrality: making decisions based on facts, and applying rules consistently. It also involves judgments about the quality of interpersonal treatment: respect, politeness, consideration of one's views."[28] Tyler further notes the "widespread suggestion that many among the American public lack high levels of trust and confidence in the legal system" and the particularly destructive impact that this distrust has in minority communities.[29]

The use of criminal informants is a powerful example of procedural justice failure. By its very nature, informant use is based on shaky facts and involves the inconsistent and nonneutral application of rules. Tyler's theory helps explain how informant practices can undermine public perception of police legitimacy, thereby discouraging trust and cooperation.

A final contributor to the distrust problem flows from the more general fear that the police cannot or will not protect residents from crime in general, and from witness intimidation in particular. Urban America is famously underprotected, with understaffed police departments, slow 911 responses, and high official tolerance for low-level offenses like car theft and assault. Urban residents, particularly African Americans, suffer from higher crime victimization rates than other populations.[30]

In those "hardest-hit neighborhoods, people describe how fear, and the conviction that serious crimes are not solved, make them reluctant to confront homicide, unwilling to cooperate with authorities or act as witnesses, and disinclined to place their faith in the police." "We know no one will protect us," explains one Los Angeles resident. "We have to protect ourselves."[31] Potential victims—mostly black and Latino young men—see the police as "unreliable and hostile" and conclude that they will not be protected, leading to an escalation of the cycle of violence. Residents' unwillingness to talk to police is thus directly connected to their perception that police are insufficiently responsive.

On the flip side of the coin, this public reluctance makes it harder for police to do their jobs. Police describe their alienation from residents, their fear of going into high-crime areas,[32] and their conviction that "the people here hate us."[33] As residents grow unwilling to cooperate, police grow dispirited about their ability to solve crime.

This double bind was tragically expressed in the case of Baltimore resident Angela Dawson. In 2002, Dawson called 911 and 311 repeatedly to try to get the drug dealers off her block. According to *Baltimore Sun* reports, police response was weak to nonexistent. The dealers about whom Mrs. Dawson complained were at best chased away, and sometimes the police did not respond to calls at all. Although the police were told of threats against the family, no additional protection was provided. An individual who assaulted Mrs. Dawson was arrested and released the next morning. After months of police inaction, dealers arranged a firebombing in retaliation for the family's complaints. Mrs. Dawson and five of her children died in the fire. The Dawson family sued the city for promising protection to city residents that it never delivered.[34]

Among its many lessons, the Dawson tragedy teaches that witness noncooperation flows in part from the accurate perception that police do not always protect residents of high-crime communities. The problem is not merely the perception that police cannot protect

witnesses from threats but the more general experience of underenforcement and underprotection that has plagued inner-city America
for decades. For some, the "stop snitching" sentiment includes this
simmering sense that cooperating with police may well be futile.

III. Witness Intimidation

The problem of witness intimidation is an old and pressing one. All
fifty states as well as the federal government make witness intimidation a crime, and approximately one-third of all states have witness
protection programs. While there has been increased attention to
the phenomenon because of "stop snitching," the problem has been
around for a long time. As Police Chief Joseph Pizzuti of Mt. Vernon,
New York, explains, "People don't cooperate for a number of reasons.
They are afraid of reprisals. They don't trust the police to keep their
identities secret. They don't want to have to worry about testifying."
Pizzuti adds, "I don't think it is a new culture, I just think it has gotten press recently. The street has always been a code of don't cooperate with the police."[35] Sociology professor Peter Moskos, former Baltimore police officer, agrees: "This culture [of noncooperation] has
been there . . . for decades. I think what's new is the 'stop snitching'
DVD that came out in 2004 that brought it to the attention of mainstream society. But there's nothing new going on in the ghetto."[36]

Even in Baltimore, witness intimidation was an issue before the
DVD hit the streets. Baltimore City state's attorney Patricia Jessamy
says that she noticed an increase in witness intimidation in Baltimore
in 2002, prompting her to propose a bill in 2004 that would increase
penalties for witness intimidation and make it easier for law enforcement to use statements of witnesses who fail to show up to court. The
bill originally failed, but passed the next year after Jessamy sent cop-
ies of the "Stop Snitching" DVD to all Maryland legislators.[37]

A decade before "stop snitching" became a term of art, national
law enforcement professionals were concerned about the connections
among gangs, policing, and community reluctance to cooperate. In
the mid-1990s, the National Institute of Justice released two reports

indicating that witness intimidation was a serious and growing problem.[38] The reports found an increase in witness intimidation associated with gang and drug activity in certain neighborhoods, particularly in connection with the crack cocaine trade. In gang-dominated
neighborhoods, some prosecutors estimated that over 75 percent of
violent crimes might involve witness intimidation. Fear of retaliation,
moreover, was not necessarily linked to actual threats. Rather, the reports found, it can persist on a community-wide basis depending on
general levels of crime, violence, and insecurity.

The reports also noted that fear is not the only factor in witness
reluctance. "Strong community ties and deep-seated distrust of law
enforcement may also be strong deterrents to cooperation." In particular, "typically, victims and witnesses are the children of the gang
member's friends or relatives, members of the same church, class-
mates, or neighbors."

Importantly, the reports explained that witness reluctance to come
forward was neighborhood-specific:

> In neighborhoods not plagued by gangs and drug sales, fear and in-
> timidation play a much less significant part in the failure to cooperate
> with police and prosecutors. . . . [V]ictim and witness intimidation is
> *endemic* in neighborhoods infested with gang activity and drug sales
> and virtually *invisible* to people outside these neighborhoods. The
> majority of citizens outside gang-dominated neighborhoods learn
> about victim and witness intimidation only through the media.[39]

This discrepancy in the perceptions of residents of different neighborhoods explains some important dynamics. It shows how the intersec-
tion of crime rates, race, social vulnerability, and policing experiences
can create radically different criminal justice experiences: in some
neighborhoods, that matrix generates trust in police that supports
cooperation, whereas in other neighborhoods, that matrix generates
distrust that undermines police-community relations.[40]

This dynamic also helps explain why reactions in high-crime neighborhoods may seem puzzling to people who live in communities with
different histories. Mainstream media and its consumers, for example,

often have difficulty understanding urban perceptions of "stop snitching," finding inexplicable the idea that law-abiding people might resist cooperating with the police. The national puzzlement over "stop
snitching" is thus in part a product of this cultural and experiential
divide between neighborhoods.

Today, in some areas the intimidation problem is worsening along
with increases in gang violence and organization. In Philadelphia in
2006, Tyreese Gaymon-Allen was killed in retaliation for identifying his
cousin's killer.[41] According to a 2007 *Baltimore Sun* report, "Three years
after Baltimore drew national attention with the release of the street-
produced DVD Stop Snitching, witness intimidation remains one of the
biggest impediments to solving and successfully prosecuting homicides
and shootings in the city and beyond."[42]

In Salinas, California, the unsolved homicide rate is 65 percent,
twice the national average, which police attribute to witness reluctance to come forward.[43] In the high-crime neighborhood of South
Los Angeles, police report struggling to get and keep witnesses, with
hundreds of homicides still unsolved, even as the city's overall homicide rate declines.[44] Police and prosecutors in large cities such as Milwaukee, Philadelphia, Atlanta, and Chicago complain of insufficient
witness protection funds.[45] In a 2007 report entitled "Snitches Get
Stitches: Youth, Gangs, and Witness Intimidation in Massachusetts,"
researchers found that reluctance to be perceived as a snitch was a
large deterrent to youth cooperation with police.[46]

Widespread fear impedes not only law enforcement but sometimes
news reporters attempting to document it. According to one reporter
writing in 2008, "Investigative reporters in all corners of the country
are increasingly encountering the Stop Snitching campaign . . . that
makes their jobs that much more difficult." Describing numerous instances in which residents refused to talk to reporters, and a few cases
in which reporters themselves received threats, the author concludes
that "what has long represented a substantial hurdle for law enforcement is now increasingly hindering news-media efforts as well."[47]

In some of these areas, the "stop snitching" motto—borne on t-
shirts or graffiti—has become a recognizable tool of civilian witness intimidation. In Cleveland, gang members hung "stop snitching" t-shirts

on street signs after the murder of eighteen-year-old Shawrica Lester in 2007.[48] When Mia M. decided to testify about a murder she witnessed in Baltimore, she was threatened at gunpoint; a man accosted her on her way home to remind her that "snitches get stitches."[49]

By contrast, officials in other jurisdictions indicate that actual witness intimidation is rare, although potential witnesses harbor general fears. As one Georgia prosecutor put it in 2007, "I don't think [retaliation] is a significant problem here. A lot of times, the intimidation is the perception or assumption by the person that they will be retaliated against."[50]

In some places, cooperation is even improving. In Milwaukee, one of the first cities to see the t-shirts, police now attribute their impressively high homicide clearance rates to community members coming forward to report crimes.[51] In Boston, a new anonymous text-messaging crime tip program instituted in 2007 garnered a massive community response, with a five-fold increase in tips from the year before. "I think change comes gradually, it never happens overnight," mused CrimeStopper chief officer Mike Charbonnier. "We're beginning to tap into the stop snitching culture."[52]

In sum, witness intimidation is a long-standing problem associated primarily with gangs, drug trafficking, and focused inner-city violence, and varies greatly between locales. This history has been obscured by the fact that when the "stop snitching" DVD and t-shirts first appeared, many commentators treated them as a direct cause of increased witness intimidation. Police and prosecutors blamed the "stop snitching movement" for their difficulties in recruiting witnesses and solving serious homicides, while the press attributed instances of intimidation to a "stop snitching" culture. From headlines across the country:

Witnesses clam up—and crimes go unsolved. Failure to make arrests in 12 city homicides blamed on "stop snitching" culture, misuse of police informants. (Indiana)[53]

Anti-snitching message frustrates authorities, stalls felony cases. (Florida)[54]

"Stop Snitching'" campaign silences witnesses, lives. (California)[55]

Snitching stigma may hinder police. (Pennsylvania)[56]

Anti-snitch campaign riles police, prosecutors. (*USA Today*)[57]

Such headlines imply that a new cultural phenomenon is to blame for witness reluctance. But a decade of research suggests that popular interest in "stop snitching" is itself a symptom of increased fear and insecurity in high-crime neighborhoods. In locales with substantial histories of gang violence, personal insecurity, and police distrust, the reluctance to cooperate with police has deep roots.

IV. The Role of Rap and Hip Hop

One of the reasons why "stop snitching" has gotten so much mainstream attention is its connections with hip hop, rap music, and other high-profile forms of culture and celebrity. Lil' Kim and Busta Rhymes received ongoing media coverage for their refusal to cooperate with police. Cam'ron's comment on *60 Minutes* that he wouldn't turn in a serial killer has been replayed and requoted dozens of times by journalists.

Some rap artists have expressly embraced the "stop snitching" ethos. Songs by artists such as Lil' Wayne, The Diplomats, Scarface, and Coco Brothers exhort listeners to "stop snitching."[58] The rapper The Game entitled an entire mix tape "Stop Snitchin Stop Lyin" with one track entitled "Stop Talkin' to the Cops."[59]

The songs often disparage the lenience earned by criminals who snitch. The song entitled "Tell, Tell, Tell (Stop Snitchin)," performed by Project Pat and featuring Young Jeezy, contains the following lyrics: "Police say they'll let me go if I gave up on my dawg / Don't try to observe the truth, I don't break no ghetto laws / I don't put pressure mane on others to ease pain / Or brothers put in chains, help mothers to go insane."[60] Chamillionaire's song "No snitchin'" includes the lyrics, "He was lookin' at a 30 but he only did 10 / how your years turn to months, can he tell you dat and / He ain't really gotta answer, just the sweat in his hands / Will he make it out to make it, mmm well it depends / Everybody know the info you was tellin ya friends."[61]

Like all cultural phenomena, however, rap and hip hop are not monolithic. Other artists have responded very differently to the "stop snitching" idea, disagreeing with the ethic as well as the media's portrayal of the issue.

Rapper Chuck D of Public Enemy, for example, condemned the "no snitching" campaign as a cheap knock-off of a historic civil rights concern. "The term 'snitch' was best applied to those that ratted revolutionaries like Huey P. Newton, Bobby Seale, Che Guevara," he said. "Let's not let stupid cats use hip-hop to again twist this meaning for the sake of some 'innerganghood' violent drug-thug crime dogs, who've sacrificed the black community's women and children."[62]

Davey D., a hip hop commentator and editorialist for the *San Jose Mercury News*, considers "stop snitching" to be a form of protest against unfairness within the criminal system.

> [M]any within hip hop were angry with Cam'ron because he squandered an opportunity to articulate to the nation what was really at the heart of the "Stop Snitching" movement. Cam'ron failed to talk about rampant police misconduct and abuse resulting in so many people being incarcerated on the basis of false testimony by government informants who have been compromised or in many cases coerced to sell people out.[63]

Hip hop artist Immortal Technique, president of Viper Records, says, "I've never written anything about 'don't snitch.'" Instead, he argues that the issues around "stop snitching" are centrally about distrust of the government:

> I think the government sometimes sends the wrong message to people when it gives special privileges to certain snitches, like if you're a murderer or a big drug dealer who brings in a lots of little drug dealers . . . . But if you are one of those people who engages in this illicit, illegal activity, it's almost . . . like the government is

saying it's okay as long as you're snitching for us. That's the same message that America seems to send out internationally to people. It's all right if you're an authoritarian regime. It's all right if you're a puppet democracy in name only. It's all right if you are a Muslim fundamentalist nation in Saudi Arabia. It's all right if you're all these things as long as you're our asset, or as long as you make money for us. That's, I think, the wrong message that it sends out to a lot of people and people see a double standard.[64]

Hip hop artists have also participated in wider reform efforts. In 2006, the ACLU held a roundtable forum in Atlanta to discuss the use of criminal informants. A major theme was the connection between the "stop snitching" ethos and the impact of drug enforcement, crime, and socioeconomic disadvantage in black communities. Numerous hip hop artists as well as community activists, attorneys, professors, and law enforcement officials participated in the two-day session. Dr. Marc Lamont Hill, professor of American studies and hip hop expert, opined that "the dichotomy of Start Snitching or Stop Snitching is a false choice." Describing the decision not to cooperate with police as a potential "act of resistance and challenge to the state," he criticized the music industry's mass marketing of the "stop snitching" concept and argued for a deeper political analysis.

> Part of our job is to engage in political education that includes, in fact begins with, a theory of the state. . . . There are people in our communities who do not believe that the law could ever be just and fair, and there are others who do. We should start to engage with this conversation about the role of the state in criminal informant policy.[65]

The group's general conclusion was that "stop snitching" constitutes one facet of the larger challenge of community security, policing, and civil rights in socially disadvantaged neighborhoods.

In sum, while musicians and other celebrities play a crucial role in purveying and interpreting ideas, "stop snitching" was not a rapper's creation, nor will it disappear if musicians stop talking about it. While it has become common practice to attribute "stop snitching" to hip hop culture, the diversity of views within the music community alone reminds us that such an equation can never fully explain the phenomenon. Instead, rap and hip hop's engagement with "stop snitching" should be seen as a sign of turbulent times in high-crime communities and in the criminal system itself.

V. What Does "Stop Snitching" Mean?

To some, "stop snitching" is a personal statement. Margarito Martinez, age twenty-three, of California, bought his "stop snitching" t-shirt in Mexico City. "To me, it means 'Take care of yourself and don't judge other people.'"[66]

To others, it's a sign of deep fear. "I'm not snitching on nobody, I swear to God!" said a fourteen-year-old girl in Omaha, Nebraska. Her thirteen-year-old friend agreed: "You can get killed out here if you snitch."[67]

To others, it was a cultural moment that passed. "I think the fashion of it is dead," remarked Marco Antonio Ennis, the Boston designer whose marketing of the shirts years before launched the controversy in that city. A local Boston chain no longer sells the unprofitable shirts: "They died out," explained the clerk.[68]

Despite its wide variety of meanings, "stop snitching" remains a public policy challenge. Witness intimidation, widespread distrust of police, and reluctance to cooperate are symptoms of a twenty-year policy at the heart of the war on drugs: concentrated use of criminal informants in high-crime, socially vulnerable communities. The resonance of the "stop snitching" motto reflects people's experiences with a legal system in which criminal deals are commonplace, in which offenders are forgiven in exchange for information, in which civilians lack protection, and in which snitching is associated with crime, violence, and unreliability. While the t-shirts and mottos may fade away, the underlying problems of violence, fear, and noncooperation will remain as long as this particular social reality persists.

CHAPTER 7

How the Other Half Lives

White Collar and Other Kinds of Cooperation

> A fundamental and distinguishing feature of our society is that means, as well as ends, have a moral component. Covert practices entail short- and long-run risks that are not found with more conventional tactics and that must give us pause. Their significance goes far beyond their use in any given case. Secret police behavior and surveillance go to the heart of the kind of society we are or might become. By studying the changes in covert tactics, a window on something much broader can be gained.
> —Professor Gary Marx[1]

LIKE JUSTICE ITSELF, informant practices are deeply connected to their social and economic surroundings. As the last two chapters described, snitching practices in poor urban neighborhoods are fundamentally shaped by the typical poverty and vulnerability of suspects, and more generally by the lack of resources that residents of such communities bring to bear in their interactions with law enforcement.

While informants are central to street- and drug-crime enforcement, the government deploys informants in a broad range of investigations, most prominently against corporate fraud, organized crime, political corruption, and, increasingly, terrorism. Even as it retains its fundamental character, snitching in these realms takes on new characteristics and implications for offenders and law enforcement alike. Because informant practices are heavily influenced by local institutional realities, they change in response to the shifting cultures and power dynamics of the criminal process.

With the exception of terrorism, the use of informants in non-drug, non-street crime arenas is characterized by greater regulation and oversight, better protections for suspects, greater involvement of defense counsel, and more public transparency and accountability. While these realms experience their share of debacles and corruption, even these can lead to public attention and efforts at reform.

These strengths flow from a panoply of facts: suspects in these arenas tend to be wealthier, whiter, and better educated, with more personal resources and better access to counsel, while target institutions such as corporations or political associations themselves have legitimate functions in society that law enforcement may be loath to undermine by more aggressive tactics.[2] The resulting cultures of investigation and prosecution are more sensitive to the possibility of litigation and public exposure. Or, as Professor Marx wrote bluntly twenty years ago, "When lower-status drug dealers and users or prostitutes were the main targets [of covert operations,] the tactic tended to be ignored, but when congressmen and business executives who can afford the best legal counsel became targets, congressional inquiries and editorials urging caution appeared."[3] All these factors add up to significantly differing informant practices, creating a kind of rich man's version of the informant experience.[4]

At the same time, snitching is still snitching. So-called white collar crime, organized crime, and other forms of informant use share many of the fundamental characteristics—and dangers—of their street and drug counterparts: loosely negotiated deals trading lenience for information in which culpable offenders are let off the hook; relaxation of traditional criminal procedure rules and weakening of the role of defense counsel; increased secrecy and lessened public accountability; and, perhaps most importantly, the vast power that accrues to the government when suspects agree to cooperate. In other words, the rich man's version of snitching still looks a lot like the poor man's version.

This chapter surveys the most prominent arenas of non-drug-related informant use: organized crime, political crime, white collar or business crime, and terrorism. While each arena is in many ways unique, with its own peculiar rules and practices, taken together they complete the picture of the influential role of informant use throughout the American justice system. Their relative strengths further suggest that the heightened regulation, transparency, and role of counsel in these arenas could profitably be imported into the less regulated world of street and drug snitching to ameliorate some of its most dangerous features.

I. FBI Informants and Organized Crime

> Without informants, we're nothing.
> —Clarence Kelley, FBI Director (1973–1978)[5]

The hallmark of a typical FBI confidential informant or "confidential human source" is that he is identified and cultivated, perhaps over the course of years, by a particular law enforcement "handler," in secret. The informant may be part of a criminal organization or a legitimate corporation or group, or it may be his task to infiltrate, and his job is to provide the FBI with ongoing information about that entity and its criminal doings. Other informants may take the opportunity to exit the criminal organization by becoming a witness against it. The informant may be rewarded in several ways, including monetarily, with lenience for past crimes, or by being permitted to continue committing criminal offenses.[6] In its 2008 budgetary request, the FBI states that it maintains over fifteen thousand confidential human sources.[7]

In 2006, the Department of Justice issued the FBI its own special set of guidelines, entitled "The Attorney General's Guidelines Regarding the Use of FBI Confidential Human Sources."[8] These FBI Guidelines are similar to the more general Confidential Informant Guidelines issued by the Justice Department in 2002, which at the time governed the FBI as well as the DEA, the U.S. Marshals Service, and the INS.[9]

The guidelines create documentation, authorization, and ongoing evaluation requirements for FBI agents who want to create or use a confidential informant (CI) or confidential human source. For example, the guidelines require an agent who wants to create a CI to submit a comprehensive "validation report" to her field manager, and, if approved, to register that CI in a file containing, among other things, documentation of any promises or benefits made to the CI. The CI must be formally informed of the terms of the cooperation, including the fact that the CI must be truthful, and that the CI may not engage in any additional criminal activities other than those officially authorized by the agency. High-level informants require additional written approvals from a Human Source Review Committee. The agency must conduct annual suitability reviews. The guidelines also limit investigative officials in other ways: for example, agents lack authority to confer immunity from prosecution on any informant—only a prosecutor can do that. Agents also may not socialize with informants, or exchange gifts.[10]

First promulgated in 1976, the guidelines have gone through a number of iterations. As a result of the Boston Bulger/Flemmi scandal described in chapter 1, the guidelines were significantly strengthened in 2002 with additional rules and reporting requirements. The impact of these changes, however, is unclear. In 2005, the Department of Justice Office of the Inspector General (OIG) issued a report concluding that the FBI did not fully comply with those strengthened guidelines, finding full compliance in only 13 percent of cases examined.[11]

Due to the secrecy and lack of public records, it is impossible to say precisely how many cases the FBI has been able to solve on the basis of its use of CIs. In general, the government has long maintained that certain kinds of cases would be impossible to investigate or prosecute without informants. Moreover, anecdotal evidence indicates that informants are an important and fruitful tool. Mafia assassin Jimmy Fratianno, who spent the 1980s in witness protection, helped convict numerous mob members.[12] The FBI has disclosed additional informant-driven successes: a three-year grand jury investigation of organized crime that led to six convictions and a $500,000 forfeiture; the investigation of three violent gangs in a northeastern city that led to thirty-five cases involving fifty-four gang members; and a two-year undercover operation that led to the indictment of four Houston City Council members.[13]

For the same reasons of secrecy and lack of documentation, it is likewise impossible to say just how often high-level confidential informants run amok, leading to new crimes, corruption, or failed cases. But individual incidents reveal the sorts of problems that the government has contended with over the years. For example, Salvatore "Sammy the Bull" Gravano was one of the FBI's most infamous, successful, and problematic informants. A mafia hit man who confessed to nineteen murders, his 1992 testimony helped the FBI obtain nearly forty convictions, most notably that of John Gotti. The government then released Gravano and relocated him to Arizona in the witness protection program. There, he rejoined organized crime and in 2001, pled guilty to running a multi-million-dollar Ecstasy ring. In 2003, he was charged with ordering the killing of Detective Peter Calabro, but charges were dismissed when the government's sole witness died.[14]

Secrecy exacerbates the problem of informant criminality, particularly when prosecutors and law enforcement agents do not share information. Starting in 1982, Jackie Presser, president of the International Brotherhood of Teamsters Union, was under investigation by Justice Department prosecutors for stealing union money through the creation of nonexistent "phantom" employees, or "no shows." It turned out that Presser had been an FBI informant for ten years and that the FBI had authorized him to hire the "no shows." Charges against Presser were dropped, and Presser's FBI handler was indicted for lying to protect Presser.[15]

These examples illustrate some of the now-familiar dangers in using high-level informants to infiltrate criminal or corrupt organizations. Such dangers include the ongoing criminal activity of the informants themselves, the close ties developed between agent and informant, and the lack of information sharing within the government. All too often, the left hand does not know what the right hand is doing, and the extent of the informants' criminality is known only to a few.

At the same time, these violent, corrupt informants often provided extremely valuable and accurate information. Unlike the informal encounters that so often characterize street snitching, these FBI informants had ongoing relationships with their handlers and often the handlers knew a great deal about their informants' misdeeds. The revised DOJ guidelines are premised on this model: they are designed to preserve valuable information sources while strengthening the accountability and oversight of handlers and informants alike.

FBI informant failures have triggered national scrutiny. In 2004, the U.S. House of Representatives Committee on Government Reform conducted extensive hearings on the FBI's use of mafia informants who had committed and continued to commit murder while in the FBI's employ. The resulting report comprehensively documented not only those informants' wrongdoings but also the cover-ups, perjury, and other malfeasance committed by FBI and other law enforcement officials in connection with their informant relationships.[16]

In July 2007, the U.S. House Judiciary Committee held a congressional hearing on law enforcement use of confidential informants. The hearing addressed numerous concerns, one of them being the FBI's continued mishandling of its CIs. Congressmen Daniel Lungren (R-CA) and William Delahunt (D-MA) separately lambasted FBI assistant director Wayne Murphy for the FBI's failure to control its informants, and, in particular, the agency's failure to inform state and local law enforcement when FBI informants commit additional crimes. Rep. Lungren, former California attorney general, was particularly concerned about the impact on state law enforcement.

> LUNGREN: [I]s there a policy in the FBI to share information with local and state law enforcement officials when you have become aware, that is, the FBI, that your confidential informants have engaged in serious violent felony activity, not all criminal activity, serious violent felony activity in the jurisdiction of the local or the state authorities[?]
>
> MURPHY: It is my understanding, Congressman, that there is not a specific documented policy, directly to answer your question, sir. . . . Our process and approach is to take onboard criticism and observations about how we conduct our procedures and to consider whether or not we have appropriate measures in place to ensure and preserve the integrity of our process.
>
> LUNGREN: Yes, all I can say is if I were still a law enforcement officer in the state of California and you were to tell me that the FBI was reserving judgment as to whether you could tell me

that you have C.I.s in my jurisdiction that are committing serious violent felonies, I would be more than offended.[17]

As of this writing, Reps. Lungren and Delahunt are working on a bill
that would require the FBI to report to state law enforcement serious
violent felonies committed by its informants and would impose criminal penalties on agents who fail to do so.[18] In a radio interview, Rep.
Delahunt stated his concerns: "What is totally unacceptable is having violent criminals out on the street, preying on American citizens
everywhere, while there is information that isn't being disclosed to
local and state law enforcement authorities that have the primary responsibility in this country to protect us from violent crime." General
counsel for the FBI, Valerie Caproni, responded that the bill would
severely hamper the FBI's ability to deploy informants at all: "I don't
think if [this bill] was passed we could get agents to run informants,"
she worried.[19]

This brief overview of informant use by the FBI and in high-level
federal investigations presents a picture that differs in important re-
spects from typical street-crime and drug-informant practices. This
is an arena characterized by documentation, regulations, and, eventually, oversight of individual agent decision making. It is a smaller,
more focused arena, with higher-level crimes, more sophisticated investigations, and fewer informants to manage. It is also characterized
by a different kind of informant, often with resources and leverage
that make them formidable players in their own right.

The problems that plague this law enforcement world are also different. Wrongful convictions still occur, crime is still tolerated, and
informant-handler relationships still sometimes lead to corruption.
But it is harder for such miscarriages of justice to slip beneath the radar. And when they do surface, the high-profile nature of the cases
and players has generated serious legislative attention.

II. Political Informants

There are two main kinds of political informants: those who belong to or infiltrate political organizations and those who expose the corruption of individual elected officials. They implicate different values and problems.

A. Agent Provocateurs and Infiltrators

The U.S. government has a long and problematic history of using informants to infiltrate and undermine political groups and associations. Over the years, the FBI has used informants to penetrate a variety of organizations, such as the Communist Party, civil rights organizations, Students for Democratic Society (SDS), the Black Panther Party, as well as white supremacist groups. These informants not only gathered information but sometimes provided their host organizations with resources, instigated actions likely to result in arrests or violence, and even, in the case of SDS, formed new chapters of the organization in order to keep tabs on the movement.[20] Sometimes these tactics have had historic consequences. FBI informant William O'Neal, recruited by the FBI from the Cook County jail, infiltrated the Black Panthers in Chicago and helped instigate the 1969 police raid that led to the deaths of Panther leader Fred Hampton and Mark Clark.[21]

The use of informants in connection with the civil rights movement has sparked special concerns. Information from two FBI informants recruited from the Communist Party was used to obtain a wiretap of Dr. Martin Luther King, Jr.[22] FBI informant Gary Rowe was a Klan member implicated in the murder of civil rights worker Viola Liuzzo in 1965.[23]

More recently, FBI informant David Gletty stirred great unrest when it was revealed that he was behind a 2006 neo-Nazi march through a predominantly black neighborhood in Orlando, Florida. The march, for which Gletty obtained the permits and was listed as the "on scene event manager," generated a great deal of anxiety in the black community as well as fears of racial unrest that triggered a major police mobilization. Local leaders complained that the government should not instigate such racially charged events. As city councilwoman Daisy Lynum put it, "To come into a predominantly black community which could have resulted in great harm to the black community? I would hate to be part of a game. It's a mockery to the community for someone else to be playing a game with the community." The FBI later issued a statement denying that it played any role in the rally.[24]

Even when informants do not actively participate in criminal activity or undermine organizations, the official infiltration of political groups can disturb democratic activities. Recently released documents indicate that the New York City Police Department used undercover officers and informants to infiltrate numerous groups—including "street theater companies, church groups, antiwar activists, environmentalists, and people opposed to the death penalty"—in preparation for the 2004 Republican National Convention, at which there were expected to be massive protests.[25]

1. First Amendment Concerns

When the government uses informants to infiltrate and conduct surveillance on political or other legitimate groups, it raises unique concerns. As a constitutional matter, it implicates the First Amendment because it can constitute interference with group members' rights of free speech and association. "[I]ndividuals maintain a first amendment right to associate for lawful political purposes free from government intrusion."[26] This right, however, does not preclude legitimate law enforcement efforts. The Supreme Court has made clear that when the government merely gathers otherwise public information and intelligence about free-speech activities and organizations, it does not infringe the subjects' First Amendment rights.[27] More specifically, lower courts have held that "[t]he use of informers and infiltrators by itself does not give rise to any claim of violation of [First Amendment] constitutional rights."[28]

But when the government becomes more active, going beyond mere data gathering or the planting of a passive informant, free speech rights may be impermissibly chilled or violated. For example, in *Handschu v. Special Services Division*, New York police used informants to infiltrate anti–Vietnam War and other political groups in the early 1970s. Those informants were used not only to collect information but also, as alleged by group members, to provoke illegal activities such as armed robbery in order to disrupt and undermine the organizations themselves. The group members sued the city to stop the practice, alleging that government "informers and infiltrators provoked, solicited, and induced members of lawful political and social groups to engage in unlawful activities . . . provided funds and equipment to further that purpose," and otherwise engaged in "excesses and abusive tactics and activities with the purpose and effect of sowing distrust and suspicion among plaintiffs and other[s] who espouse unorthodox or dissenting political and social views, thereby discouraging them from associating for that purpose."[29] The court concluded that if the allegations were true, such official practices would violate the First Amendment.

During that same period, the National Caucus of Labor Committees, a socialist political organization in Detroit, alleged that a paid FBI informant had sought to sow distrust within the organization and to discourage others from joining by, among other things, publicly misrepresenting the party's goals, inciting violence, making racist remarks, stealing mail, and letting his name be placed on the ballot for state representation as a party candidate. The court in *Ghandi v. Police Department of the City of Detroit*, concluded that the informant's "conduct, if reported accurately, strikes at the very heart of a free society. It amounts to a government informer making a direct attack upon the right of a fellow citizen to publicly express his political views while campaigning for public office."[30] More recently, the Ninth Circuit in 1989 found that when immigration officials recorded church services, thereby driving congregants away, they sufficiently harmed the churches' and congregants' interests in freedom of association to support a First Amendment claim.[31]

More broadly, infiltration raises a selection problem not present in the conventional criminal setting, which is the official identification of civic groups as dangerous or potentially criminal. When the government deems a political or religious or environmental group dangerous, thereby justifying the decision to recruit or plant an informant, we worry that the government is expressing a political bias under cover of the criminal system. In his seminal 1974 article, Professor Marx studied thirty-four cases in which information was publicly available regarding informant infiltration of political groups. Of all the groups selected for infiltration, only two were politically conservative. During the 1960s and 1970s, J. Edgar Hoover infamously used informants and agents to undermine left-leaning political organizations. In an internal agency memo, Hoover explicitly instructed his agents that "[t]he purpose of this [counterintelligence] program is to expose, disrupt, and otherwise neutralize the new Left organizations, their Leadership and adherents."[32]

In these ways, using informants for political purposes raises a different set of concerns than does the use of informants for traditional crime control. Fears about First Amendment infringement are at their height. Not only can the government's power to choose its targets represent a kind of thumb-on-the-scales favoritism, but the proactive investigative techniques associated with informants and provocateurs may undermine the political process itself. Because of the history of governmental interference with left-wing and civil rights groups, the legacy of this sort of informant has left an important mark on the public understanding of snitching.

At the same time, some of the universal problems with informant use affect this arena as well. Infiltrating informants may get away with wrongdoing in exchange for their usefulness. They may finger the innocent or entrap others into behaving in ways that they otherwise would not. When they are exposed, they may undermine public perceptions of law enforcement legitimacy. In other words, even in this unique arena, political informants carry many of the same challenges and risks as their more conventional criminal counterparts.

B. Political Corruption

Sometimes informants are used to catch corrupt politicians. Informants can be used proactively to set up illegal transactions, or they can themselves be corrupt political operatives who turn in their former associates in exchange for lenience. The second strategy has been relatively uncontroversial, but the first—the "sting"—has generated concerns about selection bias and law enforcement infiltration of the political process, similar to the concerns that plague the use of the political agent provocateur.

1. The Sting

One of the most contentious examples of the first strategy was the 1970s "Abscam" investigation. FBI agents, along with criminal informant and con man Melvin Weinberg, posed as representatives of wealthy sheiks looking for investment opportunities and approached numerous political figures with bribes. The strategy netted twenty-five indictments, including the convictions of a senior U.S. senator, four congressmen, and several local Pennsylvania and New Jersey politicians, each of whom eventually accepted between $10,000 and $50,000.[33]

The defendants argued that they had been entrapped. Although two district courts agreed, eventually all the convictions were upheld on appeal. Some of the defendants argued further that the use of Weinberg, a criminal who received lenience for his mail fraud charges in exchange for organizing the sting, was improper. This argument also failed. As the U.S. Court of Appeals for the District of Columbia put it,

> Successful creation of an "elaborate hoax" such as Abscam may well require employment of "experts" such as Weinberg to give the operation an aura of "credibility" and "contacts" with criminal elements. The employment of a convicted confidence man in Abscam is analogous to the entirely proper employment of a convicted seller of drugs to purchase drugs from a suspected distributor. As the Second Circuit stated: "[U]se of dishonest and deceitful informants like Weinberg creates risks to which the attention of juries must be forcefully called, but the Due Process Clause does not forbid their employment, detail their supervision, nor specify their compensation."[34]

Although the Abscam convictions were deemed legally sound, deeper concerns lingered that the government had crossed an inappropriate line by creating criminal opportunities to lure politicians about whom the government had no other incriminating evidence. As Professor Paul Chevigny wrote at the time, "the power to offer a temptation to crime is the power to decide who shall be tempted. It can be and often has been used as a way for the Government to eliminate its enemies, or for one faction in Government to get rid of another."[35]

2. Criminals Who Cooperate after the Fact

A more conventional and less controversial use of political informants is the practice of flipping existing offenders to reveal wrongdoing that has already occurred. Lobbyist Jack Abramoff has become the poster child for this form of political cooperation. Abramoff not only bribed politicians and their staffers but bilked several Native American tribes of millions of dollars in excessive consulting fees. As part of his 2006 guilty plea, he agreed to cooperate.[36] His assistance to date has made possible the prosecution of at least one congressman and several high-level administration officials.[37]

In exchange for his cooperation, Abramoff is currently serving a four-to-six-year sentence. This sentence represents less than half of the eleven years he could have faced on the corruption charges alone— his cooperation also earned him lenience in connection with an unrelated fraud case in which he received a six-year sentence, although in that case he could have faced as many as thirty years.[38] Despite Abramoff's massive wrongdoing and heavy attention to the case, the public record has been practically devoid of complaints about his relatively light punishment. Rather, commentators have focused on the likelihood that additional high-level elected officials will be caught as a result.[39]

This treatment reflects the intuition that the Abramoff case represents the best version of the snitch compromise. Informant use inherently involves the toleration of crime and the lenient treatment of wrongdoers. It functions at its best when that toleration and lenience permit the prosecution of more serious wrongdoers, and improved scrutiny and regulation of the arena in which the wrongdoing took place. Due in part to the Abramoff revelations, Congress created a new independent Office of Congressional Ethics.[40] Because Abramoff's deal exposed widespread unethical lobbying practices, it produced a concrete social benefit. This is snitching at its best.

It is also snitching at its least problematic. Abramoff's deal involved no proactive instigation or toleration of new criminal conduct, it was fully vetted by attorneys on both sides, the public learned a great deal not only about Abramoff himself but also about the criminal conduct at issue, and Abramoff's obligations and benefits were relatively determinate. Such constraints are characteristic of cooperating defendants who have already been charged with a crime and who, with the help of counsel, provide retrospective information about past wrongdoing. They are not characteristic of active high-level informants and infiltrators, the typical drug or street snitch, or, more generally, lower-level criminal informants who may provide the police with information over time and leverage cooperation across cases and jurisdictions.

III. White Collar Crime and Cooperation

So-called white collar or financial crime has always been treated differently from street crime. Encompassing such offenses as fraud, embezzlement, money laundering, tax evasion, and other nonviolent economic offenses, the white collar category has its own culture and poses its own challenges. For one thing, the federal government is central to white collar enforcement. Although the federal criminal system makes up just one-tenth of the entire American system, and, numerically speaking, there are more state fraud prosecutions than federal ones, federal law enforcement dominates this arena, especially with respect to large companies and high-profile cases.[41] Federal prosecutions tend to be complex and resource intensive, and often have national ramifications, setting the tone in the business community for future practices.

White collar criminal enforcement also takes place against a backdrop of extensive civil regulation and large administrative agencies that have their own enforcement mechanisms. Most wrongful business conduct may be treated either civilly or criminally. As law professor Darryl Brown points out, "Parallel statutory regimes providing civil and criminal sanctions for essentially the same conduct exist in virtually every area of white-collar wrongdoing, including health care fraud, environmental harms, workplace safety, and securities law." [42] Business organizations thus typically spend more time negotiating compliance with regulatory agencies than they do confronting criminal prosecutors. As a result, business activities take place in a highly regulated atmosphere that is already heavily layered with expectations about civil compliance and cooperation, and in which civil liability is often routinely substituted for criminal sanctions.

For decades, the criticisms of white collar criminal enforcement were that it was too lenient, that white collar offenses were not vigorously pursued, and that offenders received punishments that were too light. In March 2002, *Forbes* magazine ran a cover story entitled "White Collar Criminals: They Lie, They Cheat, They Steal, and They've Been Getting Away With It for Too Long: Enough Is Enough."[43] The story revealed that from 1992 to 2001, SEC enforcement attorneys referred 609 cases to the Justice Department for potential criminal charges. Of that number, only 187 cases were actually prosecuted, 142 individuals were found guilty, and 87 went to jail. Even the highest-profile wrongdoers served relatively low sentences. In 1986, Michael Milken was famously sentenced to ten years for an illegal insider trading scheme worth upwards of $100 million. He was eventually released after serving two years because he agreed to testify against one of his former colleagues.[44]

Critics have also long argued that the differential treatment between white collar and street crime reflects social biases—because white collar defendants tend to be whiter and wealthier, they receive better treatment and more sympathy from the criminal system than poorer defendants who are more likely to be members of racial minorities.[45] Even though business crime can impose substantial harms, depriving innocent victims of pensions or savings and costing the nation billions of dollars, white collar offenders are often considered less culpable than street crime offenders who may steal less and harm fewer people. Or, as Rhode Island justice Stephen J. Fortunato wrote more dramatically, "The gentle and genteel treatment by prosecutors (with occasional notable exceptions) of corporate thieves, swindlers, polluters, tax evaders, and hustlers is proof positive that there are two separate and distinct criminal justice systems operating in this country."[46] To be sure, white collar offenders still experience race and wealth discrimination: a recent study reaffirmed that among federal white collar offenders, black and Hispanic defendants are incarcerated more often and for longer than their comparable white counterparts.[47] But as compared to street and drug crime, the culture of white collar prosecution has tended to be more lenient and restrained.[48]

In recent years, however, in what is often called the "post-Enron era," there has been a shift in the white collar arena, with federal law enforcement and the public paying heightened attention to corporate fraud. In 2002, in response to the high-profile collapse of firms like Enron and WorldCom, the Department of Justice created the Corporate Fraud Task Force, while Congress and the Sentencing Commission increased penalties for white collar crimes.[49] The new wave of high-profile prosecutions has included such firms as Computer Associates, and the accounting firms of KPMG and Arthur Andersen. With new record-setting sentences—Enron's Jeff Skilling received twenty-four years, while WorldCom's Bernard Ebbers received twenty-five—a few even argue that the pendulum has swung too far, and that white collar offenses are being treated too harshly.[50] The recent collapse of the financial sector and the ensuing federal bailout is widely expected to generate a new wave of prosecutions.[51]

Cooperating informants are an increasingly important part of white collar investigations and prosecutions. Because many financial or paper crimes are hard to detect, it often requires cooperation on the part of a knowledgeable individual or corporation to bring them to light. White collar cooperation takes two main forms. One is the now-familiar individual cooperator who, in exchange for lenience for his own crimes, provides information about his and others' wrongdoings. Because this form of cooperation tends to be well documented and fully litigated, it has received the most attention in the scholarly literature on informants. But the white collar arena has produced an additional, distinct phenomenon, namely, cooperation by the corporation itself. When a corporate entity becomes a "snitch," it raises unique issues for law enforcement and for the entity's individual employees.

A. Individual White Collar Cooperators

The typical white collar informant is a participant in a larger scheme to steal or defraud. For example, the government's financial fraud cases against Enron's chief officers Kenneth Lay and Jeffrey Skilling were built on the testimony of numerous informants, including accountants and managers as well as CFO Andrew Fastow. Many of these witnesses were also guilty but received reduced sentences in exchange for their cooperation.[52]

When the government suspects a white collar offender, a number of things may happen that distinguish this arena from street- and drug-crime enforcement. First, the government may approach the suspect or his attorney, or send him a "target letter" revealing that he is under investigation, prior to any charges being filed. If the suspect does not already have counsel, this gives him the opportunity to get it.[53] Some companies actually provide counsel for employees facing employment-related criminal charges. The fact that white collar defendants have better and earlier access to counsel than do street- or drug-crime suspects radically improves defendant options in this arena.

Two decades ago in his landmark book on white collar defense, Kenneth Mann described the pre-indictment process as the most important service a defense attorney can provide her client. Counsel's ability to control information early on means that a defendant can shape the direction of a case and even potentially avoid indictment altogether.[54] With the advent of cooperation, this pre-indictment process becomes a time of even greater opportunity and potential negotiation for represented defendants.

As do all defendants, white collar offenders depend heavily on their attorneys during the cooperation process. A good defense attorney can evaluate the strength of the government's case, advise her client about the likelihood of success, and ensure that her client receives the greatest benefit from his cooperation. If the government eventually charges the defendant with a crime, the attorney remains the defendant's most important guarantee that the government will keep its promises and that the defendant will get maximum credit for his cooperation.[55]

Professor Richman points out that law enforcement's ability to obtain cooperation depends in part on its reputation for keeping its promises. If the government breaks its promise, the defense attorney may be the only witness who can publicize the breach. Richman tells the story of one attorney who took out a public advertisement in a national legal publication, castigating the U.S. Attorney's Office in an open letter for having broken its promises to his cooperating client. After describing the client's cooperation in detail, the letter states,

> During the sentence proceedings I stated that I was going to tell every defense lawyer in our nation not to enter any plea agreement with your office. Your office cannot be trusted. Your office cares nothing about promises and agreements. I am surprised that the eagle in the Great Seal of the United States didn't fly from the wall in horror.
> . . . Like some sleazy insurance company who refuses to pay the widow because it wants the premiums but doesn't want to honor its obligations, your office will go to any length to renege on its solemn promises.[56]

By way of contrast, when police break their promises to a street-corner snitch, no one is likely to find out. In such ways, the pervasive presence of white collar defense counsel significantly levels the playing field between suspects and the government.

Once a white collar defendant decides to become an informant, cooperation and benefits may take a number of forms. Typically the cooperation will involve engaging in proffer sessions with the government in which the defendant, with his attorney, will provide information about the scheme and others' wrongdoings. He may also be required to testify before a grand jury or at the trial of others. In addition to providing information about past wrongdoings, he may help investigate ongoing crimes by wearing a wire or otherwise engaging in proactive investigation. For example, while investigating Richard Scrushy, former CEO of Health-South, investigators wired a financial officer's necktie to secretly record conversations.[57]

Benefits may include avoiding indictment for some or all crimes that the informant has committed. He may also obtain immunity from crimes that he admits to but the government does not already know about, or crimes that the government subsequently discovers as a result of his cooperation. Finally, once he pleads guilty, he may receive reductions in his sentence depending on the value of his information.[58]

White collar cooperation agreements tend to be complex, formal, and written. They may involve careful descriptions of the kinds of immunity that a defendant is or is not entitled to, the kinds of work he is expected to do, and the recommendations that the government may make at sentencing. Because these agreements are executed over time, sometimes long periods of time, they must provide for the waiver or elimination of some bedrock rules of criminal procedure such as double jeopardy, speedy trial rights, self-incrimination rights, and others. As Professor Graham Hughes wrote in an early article on the phenomenon, "deals involving promises to cooperate are sharply different from the general phenomenon of plea bargaining. They are exotic plants that can survive only in an environment from which some of the familiar features of the criminal procedure landscape have been expunged."[59]

Another important aspect of white collar cooperation, true for drug and other conspiracies as well, is that the earlier a defendant cooperates, the better the deal he is likely to get. This "first in the door" phenomenon reflects a number of considerations. The government wants people to cooperate and therefore tends to reward those who do it early, saving the government time and effort. Early cooperators also influence the way the case itself develops, identifying new defendants, becoming witnesses, and shaping the government's investigative and litigation strategies.[60] Accordingly, having good legal advice and an attorney who knows how to navigate the system can make a big difference for cooperators at this stage.[61]

In sum, individual white collar informants look something like street crime informants, but with significant differences. Both provide information about wrongdoing, and both receive lenience for their crimes. But white collar informants tend to be passive rather than proactive, revealing wrongdoing rather than continuing to engage in criminal activities in order to provide more evidence. They tend to have counsel from a very early stage with the concomitant ability to get better deals. They also tend to have more formal agreements with the government with respect to their obligations and expected rewards. Finally, the public is more likely to learn about them when the investigation becomes public, when they testify, or when they are sentenced. In other words, because white collar defendants are better able to defend themselves and the cooperation process is better regulated, white collar cooperation is less likely to succumb to the dangers of the snitch deal—unreliability, ongoing criminality, secrecy, and the victimization of innocent bystanders as well as vulnerable informants.

B. Corporate Cooperation

When a business entity engages in illegal conduct, the entity itself may be prosecuted. This practice was thrust into the spotlight during the 2002 prosecution of accounting firm Arthur Andersen for its obstruction of justice during the SEC investigation of Enron. Although the conviction was overturned on appeal before the Supreme Court,[62] the company had already gone out of business, sending a wave of anxiety through the business community.

Federal prosecutions are currently governed by the "Filip Memo," a memorandum written in 2008 by then–deputy attorney general Mark Filip that replaced a similar memo written by Filip's predecessor, Paul McNulty. The memo outlines the considerations and procedures that prosecutors must follow when developing a case against a business organization.[63] Specifically, in deciding whether to indict a company, prosecutors must consider a list of nine factors that include "the corporation's timely and voluntary disclosure of wrongdoing and its willingness to cooperate in the investigation of its agents," as well as "the corporation's remedial actions, including any efforts to . . . cooperate with the relevant government agencies." The Filip memo expressly permits cooperating corporations to avoid prosecution altogether: "the corporation's timely and voluntary disclosure of wrongdoing and its cooperation with the government's investigation may be relevant factors" in deciding whether to file charges.[64]

Corporate prosecutions and cooperation are also heavily shaped by the U.S. Sentencing Guidelines, which provide that a cooperating corporate entity, like an individual, may receive a reduced sentence, i.e., a smaller fine. Every corporate defendant receives a "culpability score." By cooperating, a corporation can lower its score and thus its sentence. For example, the guidelines provide for a lower culpability score if "the organization had in place at the time of the offense an effective compliance and ethics program," and if the corporation's cooperation regarding its own wrongdoing was both "timely" and "thorough."[65] Like individual defendants, corporations can seek additional departures from the guidelines by providing substantial assistance in the investigation or prosecution of another organization.[66]

In addition, different divisions within the Justice Department have their own individualized cooperation policies. For example, "the Antitrust division has established a firm policy . . . that amnesty is available only to the first corporation to make full disclosure to the government."[67]

Two controversial features of corporate cooperation bear further elaboration. The first is the use of deferred prosecution agreements (DPAs). The second is the situation in which a corporation cooperates by investigating and turning in its own employees.

1. Deferred Prosecution Agreements
Cooperation has become the central means by which a corporate defendant can avoid a conviction and, as with the demise of accounting giant Arthur Andersen, the threat of economic death. Because a criminal conviction can ruin a business, companies will go to great lengths to avoid it. For a company under criminal investigation, an attractive mechanism for avoiding prosecution is a deferred prosecution agreement, or DPA. Over the past few years, AOL, the accounting firm KPMG, Computer Associates, British Petroleum, Union Bank of California, Pfizer, and Bristol Meyers Squibb have all avoided prosecution by entering into DPAs. In 2007 alone, the Justice Department

entered into thirty-five such agreements, although that number fell in 2008.[68]

The benefits of the practice are significant: an offending company can stay in business, preserving jobs and economic stability in the market, while the government can force the company to change its illegal practices. The practice is also controversial on many fronts: some argue that it gives the government too much power over businesses, while others maintain that it lets too many criminal corporations off the hook.[69]

A DPA is an agreement between the government and the business organization in which the organization agrees to engage in certain remedial, cooperative measures in exchange for which the government promises not to go forward with the prosecution. There is a comparable arrangement for individual defendants, referred to as "pretrial diversion," which is typically available only to a limited category of minor or first-time offenders.[70] By contrast, corporate DPAs are increasingly being used to resolve high-level frauds and widespread corporate malfeasance.

A DPA may require a corporation to do any number of things, including cooperate with the ongoing investigation, pay fines or penalties or make restitution, hire a monitor, and admit and accept responsibility for wrongdoing. Businesses are typically willing to go to great lengths in order to comply and avoid prosecution. Or, as *Forbes* magazine describes it, in response to "the mere threat of indictment, [companies are] handing over internal documents, waiving the privilege that normally shields attorney-client communications and ratting out individual employees as targets for prosecution."[71]

Because DPAs require admissions, it is difficult if not impossible for a corporation to change its mind and subsequently defend against the allegations. This gives the government a great deal of power over the course and details of corporate cooperation. As one court put it in the KPMG case, "Anything the government regards as a failure to cooperate . . . almost certainly will result in the criminal conviction that KPMG has labored so mightily to avoid, as the admissions that KPMG now has made would foreclose a successful defense."[72] In other words, once a corporation decides to cooperate, it effectively hands the government a great deal of authority over its operations, even operations that may not bear directly on the alleged wrongdoing.

Law professor Lisa Griffin, a former federal prosecutor, concludes that the government's current reliance on DPAs suffers from a variety of flaws. She argues, for example, that prosecutors are using DPAs to meddle in corporate governance far beyond the needs of the criminal investigation, engaging in forms of "corporate-wide behavior modification" that may not represent good business practices. She also notes the lack of judicial review of such agreements, under which the government obtains effective control over these entities with little external check or scrutiny.[73]

The government has responded to at least one criticism of its white collar cooperation policies. Pursuant to the McNulty Memo, predecessor to the Filip Memo, DPAs routinely pressured companies to waive attorney-client privileges and work-product protections in order to provide the government with full access to company records and internal investigations. In a conventional prosecution, an individual or corporation cannot be forced to reveal to the government confidential communications with counsel. But corporate cooperation agreements routinely required "voluntary waivers" of such privileges. In practice, this meant that corporate counsel might share confidential information with the prosecution about company practices and documents, or conversations with individual employees.[74] It also led to a number of high-profile prosecutions of corporate actors, such as Sanjay Kumar, CEO of Computer Associates, who lied to their own corporate counsel during internal investigations. [75]

The public outcry over these "compelled-voluntary waivers" led the government to change its policies. Numerous critics, including members of Congress and one appellate court, found it unethical and contrary to established adversarial procedures for the government to deprive corporations of their attorney-client and work-product privileges as the price of cooperation. Congress is currently considering legislation that would prohibit such arrangements.[76]

The Filip Memorandum disavowed these features of corporate co-operation deals. In revising the prosecutorial cooperation guidelines, Filip based his decision expressly on the fact that

> a wide range of commentators and members of the American legal community and criminal justice system have asserted that the Department's [previous] policies have been used . . . to coerce business entities into waiving attorney-client privilege and work-product protection. . . . [T]he contention from a broad array of voices is that the Department's position . . . has promoted an environment in which those protections are being unfairly eroded to the detriment of all.[77]

By taking the waiver tool off the table, the Filip Memo stands out as a rare instance of law enforcement self-restraint in the cooperation arena.

Like street crime cooperation, white collar cooperation gives the government largely unfettered power over suspected individuals and entities. And like street informing, corporate cooperation offers its own temptations to government officials. In 2008, the House Judiciary Committee summoned former U.S. attorney general John Ashcroft to explain how he received a no-bid contract worth between $28 and $52 million to serve as the monitor for a DPA involving the medical supply company Zimmer Holdings. Zimmer hired Ashcroft at the suggestion of Christopher Christie, the U.S. attorney in New Jersey investigating the company, who had formerly worked under Ashcroft at the Justice Department. The week prior to Ashcroft's testimony, the Justice Department announced new guidelines to prevent the appearance of this sort of conflict of interest. Under the new guidelines, DPA monitors must be selected by committee and approved in Washington by the deputy attorney general.[78]

Corporate cooperation is thus characterized by an increasingly powerful government sending companies scrambling to comply with their DPAs. In this sense, despite the vast differences, corporate snitches have something in common with their individual counterparts: the decision to cooperate cedes enormous power to the government and permits law enforcement to control aspects of an individual's or a company's existence that would otherwise be beyond the reach of the criminal law.

Corporate cooperation shares another troublesome feature with its street counterpart: by permitting companies to cooperate, the government forgives their wrongdoing and forgoes the possibility of criminal punishment. As with the use of individual informants, the routine use of corporate cooperation can undermine important law enforcement goals. For example, it suggests that the government is less serious about punishing white collar malfeasance. It may even encourage wrongdoing, on the theory that companies know that they will eventually be able to cut a deal. According to some, the increased use of DPAs has already had these kinds of negative effects:

> Some lawyers suggest that companies may be willing to take more risks because they know that, if they are caught, the chances of getting a deferred prosecution are good. "Some companies may bear the risk" of legally questionable business practices if they believe they can cut a deal to defer their prosecution indefinitely, [law professor Vikramaditya] Khanna said. Legal experts say the tactic [of using DPAs] may have sent the wrong signal to corporations—the promise, in effect, of a get-out-of-jail-free card.[79]

Such concerns are common in the world of street crime and drug enforcement. Pervasive snitching deals have inculcated the idea that drug dealers can stay in business as long as they remain useful to the government. It was a murder case that prompted Judge Stephen Trott to make his oft-quoted lament: "Never has it been more true than it is now that a criminal charged with a serious crime understands that a fast and easy way out of trouble with the law is . . . to cut a deal at someone else's expense."[80] These destructive lessons of informant culture are now working their way into the rarified world of corporate crime.

2. The Employer-Employee Problem

A set of separate concerns unique to organizational cooperation has to do with the relationship between corporations and their employees. On the one hand, part of corporate cooperation involves identifying individual wrongdoers in the organization and revealing them to the government. On the other hand, this can tempt corporations to fulfill their obligations to prosecutors by sacrificing individual employees, or selectively sacrificing some while protecting others. Professor Griffin points out that the use of DPAs appears to have shifted liability away from corporations and towards individuals: since July 2002 there have been over one thousand individual white collar convictions although almost no corporations have been charged.[81]

One problem with this dynamic flows from the potential unfairness to individual employees. Because companies have significant power over their workers—particularly the ability to discipline or fire them—they can pressure workers to cooperate or provide information in ways that the government could not do directly without implicating the individuals' constitutional rights. Individual employees suspected of wrongdoing may have few means of defending themselves against the joint forces of their employer and the government.[82]

For example, in its investigation of KPMG for abusing tax shelters, the government indicated that in deciding whether or not to indict the company, it would consider the company's long-standing practice of providing employees with legal fees in connection with legal matters arising out of their employment. In its effort to avoid indictment, the company changed its practice, informing employees that it would not pay their legal fees unless they cooperated with the government. The district court described what followed:

> The government took full advantage. It sought interviews with many KPMG employees and encouraged KPMG to press the employees to cooperate. Indeed, it urged KPMG to tell employees to disclose any personal criminal wrongdoing. When individuals balked, the prosecutors told KPMG. In each case, KPMG reiterated its threat to cut off payment of legal fees unless the government were [sic] satisfied with the individual's cooperation. In some cases, it told the employees to cooperate with prosecutors or be fired.[83]

In 2006, the court concluded that the government's tactics interfered with KPMG employees' right to counsel, requiring the dismissal of some of the indictments. The court also found that some of the statements taken from some employees under these circumstances were coerced and therefore inadmissible.[84] The Filip Memo subsequently disavowed the use of such tactics.[85]

The ability of cooperating corporations to direct governmental attention toward particular employees raises a final problem: the risk that individual employees will take the fall for corporate-wide or high-level wrongdoing. In effect, by sacrificing lower-level employees, the corporation can protect itself, or high-level decision makers who might otherwise be personally liable.[86] This dynamic mirrors the same, well-known problem with informants in drug organizations. High-level operatives are better able to leverage cooperation to protect themselves, while low-level dealers and users who have little information and less protection may be sacrificed. This dynamic ensures that while cooperation in either realm often produces convictions, culpable organizations and their leadership—be they corporate or criminal—may be able to manipulate cooperation to evade punishment.

C. White Collar versus Street Snitching

The foregoing picture reveals a set of white collar cooperation practices that differ significantly from street crime and drug informing. First and foremost, the bulk of corporate activity is perfectly legal. Unlike a drug ring, society has an interest in protecting productive business organizations, even those that have committed crimes. As the Filip Memo points out, one of the factors that prosecutors must consider in initiating a corporate prosecution includes "collateral consequences, including whether there is disproportionate harm to shareholders, pension holders, employees, and others not proven personally culpable, as well as impact on the public arising from the prosecution."[87] Moreover, the activities that constitute fraud or other offenses may be very similar to legal operations, and therefore hard to distinguish and punish. This fact shapes all law enforcement practices in the business arena, including strategies for and the significance of cooperation.

Another important set of differences flows from the fact that white collar investigations and cooperation tend to be well documented, involving lawyers on all sides. The existence of witnesses, experts, and paper trails helps to eliminate unreliability, additional rule breaking, and reneging. It also enables courts and the public to figure out what happened afterwards. These attributes are in stark contrast with the secretive, informal, unwitnessed negotiations that so often characterize street and drug informing.

Importantly, white collar defendants, be they corporate or individual, tend to be wealthier, better educated, and better able to defend themselves against government demands than street crime defendants.[88] This ability goes above and beyond the individual defendant's ability to fully litigate his own case. As illustrated by the uproar over compelled waivers, white collar defendants and their defense bar can muster significant public and institutional support. As a result, government strategies are likely to be more cognizant of legal rules because those rules are more likely to be challenged and litigated. These strengths—better documentation, accountability, and counsel—inspire some of the reforms proposed in chapter 8.

At the same time, white collar informing shares important characteristics with its street counterpart. Both confer a vast amount of discretionary, unreviewable authority on law enforcement. Both exacerbate power inequalities among potential offenders, as well as between vulnerable offenders and the government. In both arenas, the decision to permit cooperation means that the government is tolerating and forgiving crime, and sometimes even creating an atmosphere in which crime may flourish. And both deprive courts, and thus the public, of significant amounts of power over and information about the operations of the executive.

Finally, the pressure to cooperate in the corporate context risks fraying the networks of trust on which business entities depend for success. Like a neighborhood, "a corporation is a collective enterprise"[89] that can be weakened by the specter of informant use. In the same way that heavy concentrations of informants threaten social networks in high-crime communities, the fear that corporate entities or individual employees may turn on each other can erode the trust and loyalty that businesses need in order to flourish.[90] Despite their significant differences, therefore, white collar and street crime cooperation involve many of the same dangers.

IV. Terrorism

terrorism = "activities that . . . involve acts dangerous to human life that are a violation of the criminal laws of the United States or of any State, [that] appear to be intended—(i) to intimidate or coerce a civilian population; (ii) to influence the policy of a government by intimidation or coercion; or (iii) to affect the conduct of a government by mass destruction, assassination, or kidnapping . . . ."

> —United States Criminal Code, chapter 113B—
> Terrorism, Definitions[91]

The terrorist attacks of September 11, 2001, affected many aspects of the U.S. legal system. From Guantanamo Bay to the establishment of military tribunals to increased demands for executive authority and secrecy, the threat of terrorism continues to influence the legal and criminal landscape.

An important feature of that landscape is the increasing centrality of informants and other forms of undercover operations. The tactic is an old one: it was paid informant Emad Salem who infiltrated a group of terrorists planning the bombing of numerous New York buildings, including the United Nations, and whose tapings and testimony enabled the 1995 prosecution of the group's leader, Sheik Omar Abdel Rahman.[92] Since September 11, 2001, however, there has been an explosion of attention, funding, and organizational commitment to developing informants in terror investigations.[93]

Any discussion of terrorism informants must begin with a caveat: much of the government's activities in this area is classified or otherwise nonpublic. In addition, terror investigations place a premium on ongoing data collection and prevention rather than generating criminal cases. Therefore, general statements about how the government uses informants, or what the costs and benefits have been, must be tempered by the acknowledgment that data is simply unavailable. Moreover, the preventative effects of informant use are difficult to measure: we do not know what would have happened had the government not intervened. This section, therefore, does not try to comprehensively describe or evaluate terrorism informant use and practices, but attempts a more modest task: outlining the general law and rules governing informants in this area, perusing the public record for the kinds of data that has become available, and thinking about useful parallels between terrorism-related informant use and other kinds of informants about which we have more information.

The basic rules governing terrorism informants are familiar ones. As a general matter, law enforcement has wide discretion to create, deploy, and reward informants, and the ability to keep much of that process off the public record. These standard characteristics, however, are heightened for terrorism informants, who can be created and used by their handlers in a wide variety of ways, across jurisdictions and countries, often over the course of many years, with few constraints. The rewards for such informants are also familiar: they include money, lenience for crimes committed, material support for political or economic activities, preferential immigration treatment, witness protection, and, more elusively, the freedom and power that can come with having a relationship with the U.S. government. The State Department, for example, runs a Rewards for Justice program that can pay up to $5 million for information leading to the arrest or conviction of any individual for the commission of an act of international terrorism.[94] The Responsible Cooperators Program provides incentives for aliens to give information about terrorism activities, including the "S" visa—sometimes referred to as the "snitch visa"—for aliens who provide "critical reliable information" regarding terrorist or criminal activity.[95]

Above and beyond these general similarities, some special rules govern terrorism informants that make their use more flexible and clandestine than the use of conventional informants. This additional flexibility flows from deep sources, primarily the greater authority vested in the executive when national security matters are at stake.[96] The Supreme Court has been particularly protective of executive authority to keep national security matters confidential, noting that such executive decisions should be given the "utmost deference."[97] Moreover, terrorism investigations and cases are not always handled as criminal matters, but may be treated as military or foreign-intelligence investigations to which traditional criminal procedure protections do not apply.[98] For example, the Fourth Amendment's warrant requirement may not cover noncriminal national security investigations regarding foreign powers, organizations, or individuals at all.[99] Likewise, national security and classified information is more protected and therefore more difficult to discover.[100]

Surveillance in the terrorism or national security context is governed primarily by statute and by executive guidelines. The Foreign Intelligence Surveillance Act (FISA) governs national-security-related electronic surveillance, wire taps, and other processes for obtaining information.[101] FISA created the Foreign Intelligence Surveillance Court (FISC), a secret court to which the government can apply for warrants and wiretaps in national security cases. In addition, the PATRIOT Act expanded the government's authority to use "national security letters" to obtain information from third parties such as phone companies.[102] These national security investigative techniques are on the rise: in 2003, the number of FISA surveillance orders exceeded the number of traditional wiretaps nationwide.[103]

The government's stepped-up surveillance has generated heated debates over the propriety of these special forms of information gathering and their impact on civil liberties and privacy. But even though informants are a crucial part of the government's antiterrorism investigative strategy, they have generally escaped these kinds of criticisms. This is in large part because informants tend to escape regulation altogether: as in the traditional criminal context, law enforcement needs no judicial or other permission to deploy them in the national security arena; they leave little or no paper trail; and they tend to slip beneath the public radar.[104]

A variety of federal agencies use informants to investigate terrorism and other national security threats. They include the Pentagon, the CIA, Treasury, Customs, the FBI, and the DEA. Information regarding the ways in which intelligence agencies, both civilian and military, use and reward informants is often classified.[105] Public information, therefore, tends to pertain to the FBI, and to a lesser extent the DEA. This is because these agencies primarily investigate traditional criminal offenses: their use of informants is thus more publicly regulated than those of agencies whose primary missions are national security related. FBI and DEA informants may also start off as drug or other kinds of informants, and then morph into terrorism sources, and are thus subject to greater controls and disclosures.

Several sets of guidelines govern the FBI. The first is the Attorney General's Guidelines for FBI National Security Investigations and Foreign Intelligence Collection.[106] These guidelines cover the general parameters of national security investigations, data collection, and threat assessment. They include a wide variety of rules such as the requirement that the Attorney General's Office be apprised of investigations, internal reporting requirements, and guidelines for dealing with foreign, state, and local governments. While the guidelines do not specifically refer to informants, they contemplate the use of human sources and thus provide the FBI with guidance in that arena.

The second set is the Attorney General's Guidelines on General Crimes, Racketeering Enterprise, and Terrorism Enterprise Investigations, promulgated in May 2002 by Attorney General John Ashcroft.[107] While these guidelines require compliance with the more specific Attorney General's Guidelines Regarding the Use of Confidential Informants, they make at least one important change with respect to informant use, which is that they authorize the development of informants and other investigative tactics at the earliest stages of suspicion. Previous guidelines had required more evidence and further investigation before such tactics could be used.[108]

The attorney general's 2006 informant guidelines govern the use of all FBI confidential human sources, including investigations using domestic terrorism informants. They do not apply to the development of informants in foreign countries. The guidelines contain a few special reporting and confidentiality rules for terrorism-related informants. For example, terrorism-related sources are not vetted by the Human Source Review Committee, but rather are referred to a special national security division. In addition, the identities of those informants are typically not revealed, even to federal prosecutors and reviewers.[109]

As this brief overview makes clear, the FBI and other law enforcement agencies have a great deal of flexibility in the ways in which they can use informants to obtain terrorism-related information. Because of the increased secrecy and ongoing nature of investigations, there is even less public data on the ways in which terrorism informants are used than there is for traditional criminal informants. Nevertheless, recent press and public attention to the phenomenon has produced a few cases that suggest the contours of some common practices.

The FBI considers informants central to its efforts to investigate and prevent terrorist violence. According to one former FBI operative, "you can't get from A to B without an informant."[110] The few public terrorism prosecutions since 9/11 typically involve informants. But beyond recognizing that informants are central to the effort, the wide variety of practices defy clear categorization. Some terrorism informants are foreign nationals who have long-standing—and sometimes on-again-off-again—relationships with the U.S. government. Some are U.S. drug dealers who turn into informants to escape traditional criminal liability. Some are U.S. residents who live in communities that the FBI wants to investigate. Some are in it for the money. And some are all of the above.

Results likewise defy easy evaluation. Some informants produce critical, reliable information that permits the government to prevent terrorist activities. Some take the government for a ride, earning money and/or lenience while producing information of little value. Some work so hard to generate cases and information that the resulting prosecutions look more like entrapment than prevention. And some do all of the above.

There have been a number of successful investigations and prosecutions, although even these have been controversial, largely because of the difficulty in discerning the true extent of thwarted threat. For example, it was a convicted drug dealer-turned-informant who posed as a terrorist and prevented a plot to blow up fuel tanks at John F. Kennedy Airport in New York. Although many hailed this as an excellent example of preventative investigation, some criticized the case because it appeared that the main suspect lacked the resources or ability to actually carry out the plot.[111]

For some terrorism suspects, it is difficult to discern whether they would actually have proceeded without the instigation or support of the informant. In May 2006, for example, informant testimony led to the conviction of a man plotting to blow up a busy New York subway station. Critics charged that the young man was not a real threat and that the informant goaded him into making incriminating statements. The informant, Osama Eldawoody, who earned over $100,000, including relocation costs, is now in hiding.[112]

Similarly, tapes played at a 2006 hearing revealed the large role that an FBI informant played in developing the case against seven men accused of plotting to blow up the Sears Tower in Chicago. The suspects were taped reciting oaths to al Qaeda, using words given to them by the informant, leading some to worry that the informant exaggerated the threat posed by the men.[113]

Like traditional criminal informants, active terrorism informants pose the threat of ongoing criminal activities. For example, Ali Mohamed, an Egyptian-born U.S. citizen, pled guilty to terrorism charges in 2000, after having served as a double agent. He worked briefly for the CIA, and then spent years providing information to the FBI, even as he continued his own deep involvement in al Qaeda training, fund raising, and support. His connections to the FBI gave him freedom to pursue his al Qaeda–related goals, including the planning of the 1998 bombing of the U.S. Embassy in Nairobi. It also gave him insight into the U.S. government's antiterrorist efforts. A former State Department official called the case "a study in incompetence, in how not to run an agent."[114]

Terrorism informants also raise the familiar specter of unreliability and weak cases. After winning two high-profile terrorism convictions and claiming that it had thwarted a sleeper terrorism cell in Detroit, the U.S. Justice Department took the highly unusual step of repudiating its own case and having the charges thrown out. The cases were based on bad evidence obtained from a single informant who was attempting to avoid fraud charges in another case. Although recognizing that their case rested on weak evidence, prosecutors had hoped to leverage the prosecution in order to get additional suspects to cooperate.[115]

An additional problem with terrorism informants appears to be the perception that the U.S. government doesn't keep its promises. In a 2002 article, *U.S. News & World Report* reported that numerous informants had complained that the government had mistreated them, and had even sued to try to get promised benefits, including health care, immigration status, and money.[116] One valuable Yemeni informant, Mohamed Alanssi, who helped the United States investigate over twenty cases, set himself on fire in front of the White House to protest his treatment by the FBI.[117]

This brief sketch indicates that, despite their special character, terrorism informants present many of the same benefits and challenges as do criminal informants. On the one hand, they offer unique information and access that is often impossible to get in other ways. On the other, they pose threats of unreliability, further crime, corruption, and the danger that they may continue to operate as criminals even as they cooperate with the government.

Some of the risks of informant use are actually heightened in this arena. Handlers may be less able to track, control, or even understand the behavior of their international operatives. Secrecy is at its height, so the opportunity for abuses—by government agents as well as informants—is correspondingly greater. Moreover, because of terrorism's international character, the handling or mishandling of such individuals can implicate diplomatic and international relations as well as crimes committed in other countries.

While terrorism informants are shrouded in secrecy and thus difficult to evaluate, the insights that we glean from traditional informants can help us think about informant use in this even more clandestine, less regulated world. Indeed, the 2007 congressional hearing on informants reflected this connection: the hearing was held jointly by the Subcommittee on the Constitution, Civil Rights, and Civil Liberties, as well as the Subcommittee on Crime, Terrorism, and Homeland Security, in recognition of the fact that both domestic and national security interests are implicated by informant practices. Noting several instances in which informants were used to thwart terrorist attacks, Rep. Lungren cited the need to improve terrorism-informant practices as an important reason for additional hearings and new legislation.[118]

The central lesson from the world of traditional criminal investigation is that informants are at their most dangerous when the government permits them to commit new crimes, off the record, without regulation or public transparency. The pressure for such compromises is at its height in terrorism investigations because active informants provide the most valuable information. Experiences with criminal informants suggest, however, that these compromises are the most expensive and deserve to be resisted. While many of the reforms described in the next chapter may be inappropriate in the terrorism context, the principles behind them—the need for more reliability and accountability, and less violence and crime—are equally present. In a sense, fostering these principles in the antiterrorism arena is even more vital because the stakes are so high.

CHAPTER 8

Reform

Crime is contagious. If the government becomes a lawbreaker, it breeds contempt for law; it invites every man to become a law unto himself; it invites anarchy. To declare that in the administration of the criminal law the end justifies the means—to declare that the government may commit crimes in order to secure the conviction of a private criminal— would bring terrible retribution.

—Justice Louis Brandeis[1]

USING INFORMANTS IS complicated. Not only does it implicate many formal laws and procedures; it engages core features of American law enforcement culture. It is connected to inequalities and vulnerabilities in communities and institutions; and it reflects systemic racial, economic, and social biases. Its impact is simultaneously legal, historical, cultural, and personal. Because informant use and its problems are rooted in so many different social institutions, they cannot be fixed solely by changing legal rules.

This is true for many challenges facing the criminal system. The justice process is not controlled by law alone; rather, it is influenced by social context and economic realities, the ways in which individual police, prosecutors, and judges apply the law, and even ineffable things such as the way crime and justice are publicly perceived. Some challenges have little to do with law at all. Chief Judge Abner Mikva once commented that "the criminal justice system is not enough—or even the most relevant institution—to deal with our crime problems. It makes about as much sense to look to prisons to solve our chronic crime problem as it would be to build more funeral parlors to solve a cholera epidemic."[2]

Stricter legal rules, moreover, do not always effectively improve the outcomes of the criminal process. This is not only because rules can be evaded but also because strict rules can drive officials towards less regulated, more secretive practices. For example, the existence of strong criminal procedure protections at trial can drive prosecutors to avoid trials altogether in favor of plea bargaining, over which they have more control.[3] Likewise, Professor Gary Marx argues that one of the reasons why U.S. law enforcement relies more heavily on covert operations than do its European counterparts is that other American police activities are more stringently regulated.[4] Accordingly, while stricter rules can improve some features of informant use, they may also drive some informant practices even further underground.

These are arguments not against regulation or for accepting the status quo, but for thoughtful reform sensitive to the realities of the American criminal process. The more heavily we rely on the criminal process to intervene in people's lives and to regulate the workings of communities and institutions, the more significant our legal rules become. Such rules, and the commitments behind them, influence not only the experiences of criminal suspects and the outcomes of criminal cases, but our collective experiences of governance. As Professor Simon puts it, "When we govern through crime, we make crime and the forms of knowledge historically associated with it— criminal law, popular crime narrative, and criminology—available outside their limited original subject domains as powerful tools with which to interpret and frame all forms of social action as a problem for governance."[5]

Accordingly, even though legal reform can only be a partial response to the complex challenges of informant use, it is vital not only in pursuit of improvements within the criminal process but for its social influence as well. Because informant use engages so many aspects of the larger criminal justice project, efforts to improve the accuracy, fairness, and transparency of informant use are also steps towards a fairer, more responsive legal system and democracy.

Informant reform is just beginning. Over the past few years, all around the country, state, local, and federal officials have begun to grapple with different facets of informant use and have proposed or instituted a wide variety of new rules: some address the ways in which informants are used as witnesses, while others take aim at witness intimidation, while still others focus on police investigative practices. While these efforts are largely piecemeal, taken together they represent the start of a more general public dialogue about criminal informants, their benefits and dangers, and the appropriate extent of restrictions on and public scrutiny of law enforcement practices.

This chapter proposes a comprehensive approach to the legal reform of informant use. Some of the specific proposals below have been adopted in numerous jurisdictions, while some have not yet been considered anywhere. Some proposals would be easy to implement, while others would require significant changes in law enforcement operations. Some are likely to be immediately effective, while others are admittedly partial and imperfect. Taken together, they provide a potential framework not only for new legislation and the reform of existing laws but for rethinking the appropriate role of informant use within the American criminal process.[6]

As a whole, the approach has four central aims:

1. increase legislative and public knowledge about criminal informant practices;
2. strengthen police and prosecutorial accountability, both internal and external, for informant practices;
3. improve the accuracy of information obtained from informants and fairness to defendants against whom informants are used; and
4. calibrate informant practices more closely to the goals of crime prevention, violence reduction, social and racial equality, and personal and community security.

I. Defining Informants

Proposal: Define "criminal informant" as any criminal suspect or defendant who provides information in exchange for an inducement or benefit. Such a definition includes all suspects and offenders with powerful incentives to fabricate evidence in exchange for lenience, money, or other benefits for themselves or someone else.

Laws pertaining to informants must first define them. Many people give information to the government for different reasons, including victims, whistleblowers, experts, investigators, and citizen bystanders. The above definition encompasses all criminal offenders receiving benefits while excluding other types of information sources.

In 2008, for example, Nebraska amended its criminal code to broaden its definition of "informant" to include any criminal suspect, whether or not he is detained or incarcerated, who "received a deal, promise, inducement, or benefit." The legislature reasoned that "[t]here is a compelling state interest in providing safeguards against the admission of testimony the reliability of which may be or has been compromised through improper inducements."[7]

In some other states, however, informant reforms have been limited to a subcategory of criminal informants: in-custody informants or "jailhouse snitches." This is in part due to the high-profile nature of jailhouse informant unreliability, which has focused legislative attention on this particular class of snitch. While jailhouse snitches have strong incentives to fabricate evidence, however, they are far from the only category of informant that does. The same motivations that lead in-custody informants to lie create the risk of fabrication in suspects who remain at large. In fact, jailhouse informants are often easier to check up on and track down because they are identifiable and leave a paper trail. The noncustodial informant may disappear long before his identity and information can be verified.

By adopting a broad definition of "informant," legislatures can ensure that reliability and accountability reforms will apply to the entire problematic class of criminal informants, not just those who happen to be incarcerated at the time they provide information to the government.

II. Data Collection and Reporting on Informant Creation and Deployment

> *Proposal*: Law enforcement agencies should keep aggregate data on the number of informants they create, the crimes those informants help solve, the crimes those informants themselves commit, and the benefits conferred on those informants in exchange for their information. The data should include the race, ethnicity, gender, and location of informants so that the differential impact on particular communities can be tracked. Like public tax data, such aggregate informant data would not include information that could be used to identity individual informants.

While the use of criminal informants is pervasive throughout state and local law enforcement, most jurisdictions lack any mechanism for keeping track of the number of informants used by the government or their productivity. This makes it impossible to evaluate whether informant use actually makes communities safer, how many crimes informants help solve, and how many crimes they commit themselves. This is a particularly pressing problem for poor, high-crime neighborhoods in which drug informants and their harms are concentrated. These communities and their representatives need data in order to analyze their experiences with informant policies.[8] States should therefore keep data on their use of informants so that criminal justice policymakers and legislatures can make better public policy decisions about informant use. Such data would also let the public see how law enforcement works in their communities and permit a more informed public dialogue about law enforcement tactics.

Informant data collection builds on existing laws and regulations. States and localities are already required to provide the FBI with a wide array of crime statistics in order to obtain federal funding. These existing reporting requirements can be expanded to include informant-related information.

The FBI already has in place an approximation of this mandate. FBI informants are kept track of, including their value to investigations as well as other crimes they commit. According to the Office of Inspector General,

The FBI tracks the productivity of its [confidential informants] by aggregating their "statistical accomplishments," i.e., the number of indictments, convictions, search warrants, Title III applications, and other contributions to investigative objectives for which the CI is credited.[9]

The FBI is separately required to report annually to the Department of Justice "the total number of times each FBI Field Office authorized a Confidential Human Source to engage in Otherwise Illegal Activity, and the overall nationwide total."[10]

The purpose of such data collection is to permit a better public and governmental understanding of informant use, to identity its true costs and benefits, and to inspire public debate. The purpose is not to endanger individual informants or officers, or to impede law enforcement investigations. For that reason, public data should be reported in the aggregate without the inclusion of individual identifying information. Such individual identifying information should be created and retained by law enforcement agencies for their own monitoring and evaluative purposes.

III. Informant Crime Control and Reporting

The central compromise and danger of criminal informant use is the official toleration of crime. This danger can be mitigated in a number of ways.

A. Legislative Limits on Crimes for Which Cooperation Credit Can Be Earned

Proposal: Legislatures should consider restricting cooperation benefits in connection with certain crimes, so that offenders who commit particularly heinous or otherwise problematic crimes cannot work off their liability by becoming informants.

As the law currently stands, there is no crime for which punishment cannot be mitigated through cooperation. Federal defendants in every category receive cooperation credit, from murderers to child pornography offenders.

In 2008, New York assemblyman Joseph Lentol proposed legislation that would limit the ability of defendants to trade testimony for lenience for certain crimes. The proposed bill would mandate that "no prosecuting attorney shall offer a dismissal of or refuse to bring charges for the crimes of murder, manslaughter, rape, or kidnapping, in exchange for the testimony of a person."[11]

Limiting crimes for which cooperation can be earned could potentially have two salutary effects. The first would be that offenders in that class would no longer be able to anticipate sentence reductions for turning in their accomplices or acquaintances and therefore might be less likely to commit the offense in the first place. The second is a more general message sent by elected representatives to the public and law enforcement alike: that the law means what it says. Such a limitation could ameliorate the public impression created by widespread snitching that liability—even for the most serious crimes—is negotiable and contingent.

To be clear, this approach is piecemeal and does not solve deeper, systemic problems with informant use. Indeed, the caustic effects of street snitching, particularly in high-crime communities, suggest that low-level snitching deals for petty crimes may be the most problematic in the aggregate. At the very least, however, legislatures should decide whether cooperation should retain its status as the omnipresent exception to every criminal law.

B. Limits on Crimes That Can Be Committed by Active Informants

Proposal: No informant should be authorized, before or after the fact, to commit a crime of violence against another person.

Violent crimes committed by informants impose particularly heavy costs because they involve the victimization of other people who are then deprived of the full protection of the law. The FBI Guidelines already stipulate that no agent can authorize an informant to commit a crime of violence. The District of Columbia has a similar statutory requirement that informants shall be "directed to refrain . . . from participating in unlawful acts or threats of violence."[12] Such an express requirement should be widely adopted.

C. Reporting Informant Crimes

Proposal: Investigative agents who know that their informant has committed a serious or violent crime should be required to report that crime to state or local law enforcement authorities in that jurisdiction.

One of the challenges of informant criminality is the secrecy with which it is treated by law enforcement handlers. The draft bill by U.S. Representatives Lungren and Delahunt, for example, requires FBI agents to report their informants' serious violent felonies to local law enforcement. This bill provides a potential model for all agencies and jurisdictions. Such a rule would not only help check informant criminality but would also reestablish crime control as a priority over the maintenance of information sources.

IV. Protecting Informants

Informants themselves are often vulnerable, to physical threats as well as psychological exploitation. They may afraid to testify, but they may also be afraid not to cooperate. Such pressures undermine not only their reliability and availability as witnesses but also their personal autonomy and security. There are a variety of ways to increase informant protections.

A. Witness Protection

Proposal: Strengthen state witness protection programs.

The federal government's Witness Security Program (WITSEC) is the model for the rest of the country. Affording short- as well as long-term protection for cooperating witnesses, it is comprehensive and well resourced, having provided protection for over seventy-five hundred witnesses and their families since 1970.[13] Most state and local law enforcement agencies, however, have few or no such resources.

Local witness protection may consist of as little as a couple of nights in a hotel before trial. For informants who live in close proximity to the people against whom they are testifying, such protection is ineffective. A central part of informant reform thus requires increased physical protection of testifying informants at the state and local level along the lines of the federal program.

Several states, including Maryland and Massachusetts, have passed additional measures such as increased penalties for witness intimidation. Others have created or beefed up their witness protection programs. The Maryland legislature has also made it easier to introduce into evidence statements made by witnesses who are rendered unavailable due to a defendant's misconduct. In other words, if a witness fails to show up in court, her previous statements made out of court can be used as evidence if the defendant threatened that witness or otherwise rendered her unavailable.[14]

B. Increase Availability of Counsel

Proposal: Provide legal counsel for uncharged suspects who are considering cooperation.

The informal, secretive, one-on-one negotiations between police and suspects are the source of many problems with informant use. Often characterized by unreliability, ongoing criminality, rule breaking, and coercion, the power struggles between offenders and police are rife with danger and irregularity. The traditional way in which the U.S. system handles such dangers is by giving suspects a lawyer. This not only reduces the coercive aspects of police pressure but also regularizes the exchange of information and benefits to make it more reliable, fair, and rule-bound. In the wake of the death of Rachel Hoffman—the 23-year-old informant who was killed during a controlled buy—Florida senators introduced legislation entitled "Rachel's Law," which provided that "each person who is solicited to act as a confidential informant must be given the opportunity to consult with legal counsel."[15]

Providing counsel to uncharged suspects who might cooperate already occurs in federal white collar practice. Because they are not yet charged with a crime, such suspects do not yet have the constitutional right to a lawyer. Nevertheless, as described in chapter 7, U.S. attorneys may inform suspects that they are potential targets of an investigation, or even sometimes ask the court to appoint counsel so that the suspect can discuss his options with a lawyer and so the process of cooperation can proceed fairly and smoothly. Making counsel available to cooperating offenders—and making sure that defendants who already have lawyers consult them—would likewise improve the fairness and regularity of the process.

To be clear, the realities of street and drug crime differ significantly from white collar investigations, and the interpolation of counsel into the now-routine dynamic between police and suspects would be disruptive. It would mean that at some point, police could no longer get quick, informal information from suspects who fear arrest or criminal charges. It might mean that fewer suspects would cooperate, and more might end up being charged with crimes. The point at which counsel is made available would have to be early enough to make a difference in the quality of information provided and the fairness of the negotiation, but not so early as to hamstring police in their investigative functions.

Nevertheless, courts, legislatures, and prosecutors' offices should make counsel available to avoid the irregularity, inaccuracy, and unfairness that plague direct negotiations between suspects and the government. The need for counsel is particularly strong for high-risk cooperating suspects, for example, those who are asked to engage in violent or otherwise risky operations, or suspects whom the government may ultimately use at trial.

C. Limit the Use of Juvenile, Mentally Disabled, and Addicted Informants

Proposal: Limit the use of especially vulnerable informants such as juveniles, individuals with mental disabilities, and drug addicts.

Vulnerable informants raise hard problems. They are more subject to coercion, less likely to be able to make good decisions on their own behalf, and as a result more likely to enter into bad deals or to get hurt as a result of their cooperation. For these reasons, their information may also be more unreliable. Pressuring vulnerable suspects to cooperate can also be unfair or, in some cases, deadly for the informant.

Many states already limit the use of juvenile informants. For example, California prohibits the use of informants under the age of thirteen and requires court permission for the use of informants under the age of eighteen.[16] This reform was prompted by the 1998 gang murder of juvenile informant Chad MacDonald.[17]

Individuals with mental disabilities are easily coerced as well as swayed to provide information that may not be accurate. For example, Derrick Megress, the informant in Hearne, Texas, who fingered numerous innocent residents, suffered from mental disabilities and was suicidal.[18] While it may be difficult for police to discern whether potential informants have such disabilities, particularly because mental disability often goes hand in hand with substance abuse, their use should also be curtailed.

Because it has become common, at least in some jurisdictions, to use snitch addicts in drug investigations, regulating their use represents a thorny challenge. Some police rely heavily on the practice, and decreasing their use would require changing some ingrained investigation habits. These habits, however, are worth changing. It is, of course, illegal to provide informants with drugs for personal use, but police routinely give cash to addicts knowing that they will use the money for drugs, thus exacerbating the very problem the war on drugs is supposed to combat. Snitch addicts have been at the heart of numerous debacles, from the Los Angeles Rampart scandal to the drugs-for-information revelations in Brooklyn, New York. The practice of giving drugs—or money for drugs—to addicts should be halted. In the same vein, no one in a drug rehabilitation program should be taken out, or used as an informant in a way that will threaten his rehabilitation.[19]

Some police already expressly disavow the use of addicted informants. Others have instituted reforms that indirectly reduce reliance on them. After the Tulia debacle, for example, the Texas legislature and Texas Department of Public Safety established new procedures and performance measures for drug investigations and enforcement.

The new performance measures involved a fundamental restructuring of the department's priorities under which the arrest of drug users and addicts is heavily disfavored, while the investigation and arrest of high-level traffickers is promoted and rewarded.

In his testimony before the House Judiciary Committee, Deputy Commander Patrick O'Burke of the Narcotics Service of the Texas Department of Public Safety explained the effects of the restructuring. Previously, police performance was measured by arrests, which created incentives to use snitches to produce a high volume of arrests but which had little impact on the drug trade. The new performance measures shift police priorities away from the cultivation and arrest of low-level users and towards higher-level traffickers. By measuring performance not by arrest but by drug volume and level of trafficker, Commander O'Burke testified, the police were able to interdict more drugs even as they conducted fewer arrests.[20]

V. Defense Informants

> *Proposal*: Create an independent authority to award cooperation benefits to informants who provide information or testify on behalf of the defense.

The use of criminal informants is inherently lopsided: a prosecutor can reward an information source with lenience or money, while a defendant who tries to pay or otherwise reward a potential witness will be accused of bribery or witness tampering. Because the government rewards only those informants who provide evidence supporting the government's case, there is a strong disincentive for informants to reveal information that might help the defense.

To remedy this imbalance, law professor George Harris has proposed establishing a mechanism for rewarding exculpatory testimony, in essence, for creating defense informants. He proposes that defendants or suspects with information favorable to the defense in a case should be permitted to apply directly to the court for the status of "cooperating for compensation," whereby they could receive charging or sentencing credit for having provided information in the same way that government-sponsored informants currently do.[21]

Alternatively, the state could create an independent prosecutor whose job is to field such requests. The advantage is that prosecutors hold charging powers and expertise not wielded by judges and therefore could reward defense informants in ways that are more comparable to prosecution informants. The disadvantage lies in forcing adverse witnesses to negotiate with the prosecutorial side, even if that independent prosecutor has no contact with the prosecuting attorney in that case.

Either way, whether cooperation benefits are conferred by a court or prosecutor, there needs to be greater balance between the government's ability to pay for information with the most valuable currency—lenience—and the defense's complete inability to access this powerful tool. Creating a reward mechanism for defense informants would help remedy that imbalance.

VI. Police Investigative Guidelines

> *Proposal*: All police departments should establish internal guidelines governing the creation, deployment, reward, protection, and documentation of criminal informants, modeled on existing FBI Guidelines.

The primary controls on police use of informants are self-regulatory: police departments' internal regulations governing the creation and use of informants.

The leading effort is the Department of Justice's ongoing revisions of its guidelines for informant use that bind the FBI, DEA, and other federal investigative agencies.[22] Such guidelines reflect DOJ's conclusion that effective informant use requires greater documentation, more internal review, and better-organized relationships among the various authorities that use informants and their information.

Some local police departments already regulate informant use through internal guidelines. Such guidelines may be simple or complex. They may require documentation, or prohibit the use of informants who are violent felons, addicts, or juveniles, or who have outstanding warrants. The Las Vegas Police Department, for example, has detailed written guidelines that, among other things, require officers to create informant files, mandate that informants "must be in a position to measurably assist in a present or future investigation" before they can be deployed, and require that informants be "advised in writing by the officer prior to being utilized that criminal law shall not be violated in gathering of information." In addition, "officers having knowledge of crime committed by an informant must notify their immediate supervisor to report the crimes to the section handling those cases."[23]

By contrast, in California, the Stanislaus County Sheriff's Office has no informant policies or training materials, even though it has used informants in dozens of cases, and the Lake County Sheriff's Department uses a single voucher form that merely records the amount paid to its informants, without any accompanying training or written policies for informant use.[24] While not all police departments will need guidelines as detailed as the FBI's, all departments should have written guidelines appropriate to their informant use, as well as training for officers to master them.

VII. Prosecutorial Guidelines

Proposal: All prosecutorial offices should establish internal guidelines that control the creation, deployment, reward, protection, and documentation of informants.

The federal government already has guidelines prescribing the considerations that should go into creating an informant. The U.S. Attorney's Manual, for example, which governs federal prosecutorial decisions, states that before entering into a nonprosecution agreement with a cooperating defendant, prosecutors should consider the following factors:

1. the importance of the investigation or prosecution to an effective program of law enforcement;
2. the value of the person's cooperation to the investigation or prosecution; and
3. the person's relative culpability in connection with the offense or offenses being investigated or prosecuted and his/her history with respect to criminal activity.[25]

As described in detail in chapter 7, in prosecuting corporate crime the Department of Justice follows the Filip Memo, which prescribes internal rules for entering into deferred prosecution agreements.

In 2008, the ABA approved new standards for prosecutorial investigations. Although they are not binding on any particular office, the legal profession often follows ABA standards, and the Supreme Court routinely cites them as guidance in determining best practices or ethical rules. These new standards contain ten factors that prosecutors should consider in "deciding whether to offer a cooperator significant benefits, including a limit on criminal liability, immunity, or a recommendation for reduction of sentence." Those factors include whether "the cooperator has biases or personal motives that might result in false, incomplete, or misleading information," whether "leniency or immunity for the criminal activity of the cooperator is warranted by the goals of the investigation and the public interest, including appropriate consideration for victim(s) [sic] interests," and whether "providing leniency, immunity or other benefits would be seen as offensive by the public or cause a reasonable juror to doubt the veracity of the cooperator's testimony."[26]

Once prosecutors decide to enter into an informant deal, the office should have guidelines to regulate how such cooperators can be deployed and what sorts of information should be obtained. Prosecutor offices should also maintain data systems to keep track of informants, the cases they are involved in, the deals they make, and the offenses they commit. The Los Angeles County District Attorney's Office, for example, now has specific policies covering the use of jailhouse informants that were instituted after the Leslie White scandals of the late 1980s. These policies require "strong corroboration" of jailhouse snitch information, and prohibit monetary payments over $50. They also require prosecutors to obtain permission from the office's Jailhouse Informant Committee before using an informant as a witness, and to check the Central Index of jailhouse informants to see if that informant has offered to be a witness or has been used as a witness before.[27]

Prosecutorial guidelines are primarily a matter of internal self-regulation. While state and local prosecutor offices have widely varying approaches to informants, their policies—where they exist—are typically not publicly accessible. In response to a 2006 public records request made by the ACLU, for example, forty-seven California prosecutors' offices declined to provide information regarding informant policies.[28] Moreover, such internal regulatory policies are not enforceable by outsiders. In other words, there is no legal remedy for the violation of such regulations or guidelines, except internal disciplinary actions that might follow. Nevertheless, such guidelines and internal rules are crucial to improving informant practices, since so much of informant use is delegated to the discretion and judgment of such law enforcement actors.[29]

VIII. Heightened Judicial Scrutiny

> *Proposal*: Courts should exercise their existing supervisory authority to improve accuracy and fairness in informant practices.

Although informant practices are largely an executive branch function, the judiciary has a great deal of influence in this arena. Presiding over warrant requests, motions, pleas, trials, and sentencing, judicial officers oversee crucial aspects of the informant process. While specific procedural reforms are proposed below, there is a general need for courts to take their oversight role more seriously.

For example, magistrate judges issuing warrants based on information from informants should stop accepting boilerplate assertions of reliability and the need for anonymity. Rather, magistrates should require specific facts from police to establish the reliability of their sources. Magistrates should also halt the practice of issuing warrants without ever asking police to produce the live informant. While informants need not appear in every case, the current expectation that police will never have to produce an actual snitch in court contributes to the culture of the invisible informant who can be switched around or even fabricated, a culture tragically illustrated by Kathryn Johnston's death. The realistic possibility that a magistrate might demand to meet the snitch, even once in a while, would help prevent such practices.

Trial judges should vet informants under their inherent authority to screen unreliable or prejudicial witnesses. Although the establishment of a formal "reliability hearing" process is proposed below, trial judges can already hold pretrial hearings: to screen out unfair, harmful, or prejudicial evidence and to establish "the qualification of a person to be a witness,"[30] where it appears that the probative value of an informant witness might be "substantially outweighed by the danger of unfair prejudice, confusion of the issues, or misleading the jury"[31] or, more generally, "when the interests of justice require."[32]

At sentencing, courts should strive for more transparency and consistency in the awarding of cooperation credit, so that the bases for rewards are more clearly visible and so that like defendants are treated alike. The Supreme Court's 2007 decisions in *Gall* and *Kimbrough* have imposed greater responsibility on federal courts in precisely this regard.[33] By restoring judicial discretion to consider all factors in sentencing—including cooperation—the Court shifted authority away from prosecutors and towards judges in determining cooperation rewards. While prosecutors still retain primary authority to make charging decisions and to recommend sentencing credit, trial courts now have the opportunity to establish fairer and more evenhanded approaches to the question of sentence reduction.

IX. Criminal Procedure Reforms

> You shall not bear false witness against your neighbor.
> —Ninth Commandment, Exodus, 20:16

Fueled in large part by the innocence movement, the most prominent extant approaches to informant reform come in the form of strengthened litigation procedures. Major reforms have come in four arenas: evidentiary rules such as corroboration requirements; discovery reforms to provide defendants with more information about potential witnesses; new procedural mechanisms such as reliability hearings; and special jury instructions.

Such reforms are important steps in ensuring more reliable trials. It should be noted, however, that because trials constitute such a small proportion of U.S. criminal dockets—on the order of 5 percent of felony cases—such reforms directly affect very few cases. They represent, therefore, only one piece in the larger reform puzzle. On the other hand, police, prosecutors, and defense attorneys often anticipate what will happen at trial and may alter some of their pretrial behavior. In other words, they operate in the shadow of trial.[34] The threat of more rigorous procedures down the line can affect investigations, charging decisions, and plea bargaining as well. Trial-based reforms can thus affect a broader range of cases and outcomes than the small number of cases that actually end up being litigated.

A. Discovery and Disclosure

Proposal: Prosecutors should discover and disclose to defendants all pertinent impeachment information regarding criminal informants used in the case, prior to the entry of a guilty plea or the beginning of trial.

A few jurisdictions have passed or considered heightened discovery requirements for informants whom the government intends to use as witnesses. The leading example is Illinois. In 2000, the Illinois Commission on Capital Punishment issued recommendations for increased safeguards for the use of jailhouse snitches, based on the

commission's finding that the use of such informants was a significant contributor to Illinois' wrongful capital conviction problem.[35]
The legislature adopted the reforms, including the requirement that
the government make specialized disclosures when it intends to use a
jailhouse informant as a witness in a capital case. Those rules require
disclosure to the defense of

1. the complete criminal history of the informant;
2. any deal, promise, inducement, or benefit that the offering party has
   made or will make in the future to the informant;
3. the statements made by the accused;
4. the time and place of the statements, the time and place of their disclosure to law enforcement officials, and the names of all persons
   who were present when the statements were made;
5. whether at any time the informant recanted that testimony or statement and, if so, the time and place of the recantation, the nature of
   the recantation, and the names of the persons who were present at
   the recantation;
6. other cases in which the informant testified, provided that the existence of such testimony can be ascertained through reasonable inquiry and whether the informant received any promise, inducement,
   or benefit in exchange for or subsequent to that testimony or statement; and
7. any other information relevant to the informant's credibility.[36]

Oklahoma courts have also required some enhanced pretrial disclosures.[37] Nebraska has a similar rule, requiring disclosures at least ten
days before trial.[38]

These state discovery reforms are limited in the sense that they apply only when the defendant has chosen to go to trial, namely, in a
small subset of cases. No such disclosure requirements are triggered
if the defendant decides to plead guilty, and under *United States v.
Ruiz*, prosecutors are not constitutionally obligated to disclose impeachment material to pleading defendants. While some prosecutorial offices voluntarily disclose such material, in the majority of cases
no informant disclosures may be made at all. Indeed, the government

often sweetens plea deals precisely in order to avoid disclosure of its informants.

Legislatures should amend their rules of criminal procedure to ensure that defendants receive comprehensive impeachment material in all criminal cases to be considered during plea negotiations as well as prior to trial. This would reduce the ability and temptation for the government to use the plea process to hide information about informants, particularly when they are demonstrably unreliable or have committed additional bad acts. It would also be fairer to defendants because it would permit them to make more fully informed plea decisions. Finally, such a requirement would increase general transparency by disclosing the use of informants in cases resolved by plea, namely, the majority of cases.

B. Reliability Hearings

Proposal: Upon a defendant's request, courts should hold a pretrial reliability hearing requiring the government to establish the reliability of any informant witness, or statements made by that informant, that the government intends to use at trial.

A potentially powerful mechanism for increasing informant reliability is to give courts a greater role in screening such witnesses and their information before they ever get to the jury. Requiring courts to establish the reliability of informant witnesses could prevent wrongful convictions, increase fairness to defendants, and provide better oversight of the use of unreliable criminal witnesses.

As part of its reforms, Illinois mandates reliability hearings for jailhouse snitch witnesses. Illinois law requires courts to consider the list of seven factors described above on which the government is required to provide discovery, and places the burden on the government to prove the reliability of its informant witness:

> The court shall conduct a hearing to determine whether the testimony of the informant is reliable, unless the defendant waives such a hearing. If the prosecution fails to show by a preponderance of

the evidence that the informant's testimony is reliable, the court shall not allow the testimony to be heard at trial. At this hearing, the court shall consider the factors enumerated in subsection (c) as well as any other factors relating to reliability.[39]

Oklahoma and Nevada courts have also required reliability hearings.[40]

Courts have long performed this kind of gate-keeping function when it comes to expert witnesses, holding hearings to determine whether such witnesses are sufficiently reliable to be permitted to testify. As the Supreme Court explained in *Daubert v. Merrell Dow*, "Expert evidence can be both powerful and quite misleading because of the difficulty in evaluating it."[41] Jurors are less effective than courts at screening out technical or specialized testimony, in part because experts carry a powerful aura of knowledge that can be particularly persuasive. Courts, therefore, step in to screen such witnesses to avoid confusing and misleading jurors and to ensure fair and accurate trials.

Informant reliability hearings proceed on the same premise. Informants resemble experts in that they purport to know things that others do not know, and have an aura of special—albeit criminal—knowledge that is highly influential with juries. In addition, courts are better positioned to evaluate informant reliability because judges understand the incentive structures of the criminal system and will be more familiar with the tendencies of such witnesses to lie.

As Professor Harris points out, there are other similarities between informant and expert witnesses.[42] Both are "paid" by one party, which makes them more one-sided than the typical witness. Their testimony is coached and prepared by the side that calls them, making them more difficult to cross-examine. Moreover, where theirs is the central evidence against the defendant, informant stories are hard to corroborate or contradict. This makes their testimony even more difficult to challenge on cross-examination, particularly since their own lives or liberty hang in the balance. Having courts scrutinize these witnesses outside the presence of the jury would alleviate many of these problems.

C. Corroboration

Proposal: All information from compensated criminal informants should be corroborated.

Corroboration requirements have deep roots. Under biblical law and English common law tradition, the "two witness" rule prohibited conviction on the basis of a single witness. In the United States, fifteen states have rules that require corroboration for accomplices. Such rules affect informant witnesses because accomplices so often become key witnesses against each other in exchange for lenience.[43]

In 1999, in Tulia, Texas, an undercover narcotics agent falsely charged dozens of African American residents with drug dealing, charging approximately 16 percent of the town's black population. With no corroboration or physical evidence, the government obtained numerous convictions and guilty pleas. Governor Rick Perry eventually pardoned the Tulia residents, but only after many of them had already served four years of imprisonment. The agent, Tom Coleman, was eventually convicted of perjury.[44]

In the wake of the Tulia scandal, Texas passed legislation requiring corroboration for all undercover drug operatives who are not themselves police officers. The law reads as follows:

(a) A defendant may not be convicted of an offense under Chapter 481, Health and Safety Code, on the testimony of a person who is not a licensed peace officer or a special investigator but who is acting covertly on behalf of a law enforcement agency or under the color of law enforcement unless the testimony is corroborated by other evidence tending to connect the defendant with the offense committed.

(b) Corroboration is not sufficient for the purposes of this article if the corroboration only shows the commission of the offense.[45]

In 2005, U.S. Representative Sheila Jackson-Lee introduced federal legislation entitled "No More Tulias: Drug Law Enforcement Evidentiary Standards Improvement Act." The bill would create, among other things, a corroboration requirement for drug informants and officers in federal cases. Under the new standard, no person could be convicted of a drug offense on the basis of the uncorroborated testimony of a single eyewitness law enforcement officer or someone working on behalf of law enforcement.[46]

There is a growing national consensus that corroboration should be required for jailhouse snitches. The American Bar Association voted in 2005 to urge all states to require corroboration for jailhouse informant testimony.[47] Likewise, in its 2007 policy review, the Washington, D.C.–based Justice Project recommended that all states adopt a jailhouse informant corroboration requirement. In 2007 and 2008, on the recommendation of the California Commission on the Fair Administration of Justice, the California state legislature passed legislation that would have required corroboration for in-custody informant witnesses. The bill was vetoed both times by Governor Arnold Schwarzenegger, who called it "unnecessary."[48]

D. Jury Instructions

Proposal: Whenever a criminal informant testifies at trial, the jury should be instructed to be especially cautious about believing that testimony, and warned to be suspicious of witnesses who receive benefits for their cooperation.

Some states handle the problem of informant unreliability by giving the jury special instructions. A typical instruction regarding jailhouse informants, this one from California, reads as follows:

> The testimony of an in-custody informant should be viewed with caution and close scrutiny. In evaluating this testimony, you should consider the extent to which it may have been influenced by the receipt of, or expectation of, any benefits from the party calling that witness. This does not mean that you may arbitrarily disregard this testimony, but you should give it the weight to which you find it to be entitled in the light of all the evidence in this case.[49]

Other jurisdictions requiring such instructions include Illinois, Colorado, Montana, Oklahoma, Ohio, Wisconsin, and Connecticut.[50]

Jury instructions are a classic and crucial vehicle for shaping ver-
dicts. Because jurors are the ultimate fact finders in criminal trials,
charged with the task of evaluating witness credibility and figuring
out what "really" happened, their evaluation of informant testimony
is central to the criminal process. For this reason, the Justice Project
recommends that all states adopt jury instructions warning jurors of
the special unreliability of jailhouse informants.[51]

While necessary, however, jury instructions are not sufficient to
weed out lying informants. Decades of research have cast doubt on
the efficacy of jury instructions, demonstrating that jurors often find
them confusing or counterintuitive, and that jurors often do not understand or apply instructions properly.[52] As discussed in chapter 3,
moreover, there are additional reasons to doubt whether jury instructions effectively educate jurors about informant unreliability.

In a recent study, psychologists examined the effects of giving information to mock jurors about informant witness rewards. They
found that jurors were equally likely to believe a witness, and therefore convict a defendant, even when they learned that the witness was
receiving a reward or incentive for his testimony. As the researchers
explained,

> Even though the witness in the incentive condition had an enor-
> mous motivation to fabricate evidence, jurors appeared to ignore
> this information and render verdicts that were not significantly dif-
> ferent across the *Incentive* and *No Incentive* conditions. . . . [J]uror
> conviction rates were unaffected by whether or not the cooperat-
> ing witness received an incentive in exchange for his testimony—
> despite the fact that participants perceived the witnesses who re-
> ceived incentives as less interested in serving justice and more in-
> terested in serving self-interests.

In other words, the jurors persistently believed informants who had
known incentives to lie. In addition, the witness's testimony strongly
influenced the verdict: jurors who heard the rewarded informant's testimony were much more likely to convict than jurors who heard only
other evidence of guilt.[53]

Such research suggests that merely giving jurors information about informant rewards and instructing them to be wary of informant testimony is not an effective safeguard against lying informants. Indeed, in the dozens of wrongful conviction cases studied in the Northwestern Law School report, in each case jurors believed informant testimony, even though they were often aware that the informant was being rewarded.[54] While such instructions are important, therefore, they are not enough.[55]

X. Improving Police-Community Trust and Communication

No discussion of informant reform would be complete without acknowledging the historic rift between police and community that has fueled recent controversies over snitching. At the same time, improving trust and communication between the police and high-crime communities is a challenge that goes far beyond the problem of snitching or, for that matter, law enforcement alone. But informants are an important part of the trust conundrum, and some communities have engaged in creative approaches. Boston began an anonymous tip texting program; police in Baltimore distributed "Keep Talking" DVDs to compete with the "Stop Snitching" original. Several jurisdictions have increased rewards for crime tips. More generally, community policing, in which many police departments are now endeavoring to establish closer ties with the neighborhoods they patrol, is centrally about building trust and communication.[56] These are the same ingredients needed to overcome some of the most difficult aspects of the informant problem.

As these wide-ranging proposals indicate, informant reform is an ambitious task potentially spanning the entire criminal process. But while the drive for reform is relatively new, large-scale efforts along these lines have already emerged. During its 2007 hearings, the House Judiciary Committee considered a wide range of potential reform subjects—from drug enforcement tactics to the rules of evidence to terrorism. That same year, New York State assemblyman Joseph Lentol, a former prosecutor, introduced comprehensive legislation that would incorporate nearly all of the above reforms, including discovery, reliability hearings, and public data collection requirements.[57] Florida's "Rachel's Law" includes some of these proposals as well. These recent events, and the ever-increasing attention to the problems of informant use, indicate that this public debate has only just begun.

Conclusion

The degree of civilization in a society can be judged by entering its prisons.

—Fyodor Dostoyevsky

LAW ENFORCEMENT PRACTICES confront us with deep truths about our collective civic choices. This book has unearthed numerous ways in which informant use is a problematic feature, not merely of the criminal process, but of American governance writ large: from the official tolerance and even perpetuation of crime to the heavy use of snitches in predominantly black communities to the governmental secrecy and lack of accountability that make so many other harmful features of informant use possible. This final chapter examines how snitching, as part of the criminal process more generally, has shaped the American polity in some disturbing ways.

I. Governing through Crime, Governing through Informants

Governing through crime is making America less democratic and more racially polarized; it is exhausting our social capital and repressing our capacity for innovation. For all that, governing through crime does not . . . make us more secure; indeed it fuels a culture of fear and control that inevitably lowers the threshold of fear even as it places greater and greater burdens on ordinary Americans.

—Professor Jonathan Simon[1]

The penal process is central to the way we manage our democracy.[2] Not simply a method of deterring, detecting, and punishing crime, we use criminal institutions and values to regulate a wide array of social interactions. The United States famously locks up more of our fellow citizens—both in absolute numbers and as a percentage of our population—than any other country in the world. In poor, high-crime neighborhoods, the penal apparatus so pervades daily experience that it defines the way many people understand and relate to the state. More broadly, we rely on criminal law to do the delicate work of social control far beyond the confines of the police station and the prison. From metal detectors in schools and the "policification" of teachers to the criminalization of immigration, American society increasingly accepts "crime control" as a model for regulating social relations.

The penal system also constitutes a massive institutional presence. Not only does it manage and supervise the lives of millions of offenders; it also provides jobs and injects billions of dollars into the economy, in some cases constituting the largest source of economic growth for entire towns. Far more than a collection of criminals and cases, the penal system is an ongoing social and economic process involving the management of a large segment of the population and the economy.

Using criminal informants to investigate others, and rewarding such criminals with lenience, is part of this larger governance process. As such, it implicates a range of democratic problems: When is it permissible for the government to tolerate or even facilitate crime? To what extent is a government justified in deceiving its citizens and keeping information secret from them? Which individual rights should be protected against governmental intrusion, and how much? Are any relationships sacrosanct against official exploitation? How should we balance law enforcement discretion with the realities of racial and economic inequality? Because evaluating informant use requires thinking about such questions, it forces us to revisit some of the criminal system's deepest commitments.

A note here on the word "democratic." It is a broad term with many contested meanings, and it is invoked here not to engage a debate over its proper use. Rather, it is to point out that penal policies, and the use of criminal informants in particular, raise a host of issues traditionally associated with the challenge of building a responsive, egalitarian, democratic society. In his book *Democracy and the Police*, legal scholar David Sklansky proposes a useful paradigm:

> [E]fforts to think systematically about the relationship between po-
> licing and democracy should strive to incorporate the perspective
> from which democracy is less about a stable system of collective self-
> government than about opposition to entrenched patterns of unjus-
> tified inequality.[3]

Managing crime by creating criminal informants raises issues in precisely this vein. It involves not only the formal structures of law and governance, and the efficacy of crime-fighting efforts, but the distribution of resources such as personal security and privacy. Fair and effective informant practices suggest a respon-sive government; unfair and unreliable practices indicate that governance processes may be breaking down. Snitching is, in this sense, a deeply democratic challenge.

A. The Infiltrator and the Spy: An Old Democracy Problem

In one narrow sense, the democratic tension inherent in snitching is an old story. The deployment of informants against civil rights and antiwar organizations in the 1970s generated a robust debate in this country over the propriety of such tactics in a nation committed to free speech and political freedom.[4] More generally, whenever the gov-ernment deploys covert operations to trick its own citizens, it raises the specter of official overreaching because it makes the government less accountable to its constituents. When the government does so for political reasons, it not only implicates free speech values but arouses the fear that the government may be using its law enforcement au-thority as a pretext to put its thumb on the political scales.

In other countries, snitching has been a prominent feature of au-thoritarianism. The former East German government was infamous for conducting pervasive surveillance of its own citizens through in-formants working for the state secret police, or "Stasi." Indeed, the use of informants in that context came to be seen as a paradigmatic aspect of authoritarianism precisely because it reflected such offensive disrespect for citizen privacy and autonomy.[5] The use of informants has also been associated with the Israeli occupation of Palestinian territories, and the British occupation of Northern Ireland.[6]

American criminal informant use is a different story. The widespread, uncoordinated use of criminal informants by thousands of different U.S. police and prosecutorial offices is not equivalent to the focused political strategy of the Stasi. Nor is it identical to J. Edgar Hoover's purposeful efforts to undermine left-wing political groups. But they share some important features. The official decision to infiltrate communities and families with informants, even when the putative goal is to ferret out drug deals rather than political activity, still raises problems of governmental overreaching, secrecy, and official deceit.

In his seminal 1988 book *Undercover: Police Surveillance in America*, sociologist Gary Marx contemplated the distinctions between undercover political policing and the covert policing of conventional crime. He maintained that while there are clear differences, the problems with political policing spill over into the criminal context.

> [I]t is still sometimes difficult to separate the heroes from the villains. The issue [of undercover policing] is complicated by the striking paradoxes, ironies, and trade-offs that are, or might be present: to do good by doing bad—preventing crime or apprehending criminals by resorting to lies, deceit, trickery; preventing crime by facilitating it; seeking to reduce crime by unintentionally increasing it; preventing harm at a cost of uncertainty about whether it would have in fact occurred; seeing police who pose as criminals become criminals; seeing criminal informers act as police; . . . and witnessing the double-edged nature of a tactic ever ready to backfire.[7]

Marx concluded that in the end, "Secret police behavior and surveillance go to the heart of the kind of society we are or might become." Twenty years later, as cooperating criminals roam vulnerable communities, snitching still goes to the heart of this question.

B. Criminal Snitching and the Dynamics of Power in Disadvantaged Black Communities: A New Civil Rights Challenge

Nowhere are the governance implications of criminal informants greater than in the disadvantaged urban communities in which the practice is most prevalent and least regulated. As a general matter, the heavy-handed presence of the criminal system in poor black communities has increased racial segregation, curtailed economic and personal opportunities, and become a central feature of institutionalized racial disparity. In neighborhoods with histories of police-community tension, disrespectful or inegalitarian criminal tactics add new fuel to long-simmering fires.[8] As Professor Simon puts it, "Governing this population through the criminal justice system has not provided the guarantees of security that might inspire greater investment in inner cities, but instead has further stigmatized communities already beset by concentrated poverty."[9]

The importance of law enforcement policies in such neighborhoods is heightened by the failure of other aspects of government. Because of thin social services, poor schools, and few jobs, the criminal system occupies an even larger space. For practical purposes, the penal system is much of the government here and therefore represents a larger proportion of the democratic process, its promises and its failures.

Informant use is one facet of this more general phenomenon. As discussed in chapter 5, the confluence of heavy drug enforcement and high rates of criminal-system involvement make it likely that many people are under heavy pressure to cooperate with police in these neighborhoods. This is a significant development. It means that some level of ongoing crime—and therefore victimization—is tolerated. It means that police rely on criminals to shape official decisions about whose home to enter and which people to arrest. It means that residents, even the very young, know that some criminals operate with impunity. And it means that the police are all too often perceived not as guardians of law and order but as deal makers who dispense justice on contingent, operational grounds rather than on principled bases.

The policy of pressuring suspects to snitch also has special implications for vulnerable populations prone to acquiesce to official pressure. Such populations are overrepresented both in the criminal system generally and in poor neighborhoods in particular. These include people suffering from substance abuse or mental disabilities. They include young and frightened informants like college student Rachel Hoffman, who acquiesced so easily to police authority and paid for it with her life. They also include indigent defendants—approximately 80 percent of the criminal justice population—who are represented by overworked public defenders with few resources and little time, and who are therefore more likely to see cooperation as their only viable option.

Finally, law-abiding residents of high-crime communities are key constituents of law enforcement policies. They may be senior citizens like Atlanta's Kathryn Johnston, or single mothers in public housing like Regina Kelly in Hearne, Texas. They are all vulnerable to the side effects of informant use because they cannot escape the crime, violence, and invasions of privacy that surround them.

Informant use thus highlights long-standing inequalities in the way we run our penal process. As law professor David Cole has explained more generally, we have two working versions of criminal justice: "one for the more privileged and educated, the other for the poor and less educated. . . . [P]olice officers routinely use methods of investigation and interrogation against members of racial minorities and the poor that would be deemed unacceptable if applied to more privileged members of the community."[10]

Snitching tracks this inegalitarian pattern. Informant practices in poor and minority neighborhoods are more intrusive, less regulated, and tolerate more risk and crime than practices used against white collar and other offenders who tend to be wealthier, whiter, better educated, and better represented. Although the formal law governing informants is largely the same in these arenas, differences in the way police and prosecutors exercise their discretion has led to vastly disparate enforcement cultures and consequences. As a result, many of the harms connected to snitching are concentrated in the most socially fragile areas.

For all these reasons, using criminal informants in poor urban neighborhoods constitutes a civil rights challenge—a public policy that exacerbates racial and economic inequality. This is civil rights in its broadest sense: the label is not so much a claim about legal entitlements as it is a reminder that the influence of the criminal system within vulnerable communities exceeds legal categories. After all, the penal process can make or break entire families, shaping the career expectations of children and the life expectancy of senior citizens. The nuances of law enforcement policies should be appreciated not only for their crime-fighting value or their consistency with existing legal rules but for their powerful impact on the contours of individual privacy and dignity. When using criminal informants exploits social disadvantage, or threatens the safety and well-being of the vulnerable, it becomes a governance failure of a high order.

C. Underenforcement and the Failure to Protect People from Crime

A decade ago, Professor Randall Kennedy famously argued that "the principal injury suffered by African-Americans in relation to criminal matters is not overenforcement but underenforcement of the laws."[11] He meant that even though African Americans are often treated more harshly by the criminal process, or singled out because of race, even more insidious is the tendency of the criminal system to ignore crime and violence when African Americans are the victims.

Informant practices are part of this larger underenforcement problem. When the government permits criminals to continue offending in exchange for information and cooperation, the community in which those crimes are committed suffers in a number of ways. First and most obviously, residents suffer from additional crime. But they also suffer the indignity of the official decision to permit such crimes to occur. When public institutions charged with maintaining law and order conclude that some individuals or communities are not entitled to full protection, it dilutes the deepest promises of democratic governance.

The problem of unaddressed crime and violence in poor urban communities is not, of course, reducible to any one law enforcement tactic, and certainly cannot be blamed on informant use alone. But the culture of snitching that barters away guilt and tolerates crime is representative of the larger underenforcement problem, in which thin policing and personal insecurity is an accepted fact of life in poor black and Latino communities. Ironically, these same communities are simultaneously subject to some of the harshest, most pervasive overenforcement of the criminal law, from racial profiling to mass incarceration and longer sentences. Criminal informant practices contribute to this catch-22.

The theory behind the toleration of informant crime is that it is necessary to prevent or prosecute worse crimes—that the ends justify the means. But the immediate communal harm inflicted by snitching is itself a force that needs to be better reckoned with. This is the means-ends calculation that sacrificed Kathryn Johnston to the long-term goals of drug enforcement. It is the means-ends calculation that permits dealers to remain on street corners where twelve-year-olds can see them. It is a calculation typically not tolerated in communities in which victims have greater political clout.

At the same time, informant use is not always a species of underenforcement: it can represent a positive, responsive governmental attitude towards crime and victimization. Using informants can, after all, be a powerful crime-fighting tool, an active effort to penetrate the most difficult criminal enterprises. It sends the message that criminal gangs and corrupt corporations and politicians are not beyond the reach of the law. By deploying informants, the government in effect proclaims that even the powerful and the insulated can be held accountable. Indeed, as complaints about underenforcement emphasize, when the government does nothing about entrenched patterns of criminality, it suggests disdain for the victims of that behavior. Recruiting and rewarding informants is one way in which the government can respond to those challenges.

In addition, offering offenders the ability to reduce their punishment through cooperation can be a positive policy. Cooperation can let offenders express repentance, their desire to abide by the law or to remedy harms they may have inflicted. In other words, it can permit people to turn over a new leaf.

In sum, criminal informant use is a complex governance mechanism whose character depends heavily on the way it is implemented. The impact and legitimacy of the practice turn on the way its benefits are balanced against its harms, who gains and who suffers, and how decisions about such things are made. From a democratic perspective, the processes by which such policies are implemented are as important as their outcomes.

D. The Politics of "Stop Snitching"

Until the "stop snitching" phenomenon generated national media attention in 2004, the political dimensions of criminal informant use went largely unrecognized. Today, some refer to "stop snitching" as a "movement," a "protest," or in other consciously political terms. Some disagree, focusing instead on its role in witness intimidation, while others relegate the entire phenomenon to the superficial realm of urban style.

As chapter 6 reveals, the "stop snitching" phenomenon is too diverse to be reduced to a single meaning. Nevertheless, the powerful public responses to it suggest that deep values are at stake. One reason why the "stop snitching" motto resonates with law-abiding citizens is that they feel that they have been ignored and mistreated by their government, that their victimization has not been taken seriously, and that their security and dignity have not been accorded equal treatment. When crowds melt away after witnessing a violent crime, residents often explain that they do not cooperate because they believe that the police cannot or will not protect them and that they are on their own. "Stop snitching" is, in part, about this experience of helplessness.

Part of the political resonance of "stop snitching" is also historical. Many of the commentators, activists, and artists discussed in chapter 6 understand snitching at least in part in terms of the history of the black political community: the informants deployed against the Black Panthers and the civil rights movement, and J. Edgar Hoover's racism. For them, the use of informants cannot be dissociated from the long-standing history of official efforts to undermine black political activism by turning individual African Americans against their associates. This is an important current of thought in the national dialogue about informant use, even though it is not universally shared or recognized.

In this sense, community responses to "stop snitching" represent another chapter in the national dialogue about how to police urban minority communities. This dialogue recognizes that vigorous policing may involve the destruction of privacy and liberty. It questions the propriety of government infiltrating private relationships, and the official pressuring of vulnerable individuals. It also raises questions of equality: when informant use threatens privacy, security, and autonomy in high-crime, inner-city neighborhoods, it creates suspicion that such erosions would not be tolerated in more politically powerful communities. "Stop snitching" resonates with all these historical challenges.

II. Implications

The use of criminal informants implicates crucial features of the democratic relationship between the police and the policed. This means that solutions will not emerge solely from tinkering with crime policy or from technical fixes alone. Instead, the phenomenon demands the full institutional response by which we resolve all such complex democratic matters: ongoing dialogue among all three branches of government, the press, and, most importantly, the public.

A significant barrier to this dialogue is the lack of public information about informant practices and the near monopoly that law enforcement has exercised over informant policy decisions. In order for legislatures, courts, and the public to become more involved, they need better information. Under current policies, law enforcement actors can use informants to make life-altering decisions about a wide variety of individuals, communities, and institutions. Such vital decisions should no longer be left solely to the lone police officer on the beat, or the prosecutor in her office.

Deciding the appropriate scope of informant use is a matter of principle as well as pragmatism. Legislatures might decide on principle that some features of snitching—the toleration of certain crimes, for example, or the racially disparate deployment of the practice—are unacceptable features of a justice system. More fundamentally, lawmakers might reconsider the unfettered discretion currently delegated to police and prosecutors that makes snitching and its dangers possible. Because snitching engages core features of our criminal process, it invites the rethinking of such key questions.

Even if we accept the compromises demanded by snitching, however, it makes a big difference how such compromises are handled. It matters how many snitches are used in a community, what crimes they commit, and how many they solve. It matters whether cooperating corporations are permitted to sacrifice low-level employees to save stock prices, and the extent to which cooperating high-level wrongdoers are punished. It matters whether children perceive criminal informants as acting with impunity, or whether law enforcement holds those informants accountable for their crimes. And it matters that we tolerate high levels of surveillance and intrusion in some communities that we do not easily tolerate in others. In other words, even if we accept the basic premises of snitching, the regulation and implementation of informant practices will ultimately determine the extent to which snitching is acceptable and legitimate.

Criminal informant use has long been justified by its putative end—getting convictions. But our justice system has never been, and hopefully never will be, driven solely by Malcolm X's admonition to proceed "by any means necessary." Rather, we have a proud history of regulating and restraining the criminal process—sometimes to the detriment of our ability to convict—precisely because we hold certain values to be higher than convictions and punishment. More than any single reform, it is this generalized commitment to principled regulation and restraint that needs to be injected into the arena of criminal informant use.

Ultimately, informant reform is part of larger dialogue on the appropriate limits to the penal system itself. Even as the United States uses arrest and incarceration to address a widening array of social problems, the decision to do so is increasingly destructive. The criminal process can spell the death knell for families, even entire neighborhoods, and has had a devastating effect on public images of black men as a class. An encounter with the penal system can be a life-altering event, destroying individuals' physical or psychological health and depriving them of opportunities such as education, housing, jobs, and the ability to vote. For some, committing a single crime becomes a fatal turning point that can sink an entire life, the debt to society that can never be paid.

It behooves us to remember that people who commit crimes are also human beings, parents and children, neighbors and workers. They may be sick or sad, frightened or angry, or merely suffering from bad judgment or lack of information. Even as they may victimize others, they are often victims themselves. The ways in which we permit our government to treat individuals who commit crimes, who are victims of crime, or all too often both, is a mark of our deepest democratic and humanistic capacities. The policies discussed here are, in the end, not merely about the way we manage the perennial problem of crime but about how we treat each other as fellow citizens, and how we envision a society that fosters respect and security over inequality and violence.

Notes

Introduction

1. This narrative is drawn from events reported in the *Atlanta Journal-Constitution*. See Rhonda Cook, "Chain of Lies Led to Botched Raid: Feds detail woman's death, officers' plea," *Atlanta Journal-Constitution*, Apr. 27, 2007, at 1D; Bill Torpy, "Report Says Pot Bust Led to Raid: Suspected dealer told cops there was cocaine in slain woman's home," *Atlanta Journal-Constitution*, Dec. 8, 2006, at 1A.

2. Mathew R. Warren, "Whitewashing a Cartoon Rat's Message on Snitching," *N.Y. Times*, July 18, 2008, at B2; Dorian Block, "Artistic Differences: Graffitists to sue city for mural coverup," *N.Y. Daily News*, Aug. 12, 2008, at 1.

3. Nathan Levy, "Bringing Justice to Hearne," *Texas Observer*, April 29, 2005; Wade Goodwyn, "Controversy over Federally Funded Regional Drug Task Forces in Texas," *All Things Considered*, National Public Radio, Nov. 4, 2002; Tim Carman & Steve McVicker, "Drug Crazed: Millions in federal tax dollars are being spent by narcotics task forces in Texas to nab low level users and dealers: Is this any way to wage a drug war?" *Dallas Observer*, Sept. 6, 2001.

4. Mica Astion, Shelley Penman & Sarah Lawrence, "A Summary of Multi-jurisdictional Drug Task Force Activities during Federal Fiscal Years 2005 and 2006," Mass. Exec. Office of Public Safety and Security, Office of Grants and Research, Div. of Res. & Policy Analysis, Sept. 2007, at 7, 14.

5. Alexander v. DeAngelo, 329 F.3d 912, 914–15 (7th Cir. 2003).

6. Rebecca Spence, "Case of Informant Reverberates through L.A.'s Orthodox Community," *The Forward*, Jan. 23, 2008.

7. Ryan S. King, "Disparity by Geography: The War on Drugs in America's Cities" (Washington, DC: The Sentencing Project, 2008), 2, 10–11 (available at www.sentencingproject.org/ Admin%5CDocuments%5Cpublications%5Cd p_drugarrestreport.pdf). See also chapter 5.

8. Laurence A. Benner, "Racial Disparity in Narcotics Search Warrants," 6 J. Gender, Race & Just. 183, 190–91, 196, 200–201 (2002).

9. Jonathan Simon, *Governing through Crime: How the War on Crime Transformed American Democracy and Created a Culture of Fear* (New York: Oxford University Press, 2007), 3–4.

10. See e.g., David Cole, *No Equal Justice: Race and Class in the American Criminal Justice System* (New York: New Press, 1999), 4–9. The disparate treatment of African Americans in particular is discussed in more depth in chapter 5.

11. See chapter 8.

12. Samuel R. Gross & Barbara O'Brien, "Frequency and Predictors of False Conviction: Why We Know So Little, and New Data on Capital Cases," U. Mich. Law. Sch. Public Research Paper no. 93, Oct. 2007, at 13 (available at www.ssrn.com/abstract=996629).

13. Rob Warden, "The Snitch System: How Snitch Testimony Sent Randy Steidl and Other Innocent Americans to Death Row," Center on Wrongful Convictions, Northwestern University School of Law, 2004 (available at www.law.northwestern.edu/wrongfulconvictions).

14. "Fake Drugs: Evolution of a scandal," *DallasNews.com* (available at www.dallasnews.com/s/dws/spe/2003/fakedrugs/fakedrug1103.html); see also Ross Milloy, "Fake Drugs Force an End to 24 Cases in Dallas," *N.Y. Times,* Jan. 16, 2002, at A1.

15. At the state level, such offenses comprise approximately 70 percent of all felony convictions while making up approximately 55 percent of federal convictions. Sourcebook of Criminal Justice Statistics Online, tbls. 5.44.2004 & 5.24.2006, Bureau of Justice Statistics, U.S. Dep't of Justice (2006) [hereinafter "Sourcebook Online"].

Chapter 1

1. Richard Rosenfeld, Bruce Jacobs & Richard Wright, "Snitching and the Code of the Street," 43 *Brit. J. Criminol.* 291, 303 (2003).

2. United States v. Singleton, 144 F.3d 1343, 1347, rev'd en banc, 165 F.3d 1297 (10th Cir. 1999).

3. Because the vast majority of individuals in the criminal system are male—93% of those in prison and 76% of those arrested—I routinely refer to suspects, defendants, and informants using the male pronoun. This is not intended to minimize or diminish in any way the experiences of the over one million women who are currently under the supervision of the criminal system. See Women in the Criminal Justice System Briefing Sheets, The Sentencing Project, Washington, DC, May 2007 (available at www.sentencingproject.org/tmp/File/Women%20in%20CJ/women_cjs_overview(1).pdf).

4. See Stephanos Bibas, "Transparency and Participation in Criminal Procedure," 81 *N.Y.U. L. Rev.* 911, 923–24 (2006) (describing the secretive, off-the-record quality of plea bargaining).

5. Jaxon Van Derbeken, "Informant in Officer's Slaying, Gang Killings Was Repeatedly Freed to Pursue Life of Crime," *S.F. Chronicle,* Aug. 13, 2006.

6. Graham Hughes, "Agreements for Cooperation in Criminal Cases," 45 *Vand. L. Rev.* 1, 3 (1992).

7. Dennis G. Fitzgerald, *Informants and Undercover Investigations: A Practical Guide to Law, Policy, and Procedure* (Boca Raton, FL: CRC Press, 2007), 45.

8. Stephen L. Mallory, *Informants: Development and Management* (Incline Village, NV: Copperhouse Publishing, 2000), 23.

9. Fitzgerald, *Informants and Undercover Investigations*, at 57.

10. Mallory, *Informants: Development and Management*, at 18–19.

11. Id. at 52.

12. Id. at 42–43.

13. John Madinger, *Confidential Informant: Law Enforcement's Most Valuable Tool* (Boca Raton, FL: CRC Press, 2000), 122.

14. Id. at 168.

15. Ellen Yaroshefsky, "Cooperation with Federal Prosecutors: Experiences of Truth Telling and Embellishment," 68 *Fordham L. Rev.* 917, 952–56 (1999).

16. Kurt Eichenwald & Alexei Barrionuevo, "The Enron Verdict: The overview: Tough justice for executives in Enron era," *N.Y. Times*, May 27, 2006, at A1; Associated Press, "Lea Fastow Gets a Year in Enron Plea," *N.Y. Times*, May 7, 2004, at C1.

17. Fitzgerald, *Informants and Undercover Investigations*, at 37.

18. See Stanley Z. Fisher, "'Just the Facts, Ma'am': Lying and the Omission of Exculpatory Evidence in Police Reports," 28 *New England L. Rev.* 1, 36 & n.179 (1993) (describing Chicago and New York "double file" systems in which police maintained two sets of reports and gave only the public versions to prosecutors).

19. Fitzgerald, *Informants and Undercover Investigations*, at 46.

20. Daniel Richman, "Prosecutors and Their Agents, Agents and Their Prosecutors," 103 *Columbia L. Rev.* 749, 789 (2003).

21. See Massiah v. United States, 377 U.S. 201 (1964); Miranda v. Arizona, 384 U.S. 436 (1966); George C. Thomas & Richard A. Leo, "The Effect of Miranda v. Arizona: 'Embedded' in Our National Culture?" 29 *Crime & Justice* 203, 244 (2002) (at least 80 percent of suspects waive their Miranda rights and talk to police).

22. Fitzgerald, *Informants and Undercover Investigations*, at 46.

23. John G. Douglass, "Jimmy Hoffa's Revenge: White Collar Rights under the McDade Amendment," 11 *Wm. & Mary Bill of Rts. J.* 123, 124–25 (2002).

24. Michael S. Schmidt & Duff Wilson, "Prosecutors in Balco Case Turn to Wife of Trainer," *N.Y. Times*, June 20, 2008, at D1. See Sample Target Letter, United States Attorneys' Manual (U.S.A.M.) § 9, Criminal Resource Manual, at 160 (1997), (available at www.usdoj.gov/usao/eousa/foia_reading_room/usam/title9/crm00160.htm).

25. Daniel Richman, "Cooperating Clients," 56 *Ohio St. L.J.* 69, 74 (1995).

26. See chapters 5 and 7.

27. See Introduction.

28. Jay Atkinson, "Snitch: When cops trust a pair of criminals to help catch a major heroin dealer, it reveals the tangled relationship between police and confidential informants," *Boston Globe*, Aug. 20, 2006.

29. See chapter 2.

30. Michael D. Sorkin & Phyllis Brasch Librach, "Top U.S. Drug Snitch Is a Legend and a Liar," *St. Louis Post-Dispatch*, Jan. 16, 2006, at A1.

31. Mark Curriden, "The Informant Trap: Secret threat to justice," *Nat'l L. J.*, Feb. 20, 1995, at 2; see also Fitzgerald, *Informants and Undercover Investigations*, at 22, 63–74.

32. Rhonda Cook, "Chain of Lies Led to Botched Raid," *Atlanta Journal-Constitution*, Apr. 27, 2007, at D1; Beth Warren, "Kathryn Johnston Shooting: Informant hiding out, plans to sue city, police," *Atlanta Journal-Constitution*, April 28, 2007, at 1B.

33. Matthew Dolan, "Officers in Corruption Case Guilty of Gun, Drug Charges," *Baltimore Sun*, April 8, 2006, at 1B.

34. Patrick McGreevy, "Case Not Closed Yet for LAPD: Despite progress since the Rampart scandal, the department still falls short of goals that would end U.S. oversight," *L.A. Times*, Apr. 20, 2006, at 1; Andrew Blankstein, "LAPD Eases Rules on Street Sources," *L.A. Times*, Aug. 13, 2005, at 4; Scott Glover, "Officers Allegedly Gave Drugs to Informant," *L.A. Times*, Feb. 13, 2000, at 1.

35. United States v. Burnside, 824 F. Supp. 1215, 1225, 1228, 1244, 1246 (N.D. Ill. 1993).

36. Fitzgerald, *Informants and Undercover Investigations*, at 267.

37. See Fitzgerald, *Informants and Undercover Investigations*, at 261–86; Todd Richmond, AP, "Witness Protection Programs Hurting: Programs don't have enough to keep witnesses safe," *Wisconsin State Journal*, May 1, 2008, at A1.

38. United States v. Bernal-Obeso, 989 F.2d 331, 335 (9th Cir. 1993).

39. Simon & Schuster, Inc. v. New York State Crime Victims Bd., 502 U.S. 105, 112 (1991).

40. As described further in chapter 7.

41. United States v. Jack Abramoff, Plea Agreement (D.D.C. Jan. 3, 2006).

42. Duff Wilson, "Witness in Track Doping Case Is Ready to Name Big Names," *N.Y. Times*, Apr. 13, 2008, at A1.

43. Alan Feuer & William K. Rashbaum, "Terror Case Takes Winding Path in 2 Nations' Courts," *N.Y. Times*, Aug. 9, 2007, at B2.

44. See chapter 2.

45. See chapter 4.

46. Gary T. Marx, *Undercover: Police Surveillance in America* (Berkeley: University of California Press, 1988), 2–4, 9 (describing shift in law enforcement purposes toward surveillance for its own sake). This shift towards a social control model characterizes the entire criminal system, not merely informant use. See Jonathan Simon, *Governing through Crime: How the War on Crime*

Transformed American Democracy and Created a Culture of Fear (New York: Oxford University Press, 2007), 3–5; David Garland, *The Culture of Control: Crime and Social Order in Contemporary Society* (Chicago: University of Chicago Press, 2001), 15–17.

47. Al Baker, "Drugs-for-Information Scandal Shakes Up New York Police Narcotics Force," *N.Y. Times*, Jan. 23, 2008 (documenting police practice of keeping drugs from busts to give to informants as payment).

48. Special Report: The FBI's Compliance with the Attorney General's Investigative Guidelines, Office of the Inspector General, U.S. Dep't of Justice (Washington, DC: Sept. 2005), chapter three, at 18 (available at www.usdoj.gov/oig/special/0509/final.pdf) (hereinafter "OIG Report").

49. See, e.g., Alan Maimon, "A Plot That Failed," *Las Vegas Review-Journal*, March 30, 2008, at 21A (documenting story of informant who falsified loan documents and tried to bribe a judge); United States v. Giffen, 473 F.3d 30 (2nd Cir. 2006) (businessman alleged that his bribery of foreign officials and money laundering were authorized by the U.S. government); United States v. Flemmi, 225 F.3d 78, 81–82 (1st Cir. 2000) (FBI handlers tolerated informants' extortion and murder); Michael D. Sorkin, "Top U.S. Drug Snitch Is a Legend and a Liar," *St. Louis Post Dispatch*, Jan. 16, 2000, at A1; David Rovella, "Some Superinformant: Lies, rap sheet of DEA's million dollar man starts a legal fire," *Nat'l L. J.*, Nov. 22, 1999 (DEA agents covered up their informant's tax fraud, prostitution, perjury).

50. United States v. Warren, 454 F.3d 752 (7th Cir. 2006).

51. United States v. Garcia, 193 Fed. Appx. 909 (11th Cir. 2006).

52. United States v. Smith, 481 F.3d 259 (5th Cir. 2007).

53. United States v. Abcasis, 45 F.3d 39 (2nd Cir. 1995).

54. David M. Zlotnick, "The Future of Federal Sentencing Policy: Learning Lessons from Republican Judicial Appointees in the Guidelines Era," 79 *U. Colo. L. Rev.* 1, 41–42 (2008).

55. Shelley Murphy, "Black Community Leaders Criticize Martorano Deal," *Boston Globe*, Sept. 29, 1999, at A21.

56. William J. Stuntz, "Plea Bargaining and Criminal Law's Disappearing Shadow," 117 *Harvard L. Rev.* 2548, 2564–65 (2004).

57. West's Ann. Cal. Penal Code §§ 211, 213(a)(1)(A).

58. Professor Stuntz makes the more general point that broad criminal codes and high sentences delegate power to police and prosecutors to decide who should be found guilty and of what, rendering legislative details about criminal liability nearly irrelevant. William J. Stuntz, "The Pathological Politics of Criminal Law," 100 *Mich. L. Rev.* 505, 509 (2001) ("As criminal law expands, both lawmaking and adjudication pass into the hands of police and prosecutors; law enforcers, not the law, determine who goes to prison and for how long."). Criminal informant use is a strong version of this general phenomenon.

59. Bruce A. Jacobs, "Contingent Ties: Undercover Drug Officers' Use of Informants," 48 *Brit. J. Sociol.* 36, 37 n.1 (1997) (study of U.S. city police describing "sentiment echoed by every officer").

60. Curriden, "The Informant Trap," at 4 (quoting Celerino Castillo, twelve-year veteran DEA agent).

61. Yaroshefsky, "Cooperation with Federal Prosecutors," at 937–38.

62. Curriden, "The Informant Trap," at 6 (quoting Michael Levine, 25-year veteran of the DEA and Customs).

63. Yaroshefsky, "Cooperation with Federal Prosecutors," at 938.

64. Donna Coker, "Foreword: Addressing the Real World of Racial Injustice in the Criminal Justice System," 93 *J. Crim. L. & Criminol.* 827, 837 (2003)

> (With the search warrants that were issued for neighborhoods that were predominantly African American and Latino, eighty percent relied on confidential informants. This was not the case for warrants issued in majority-white neighborhoods. . . . If, as some studies have found, drug users are more likely to purchase drugs from dealers of the same race, one expects that the racial pattern of traffic stops and searches would increase exponentially the racial disparity in search warrants. Even if there are low rates of success, significant racial disparities in warrant issuance will likely result in race disparities in drug arrests and incarceration.).

See also Laurence A. Benner, "Racial Disparity in Narcotics Search Warrants," 6 *J. Gender, Race & Just.* 183, 200–201 (2002) (attributing concentration of drug arrests in urban zip codes in part to heavy reliance on confidential informants).

65. Fitzgerald, *Informants and Undercover Investigations,* at 23–24, 36; Madinger, *Confidential Informant: Law Enforcement's Most Valuable Tool,* at 53–55; Mallory, *Informants: Development and Management,* at 48–50.

66. Morrison v. Olson, 487 U.S. 654, 727–28 (1988) (Scalia, J., dissenting) (quoting Justice Robert Jackson's view that the most dangerous and important power of the prosecutor is her ability to pick defendants). See also James Vorenberg, "Decent Restraint of Prosecutorial Power," 94 *Harvard L. Rev.* 1521, 1524–25 (1981) ("The core of prosecutors' power is charging, plea bargaining, and, when it is under the prosecutor's control, initiating investigations.").

67. Marc Mauer, *Race to Incarcerate* (New York: New Press, 2006), 114–19 (describing criminal system pyramid in which most reported crimes do not lead to arrest, and most arrests do not lead to cases or convictions); Berger v. United States, 295 U.S. 78, 88 (1935) ("The United States Attorney is the representative not of an ordinary party to a controversy, but of a sovereignty whose obligation to govern impartially is as compelling as its obligation to govern at all; and whose interest, therefore, in a criminal prosecution is not that it shall win a case, but that justice shall be done.").

68. Fitzgerald, *Informants and Undercover Investigations*, at 233 (quoting Integrity Assurance Notes, DEA, Planning and Inspection Division, vol. 1, no. 1 (Aug. 1991)).

69. Fitzgerald, *Informants and Undercover Investigations*, at 232.

70. Everything Secret Degenerates: The FBI's Use of Murderers as Informants, H.R. Rep. no. 108-414, at 1 (2004) (available at www.gpoaccess.gov/serialset/creports/everything-secret.html).

71. United States v. Salemme, 91 F. Supp. 2d 141 (D. Mass. 1999), rev'd in part, United States v. Flemmi, 225 F.3d 78 (1st Cir. 2000); Amanda J. Schreiber, "Dealing with the Devil: An Examination of the FBI's Troubled Relationship with Its Confidential Informants," 34 *Colum. J.L. & Soc. Probs.* 301, 330–38 (2001); Everything Secret Degenerates, at 2; Shelley Murphy & Brian Ballou, "U.S. Ordered to Pay $101.7 Million in False Murder Convictions: 'To the FBI, the plaintiffs' lives . . . just did not matter': FBI withheld evidence in '65 gangland slaying," *Boston Globe*, July 27, 2007, at 1A.

72. Bill Bush, "Arbitration Hearing: 2 officers keep jobs in identity dispute," *Columbus Dispatch*, April 19, 2006, at 6E.

73. "Fake Drugs: Evolution of a scandal," *DallasNews.com* (available at www.dallasnews.com/s/dws/spe/2003/fakedrugs/fakedrug1103.html); see also Ross Milloy, "Fake Drugs Force an End to 24 Cases in Dallas," *N.Y. Times*, Jan. 16, 2002, at A1.

74. Hayes v. Brown, 399 F.3d 972 (9th Cir. 2005).

75. Silva v. Brown, 416 F.3d 980 (2005).

76. Shelley Murphy, "Detective, Dealer Convicted on Drug Charges: Pair sold cocaine worth $81,000," *Boston Globe*, April 13, 2006, at B2.

77. Van Derbeken, "Informant in Officer's Slaying, Gang Killings Was Repeatedly Freed to Pursue Life of Crime."

78. Rob Warden & Patricia Haller, "Profile of a Snitch: A tragic choice," *Chicago Lawyer*, Oct. 1987.

79. Simon, *Governing through Crime*, at 143, 152.

80. Alexander v. DeAngelo, 329 F.3d 912, 918 (7th Cir. 2003) (Posner, J.)

81. Rod Settle, *Police Informers: Negotiation and Power* (Sydney, Australia: Federation Press, 1995), 250; see also Martha A. Fineman, "The Vulnerable Subject: Anchoring Equality in the Human Condition," 20 *Yale J.L. & Feminism* 1, 8, 16, 18 (2008) (pointing out that political and institutional policies exacerbate personal vulnerabilities in derogation of social equality).

82. Fitzgerald, *Informants and Undercover Investigations*, at 57.

83. Mallory, *Informants: Development and Management*, at 21, 37–39.

84. Alexander v. DeAngelo, 329 F.3d at 917 (holding that informant stated a civil rights claim when police forced her to engage in oral sex with a suspect in exchange for avoiding prosecution). See also Susan S. Kuo, "Official Indiscretions: Considering Sex Bargains with Government Informants," 38 *U.C. Davis L. Rev.*

1643 (2005) (analyzing police practice at issue in Alexander—pressuring female informants to use sex to obtain incriminating information about others in order to avoid their own prosecution—as a form of gender subordination).

85. Peter Farrell, "State Police Dismiss Detective Although He Escapes Indictment," *Portland Oregonian*, Sept. 23, 1998, at B07; Kathy Sanders, "Fort Worth Officer Put on Restricted Duty: A drug informant says he coerced her to have sex, the police say," *Fort Worth Star-Telegram*, Nov. 15, 1997, at 5.

86. Brian Ross, "Undercover Informant Found Dead," *20/20* Report, ABC News, July 25, 2008; Julian Pecquet, "Hoffman's Death Sparks Debate about Informants," *Tallahassee Democrat*, May 11, 2008, at A1.

87. S. 11-00444A-09, 2009 Sen. (Fla. 2009).

88. Henry E. Cauvin, "Witness Says Slain Girl Was Warned," *Wash. Post*, Feb. 11, 2004, at B01.

89. Todd Richmond, AP, "Witness Protection Programs Hurting: Programs don't have enough to keep witnesses safe," *Wisconsin State Journal*, May 1, 2008, at A1.

90. Joel Rubin, "Slaying of Witness Spurs LAPD Changes," *L.A. Times*, July 18, 2008, at Cal. 1.

91. Rosenfeld, Jacobs & Wright, "Snitching and the Code of the Street," at 306.

92. Tom Tyler & Jeffrey Fagan, "Legitimacy and Cooperation: Why Do People Help the Police Fight Crime in Their Communities?" Columbia Public Law Research Paper No. 06-99 (April 1, 2008), 11–15 (available at www.ssrn.com/abstract=887737).

93. Northern Mariana Islands v. Bowie, 243 F.3d 1109, 1123 (9th Cir. 2001).

94. See chapter 4.

Chapter 2

1. United States v. Dennis, 183 F.2d 201 (2nd Cir. 1950), aff'd 341 U.S. 494 (1951).

2. Peter Reuter, "Licensing Criminals: Police and Informants," in Gerald M. Caplan, ed., *ABSCAM Ethics: Moral Issues and Deception in Law Enforcement* (Cambridge, MA: Ballinger, 1983), 100–117 (describing widespread licensing of criminal activities by informants); Jerome H. Skolnick, *Justice without Trial: Law Enforcement in Democratic Society* (New York: Wiley, 1966), 129; Amanda J. Schreiber, "Dealing with the Devil: An Examination of the FBI's Troubled Relationship with Its Confidential Informants," 34 *Colum. J.L. & Soc. Probs.* 301 (2000).

3. Miranda v. Arizona, 384 U.S. 436 (1966); Rhode Island v. Innis, 446 U.S. 291 (1980); Berkemer v. McCarty, 468 U.S. 420 (1984).

4. See Massiah v. United States, 377 U.S. 201 (1964).

5. United States v. White, 2004 WL 2182188, *4 (D. Kan. 2004).

6. Town of Castle Rock v. Gonzalez, 125 S. Ct. 2796 (2005) (finding no cause of action against police who failed to enforce domestic violence restraining order); see also DeShaney v. Winnebago County Dep't of Soc. Servs., 489 U.S. 189 (1989) (finding no constitutional guarantee for any minimal level of security); see also Joseph Goldstein, "Police Discretion Not to Invoke the Criminal Process: Low-Visibility Decisions in the Administration of Justice," 69 *Yale L.J.* 543 (1960); Reuter, "Licensing Criminals: Police and Informants," at 101 (describing police discretion to license crime).

7. Section 608, Eureka Police Department, "Confidential Informants" Policy, submitted in response to Freedom of Information Act request by the ACLU of Northern California, filed with the California Commission on the Fair Administration of Justice, at 57 (Sept. 19, 2006) (available at www.ccfaj.org/documents/reports/jailhouse/expert/ACLU%20Letter%20re%20Informants-Exhibits.pdf).

8. Las Vegas Metropolitan Police Department, Informants and Associated Funds Management, section 5/206.24

9. Department of Justice Guidelines Regarding the Use of Confidential Informants, at 3–4, 14 (Jan. 8, 2001) (available at www.usdoj.gov/ag/readingroom/ciguidelines.htm) ("DOJ Guidelines"); Attorney General Guidelines Regarding the Use of FBI Confidential Human Sources, at 5–7, 27, 30, 34–35 (Dec. 13, 2006) (available at www.fas.org/irp/agency/doj/fbi/chs-guidelines.pdf) ("FBI Guidelines").

10. Daniel Richman, "Prosecutors and Their Agents, Agents and Their Prosecutors," 103 *Columbia L. Rev.* 749 (2003).

11. United States v. Abcasis, 45 F.3d 39, 43 (2d Cir.1995).

12. Fed. R. Crim. P. 12.3 (requiring defendants who "intend[ ] to assert a defense of actual or believed exercise of public authority on behalf of a law enforcement agency or federal intelligence agency at the time of the alleged offense" to notify the government in writing prior to trial).

13. United States v. Henry, 447 U.S. 264 (1980) (when jailhouse snitch deliberately elicited information from charged defendant it violated defendant's right to counsel). See also ABA Model Rule of Professional Conduct 4.2 (prohibiting lawyers from talking to represented defendants).

14. Imbler v. Pachtman, 424 U.S. 409 (1976).

15. See United States v. Williams, 47 F.3d 658 (4th Cir. 1995) (during plea negotiations prosecutor may threaten to charge defendant with more serious crimes, and carry out those threats, if the defendant refuses to cooperate with police).

16. See 18 U.S.C. § 6002 (federal immunity statute); Murphy v. Waterfront Commission, 378 U.S. 52, 77–79 (1964) (state grant of statutory immunity protects defendant in connection with federal prosecution as well); cf. State v. Edmondson, 714 So.2d 1233 (La. 1998) (cooperating defendant promised immunity in Mississippi was not entitled to immunity in Louisiana).

17. United States v. Pollard, 959 F.2d 1011, 1021 (D.C. Cir. 1992) ("Almost anything lawfully within the power of a prosecutor acting in good faith can be offered in exchange for a guilty plea.").

18. See description of proffer sessions in chapter 1.

19. Daniel Richman, "Cooperating Clients," 56 *Ohio St. L.J.* 69, 94–99 (1995); Graham Hughes, "Agreements for Cooperation in Criminal Cases," 45 *Vand. L. Rev.* 1 (1992).

20. Roberts v. United States, 445 U.S. 552 (1980) (upholding sentence that was enhanced in part on the basis of defendant's refusal to provide incriminating information about others); Bordenkirsher v. United States, 434 U.S. 357 (1978) (government could charge defendant with more serious crimes in effort to get him to plead guilty); see also United States v. Williams, 47 F.3d at 661.

21. Meda Chesney-Lind, "Imprisoning Women: The Unintended Victims of Mass Imprisonment," in Marc Mauer & Meda Chesney-Lind, eds., *Invisible Punishment: The Collateral Consequences of Mass Imprisonment* (New York: New Press, 2002), 90.

22. United States v. Armstrong, 517 U.S. 456 (1996); Thigpen v. Roberts, 468 U.S. 27 (1984).

23. See, e.g., State v. Williams, 896 A.2d 973, 976, 392 Md. 194 (2006) (because of his cooperation in drug cases jailhouse snitch received time-served for theft charge as well as the dropping of numerous other charges).

24. Parrish v. State, 12 P.3d 953, 956 & n.5 (Nev. 2000) (noting statutory provisions for awarding cooperation credit in Nevada, Florida, and Georgia).

25. 2007 Annual Report, Virginia Criminal Sentencing Commission (Richmond, VA: VCSC, 2007), 138 (available at www.vcsc.state.va.us/2007VCSCReport.pdf).

26. But see Melanie Wilson, "Prosecutors 'Doing Justice' through Osmosis: Reminders to Encourage a Culture of Cooperation," 45 *Am. Crim. L. Rev.* 67 (2008) (arguing that cooperation is "underutilized" and that prosecutors should rely more heavily on cooperation to make cases).

27. Sourcebook of Criminal Justice Statistics Online, U.S. Dep't of Justice, Bureau of Justice Statistics, tbl. 5.36.2006 (2006) (available at www.albany.edu/sourcebook/pdf/t5362006.pdf).

28. Linda Drazga Maxfield & John H. Kramer, "Substantial Assistance: An Empirical Yardstick Gauging Equity in Current Federal Policy and Practice," United States Sentencing Commission (Jan. 1998), 9–10 (available at www.ussc.gov/publicat/5kreport.pdf); Sourcebook of Criminal Justice Statistics Online, tbl. 5.36.2006, U.S. Dep't of Justice, Bureau of Justice Statistics (2006) (available at www.albany.edu/sourcebook/pdf/t5362006.pdf).

29. 18 U.S.C. § 3553(e).

30. 21 U.S.C. § 841(b)(1)(B)(iii).

31. The only exception is that first-time offenders may be eligible to receive a lower sentence under U.S.S.G. § 5C1.2.

32. U.S.S.G.§ 5K1.1.

33. Wade v. United States, 504 U.S. 181 (1992) (under U.S. Sentencing Guidelines, government motion is required to permit court consideration of defendant's cooperation).

34. United States v. Booker, 543 U.S. 220 (2005); Gall v. United States, 128 S. Ct. 586 (2007); Kimbrough v. United States, 128 S. Ct. 558 (2007).

35. Gall, 128 S. Ct. at 596.

36. See, e.g., United States v. Doe, 398 F.3d 1254, 1261 (10th Cir. 2005) ("[A] defendant's assistance should be fully considered by a district court at sentencing even if that assistance is not presented to the court in the form of a § 5K1.1 motion.").

37. Radley Balko, "Guilty before Proven Innocent: How police harassment, jailhouse snitches, and a runaway war on drugs imprisoned an innocent family," *Reason Magazine*, vol. 40, no. 1, May 2008, at 51–52.

38. Mark Curriden, "The Informant Trap: Secret Threat to Justice," 17 *Nat'l Law J.* 1 (1995).

39. 28 U.S.C. § 524(c); Joaquin J. Alemany, "United States Contracts with Informants: An Illusory Promise?" 33 *U. Miami Inter-Am. L. Rev.* 251 (2002).

40. Roy v. United States, 38 Fed. Cl. 184 (1997).

41. See Letter from Russell E. Perdock, Chief Deputy, Lake County Sheriff's Dept., to Maya Harris, ACLU of Northern California, May 30, 2006 (available at www.ccfaj.org/rr-use-expert.html) (providing sample voucher used for paying informants); Beth Warren, "Kathryn Johnston Shooting: Informant hiding out, plans to sue city, police," *Atlanta Journal-Constitution*, April 28, 2007, at 1B (describing payment arrangement for local snitch).

42. Richard Rosenfeld, Bruce Jacobs & Richard Wright, "Snitching and the Code of the Street," 43 *Brit. J. Criminol.* 291, 303 (2003); Jay Williams & L. Lynn Guess, "The Informant: A Narcotics Enforcement Dilemma," 13 *J. Psychoactive Drugs* 235 (1981) (noting that law enforcement provision of drugs to addict informants creates an ethical conflict); Stephen L. Mallory, *Informants: Development and Management* (Incline Village, NV: Copperhouse Publishing, 2000), 81 (noting that informants may skim money and/or drugs from controlled buys).

43. Terry v. Ohio, 392 U.S. 1 (1968); Rhode Island v. Innis, 446 U.S. 291 (1980); Massiah v. United States, 377 U.S. 201 (1964).

44. Title III, Omnibus Crime Control and Safe Streets Act, 18 U.S.C. §§ 2510 et seq. (governing electronic surveillance); State v. Mullens, 650 S.E.2d 169 (2007) (describing state statutory schemes); "Electronic Surveillance: Annual Review of Criminal Procedure," 36 *Geo. L.J.A.R.* 133, 157 (2007).

45. Hoffa v. United States, 385 U.S. 293, 303, 311 (1966).

46. Illinois v. Perkins, 496 U.S. 292 (1990).

47. United States v. White, 401 U.S. 745, 756, 764 (1971) (Douglas, J., dissenting); id. at 787 (Harlan, J., dissenting).

48. 18 U.S.C. § 2518(3)(c).

49. 18 U.S.C. § 2511(2)(c). See Mona R. Shokrai, "Double-Trouble: The Underregulation of Surreptitious Video Surveillance in Conjunction with the Use of Snitches in Domestic Government Investigations," 13 *Rich. J.L & Tech.* 3 (2006).

50. United States v. Nerber, 222 F.3d 597 (9th Cir. 2000).

51. State v. Mullens, 650 S.E.2d 169 (W.Va. 2007).

52. State v. Goetz, 345 Mont. 421, 191 P.3d 489 (2008); State v. Blow, 157 Vt. 513 (1991); Commonwealth v. Blood, 400 Mass. 61 (1987); State v. Glass, 583 P.2d 872 (Alaska 1978); Commonwealth v. Brion, 539 Pa. 256 (1994).

53. Brady v. Maryland, 373 U.S. 83, 87 (1963).

54. United States v. Bagley, 473 U.S. 667 (1985).

55. Giglio v. United States, 405 U.S. 150, 154 (1972) ("When the 'reliability of a given witness may well be determinative of guilt or innocence,' nondisclosure of evidence affecting credibility falls within this general rule [of Brady v. Maryland]." (citation omitted)).

56. Giglio, 405 U.S. at 151.

57. United States v. Ruiz, 536 U.S. 622 (2002).

58. Sourcebook of Criminal Justice Statistics Online, tbls. 5.46.2006 & 5.17.2006, U.S. Dep't of Justice, Bureau of Justice Statistics (2006) (available at www.albany.edu/sourcebook/).

59. D. Mass. Local Rule 116.2(B)(1)(c); Laural L. Hooper, Jennifer E. Marsh & Brian Yeh, "Treatment of Brady v. Maryland Material in United States District and State Courts' Rules, Orders, and Policies," Federal Judicial Center (U.S. Judicial Conference, Oct. 2004), 11.

60. McCray v. Illinois, 386 U.S. 300, 311–13 (1967).

61. Roviaro v. United States, 353 U.S. 53, 59 (1957).

62. Roviaro, 353 U.S. at 60–61, 628–29.

63. Crawford v. Washington, 541 U.S. 36 (2004); United States v. Lombardozzi, 491 F.3d 61, 72–75 (2nd Cir. 2007) (admitting officer's expert testimony that was based on evidence obtained from out-of-court confidential informants).

64. 18 U.S.C. § 3500; Ellen Podgor, "Criminal Discovery of Jencks Witness Statements: Timing Makes a Difference," 15 *Georgia St. U.L. Rev.* 651 (1999).

65. Ill. Comp. Stat., ch. 725, § 5/115–21.

66. Vernon's Ann. Tex. C.C.P. Art. 38–141.

67. Commission Chair John Van de Kamp Responds to Governor's Veto, Press Release, Oct. 18, 2007 (available at www.ccfaj.org/documents/press/Press17.pdf).

68. See American Bar Association, Resolution, Adopted by House of Delegates February 14, 2005 (urging nationwide adoption of corroboration

requirements and documenting current state legislation) (available at www.aba-net.org/leadership/2005/midyear/daily/108B.doc).

69. United States v. Singleton, 144 F.3d 1343, rev'd en banc, 165 F.3d 1297 (10th Cir. 1999).

70. Franks v. Delaware, 438 U.S. 154 (1978) (police reckless disregard for truth in warrant application will invalidate warrant); Napue v. Illinois, 360 U.S. 264 (1959) (prosecutor's knowing use of perjured informant testimony violated due process); Hayes v. Brown, 399 F.3d 972 (9th Cir. 2005) (prosecutor violated due process by knowingly using informant's false testimony).

71. Thomas Y. Davies, "Recovering the Original Fourth Amendment," 98 Mich. L. Rev. 547, 651 & n.288 (1999) ("The Burger Court made it virtually impossible for defendants to attack perjurious allegations in warrant affidavits."); Christopher Slobogin, "Testilying: Police Perjury and What to Do About It," 67 U. Colo. L. Rev. 1037, 1043 (1996) ("Most frequent, it seems, is the invention of 'confidential informants,' . . . a ploy that allows police to cover up irregularities in developing probable cause or to assert they have probable cause when in fact all they have is a hunch.").

72. Hampton v. United States, 425 U.S. 484 (1976) (holding that police overinvolvement would have to be "outrageous" before it would invalidate a conviction).

73. United States v. Twigg, 588 F.2d 373 (3rd Cir. 1978).

74. United States v. Russell, 411 U.S. 423 (1973) (defining entrapment defense and also recognizing availability of outrageous government conduct claim); see United States v. Berkovich, 168 F.3d 64 (2nd Cir. 1999) (noting that courts rarely find government conduct to be outrageous).

75. United States v. Simpson, 813 F.2d 1462 (9th Cir. 1987).

76. See Slagle v. United States, 612 F.2d 1157 (9th Cir. 1980) (finding drug informant to be neither an employee of the United States nor an independent contractor and therefore finding the United States not liable under the Federal Torts Claims Act).

77. Pleasant v. Lovell, 876 F.2d 787, 798 (10th Cir. 1989); see also Hoffa v. United States, 385 U.S. 293, 311 (1966) ("This is not to say that a secret government informer is to the slightest degree more free from all relevant constitutional restrictions than is any other government agent.").

78. Town of Castle Rock v. Gonzalez, 545 U.S. 748 (2005) (finding no cause of action against police who failed to enforce domestic violence restraining order); DeShaney v. Winnebago County Dep't of Soc. Servs., 489 U.S. 189 (1989) (finding no constitutional guarantee for any minimal level of policing or security); see also Linda R. S. v. Richard D., 410 U.S. 614, 619 (1973) (mother lacked standing to complain of state's failure to prosecute father for failure to pay child support where prosecution would result in prison term but not necessarily

payment, noting that "a private citizen lacks a judicially cognizable interest in the prosecution or non-prosecution of another").

79.   Ostera v. United States, 769 F.2d 716 (11th Cir. 1985); Luizzo v. United States, 508 F. Supp. 923 (E.D. Mich. 1981).

80.   Buckley v. Fitzsimmons, 509 U.S. 259 (1993) (defining qualified immunity).

81.   Alexander v. DeAngelo, 329 F.3d 912 (7th Cir. 2003) (holding that informant stated a civil rights claim under 42 U.S.C. § 1983 when police forced her to engage in oral sex with a suspect in exchange for avoiding prosecution).

82.   Id. at 918. See also Susan S. Kuo, "Official Indiscretions: Considering Sex Bargains with Government Informants," 38 *U.C. Davis L. Rev.* 1643 (2005).

83.   Shuler v. United States, 531 F.3d 930 (D.C. Cir. 2008).

84.   Imbler v. Pachtman, 424 U.S. 409 (1976).

85.   Burns v. Reed, 500 U.S. 478, 493–95 (1991). The Ninth Circuit briefly held that a wrongfully convicted defendant could sue the supervising district attorney for maintaining inadequate information-handling policies when those policies failed to disclose the use of unreliable informants in the prosecutors' office, although the Supreme Court reversed. Goldstein v. City of Long Beach, 481 F.3d 1170 (9th Cir. 2007), *rev'd* by Van de Kamp v. Goldstein, 129 S. Ct. 855 (2009).

86.   See generally Cyrille Fijnaut & Gary T. Marx, eds., *Police Surveillance in Comparative Perspective* (The Hague: Kluwer Law International, 1995), 269–89.

87.   Jacqueline E. Ross, "Impediments to Transnational Cooperation in Undercover Policing: A Comparative Study of the United States and Italy," 52 *Am. J. Comp. L.* 569, 571 (2004).

88.   Report of the Kaufman Commission on Proceedings Involving Guy Paul Morin (Ontario: 1997), 14, 599–636 (available at www.attorneygeneral.jus.gov. on.ca/english/about/pubs/morin/).

89.   Steven Skurka, "A Canadian Perspective on the Role of Cooperators and Informants," 23 *Cardozo L. Rev.* 759, 764 (2002).

90.   See M. Maguire & T. John, "Covert and Deceptive Policing in England and Wales: Issues in Regulation and Practice," 4 *Euro. J. Crime, Crim. L. & Crim. Just.* 316, 329–31 (1996); John Steele, "Police Cut Army of Informers to Get 'Value for Money,'" *The Telegraph*, Dec. 25, 2001.

91.   Ethan A. Nadelmann, "The DEA in Europe," in Fijnaut & Marx, *Police Surveillance in Comparative Perspective*, at 270–71, 280.

92.   Maarten van Traa, "The Findings of the Parliamentary Inquiry Viewed from an International Perspective," in Monica den Boer, ed., *Undercover Policing and Accountability from an International Perspective* (European Institute of Public Administration, 1997), 15–24; Jacqueline E. Ross, "Tradeoffs in Undercover Investigations: A Comparative Perspective," 69 *U. Chi. L. Rev.* 1501, 1507–8, 1511 (2002).

93.   Peter Klerks, "Covert Policing in the Netherlands," in Fijnaut & Marx, *Police Surveillance in Comparative Perspective*, 119.

94. Ross , "Impediments to Transnational Cooperation," at 574, 587–88.

95. Jacqueline E. Ross, "The Place of Covert Surveillance in Democratic Societies: A Comparative Study of the United States and Germany," 55 *Am. J. of Comparative Law* 493, 494, 505, 508 (2007); see also Peter J. P. Tak, "Deals with Criminals: Supergrasses, Crown Witnesses, and Pentiti," 5 *Euro. J. Crim, Crim. L. & Crim. Justice* 2, 10, 12–18 (1997).

96. Louise Shelley, "Soviet Undercover Work," in Fijnaut & Marx, *Police Surveillance in Comparative Perspective*, 155–56, 161.

97. Ethan A. Nadelmann, "The DEA in Europe," in Fijnaut & Marx, *Police Surveillance in Comparative Perspective*, 269–89.

98. Ross, "Impediments to Transnational Cooperation," at 569, 602.

99. Gary T. Marx, *Undercover: Police Surveillance in America* (Berkeley: University of California Press, 1988), 50.

100. This chapter benefited immensely from the expertise and editorial assistance of Kathryn Frey-Balter.

Chapter 3

1. John Madinger, *Confidential Informant: Law Enforcement's Most Valuable Tool* (Boca Raton, FL: CRC Press, 2000), 153.

2. The Honorable Stephen S. Trott, "Words of Warning for Prosecutors Using Criminals as Witnesses," 47 *Hastings L.J.* 1381, 1383 (1996).

3. Samuel R. Gross & Barbara O'Brien, "Frequency and Predictors of False Conviction: Why We Know So Little, and New Data on Capital Cases," U. Mich. Law. Sch. Public Research Paper no. 93, Oct. 2007 (available at www.ssrn.com/abstract=996629).

4. 826 F.2d 310 (5ᵗʰ Cir. 1987).

5. Jim Dwyer, Peter Neufeld & Barry Scheck, *Actual Innocence: Five Days to Execution and Other Dispatches from the Wrongly Convicted* (New York: Doubleday, 2000), 156.

6. Rob Warden, "The Snitch System: How Snitch Testimony Sent Randy Steidl and Other Innocent Americans to Death Row," Center on Wrongful Convictions, Northwestern University School of Law, 2004 (available at www.law.northwestern.edu/wrongfulconvictions).

7. Nina Martin, "Innocence Lost," *San Francisco Magazine*, Nov. 2004, at 87–88 (estimating the number of California wrongful convictions as being in the hundreds or even thousands).

8. Illinois Governor's Commission on Capital Punishment, Apr. 15, 2002, at 8.

9. Samuel R. Gross, Kristen Jacoby, Daniel J. Matheson, Nicholas Montgomery & Sujata Patil, "Exonerations in the United States, 1989 through 2003," 95 *J. Crim. L. & Criminology* 523, 543–44 (2005).

10. Radley Balko, "Guilty before Proven Innocent," *Reason Magazine*, vol. 40, no. 1, May 2008, at 42–55.

11. Report of the 1989–90 Los Angeles County Grand Jury: Investigation of the Involvement of Jail House Informants in the Criminal Justice System in Los Angeles County, July 1990, at 119–22 (available at www.ccfaj.org/documents/ reports/jailhouse/expert/1989-1990%20LA%20County%20Grand%20Jury%20 Report.pdf) (hereinafter "Los Angeles Grand Jury Investigation"). See also Robert M. Bloom, *Ratting: The Use and Abuse of Informants in the American Justice System* (Westport, CT: Praeger, 2002), 64–66.

12. Los Angeles Grand Jury Investigation, at 55, 58.

13. Id. at 58; see Massiah v. United States, 377 U.S. 201 (1964).

14. Robert P. Mosteller, "The Special Threat of Informants to the Innocent Who Are Not Innocents: Producing 'First Drafts,' Recording Incentives, and Taking a Fresh Look at the Evidence," 6 *Ohio St. J. Crim. L.* 101, 104, 164 (2009).

15. Ben A. Franklin, "Informer Is a Witness at Sentence Hearing for Teamster's Chief," *N.Y. Times*, Feb. 8, 1983, at A1; Joseph P. Fried, "Ex-Mob Underboss Given Lenient Term for Help as Witness," *N.Y. Times*, Sept. 27, 1994, at A1.

16. Paula Reed Ward, "Drug Ring Informants Get Lenient Sentences," *Pittsburg Post-Gazette*, Oct. 21, 2005, at B1; David Weiss, "Competing Gang Members Had 75 to 80 Percent of Illegal Drug Sales," *Wilkes-Barres Times Leader*, Dec. 8, 2006, at A1.

17. George C. Harris, "Testimony for Sale: The Law and Ethics of Snitches and Experts," 28 *Pepperdine L. Rev.* 1, 54 (2000).

18. See Joint Oversight Hearing on Law Enforcement Confidential Informant Practices before the House Comm. on the Judiciary Subcomm. on Crime, Terrorism, and Homeland Security and the Subcomm. on the Constitution, Civil Rights, and Civil Liberties, 110th Congr. (2007) (statement of J. Patrick O'Burke, Deputy Commander, Narcotics Service, Texas Dep't of Safety) (describing the need to measure police performance in terms other than numbers of arrests).

19. Ellen Yaroshefsky, "Cooperation with Federal Prosecutors: Experiences of Truth Telling and Embellishment," 68 *Fordham L. Rev.* 917, 944 (1999).

20. Steven M. Cohen, "What Is True? Perspectives of a Former Prosecutor," 23 *Cardozo L. Rev.* 817, 825 (2002).

21. Harris, "Testimony for Sale," at 54; Darryl Brown, "The Decline of Defense Counsel and the Rise of Accuracy in Criminal Adjudication," 93 *Cal. L. Rev.* 1585, 1600 (2005) (describing path-dependence of law enforcement decision making).

22. See chapter 2.

23. Trott, "Words of Warning," at 1383–84.

24. Alisa Bralove, "Murder-Prosecutor's Ignorance Was No Excuse for Brady Flaw," *Daily Record* (Baltimore, MD), Sept. 5, 2003.

25. Goldstein v. City of Long Beach, 481 F.3d 1170 (9th Cir. 2007), rev'd, Van de Kamp v. Goldstein, 129 S. Ct. 855 (2009).

26. Los Angeles Grand Jury Investigation, at 111–15.

27. Banks v. Dretke, 540 U.S. 668 (2004).

28. Walker v. City of New York, 974 F.2d 293 (2nd Cir. 2002).

29. Hoffa v. United States, 385 U.S. 293 (1966).

30. Trott, "Words of Warning," at 1385.

31. Trott, "Words of Warning," at 1386.

32. Zach Lowe, "Drug Arrest Reveals Police Strategy: Possession Charges Lodged as Informants Don't Testify," *The Advocate* (Stamford, CT), Nov. 26, 2007, at A6.

33. Warden, "The Snitch System," at 4–5.

34. Jeffrey S. Neuschatz, Deah S. Lawson, Jessica K. Swanner, Christian A. Meissner & Joseph S. Neuschatz, "The Effects of Accomplice Witnesses and Jailhouse Informants on Jury Decision Making," 32 *Law & Hum. Behav.* 137–49 (2008).

35. John Caniglia, "Judge to Free 15 Convicted on Drug Informant's Tainted Testimony," *Clev. Plain Dealer*, Jan. 23, 2008.

36. U.S.S.G. § 3E1.1 (rewarding defendants who plead guilty with a reduction in offense level).

37. Gross & Obrien, "Frequency and Predictors of False Conviction," at 4.

38. Id. at 5.

39. Mosteller, "The Special Threat of Informants," at 104.

Chapter 4

1. John Emerich Edward Dalberg Acton, *Lord Acton and His Circle* (Abbot Gasquet, ed., 1968), 166, quoted in United States v. Salemme, 91 F. Supp.2d 141, 148 (D. Mass. 1999).

2. Louis D. Brandeis, *Other People's Money and How the Bankers Use It* (New York: Stokes, 1914), 92.

3. Shannon Duffy, "Pa. Courts Move to Protect Informants from 'Who's a Rat' Web Site," *The Legal Intelligencer*, July 17, 2007 (available at law.com/jsp/law/LawArticleFriendly.jsp?id=1184576795741). Florida subsequently repealed the protocol.

4. Michael J. Sniffen & John Solomon, "Thousands of Federal Cases Kept Secret," Associated Press, Mar. 5, 2006.

5. See Darryl Brown, "The Decline of Defense Counsel and the Rise of Accuracy in Criminal Adjudication," 93 *Cal. L. Rev.* 1585, 1589 (2005).

6. Town of Castle Rock v. Gonzalez, 545 U.S. 748, 761 (2005) (reaffirming "deep-rooted nature of law-enforcement discretion"); see also Linda R. S. v. Richard D., 410 U.S. 614, 619 (1973) (mother lacked standing to complain of state's failure to prosecute father for failure to pay child support, noting that "a private citizen lacks a judicially cognizable interest in the prosecution or non-prosecution of another").

7. This reflects the general fact that regulated processes tend to produce more public information, whereas discretionary, unregulated processes tend not to. See, e.g., United States v. Armstrong, 517 U.S. 456, 464–66 (1996) (holding that defendants were not entitled to discovery regarding discretionary prosecutorial functions that "courts are properly hesitant to examine").

8. See Stanley Z. Fisher, "'Just the Facts, Ma'am': Lying and the Omission of Exculpatory Evidence in Police Reports," 28 *New England L. Rev.* 1 (1993).

9. Michelle J. Anderson, "Women Do Not Report the Violence They Suffer: Violence against Women and the State Action Doctrine," 46 *Villanova L. Rev.* 907, 928–29 (2001).

10. Fisher, "'Just the Facts, Ma'am,'" at 36 & n.179.

11. David Alan Sklansky, "Police and Democracy," 103 *Mich. L. Rev.* 1699 (2005).

12. Brandon Garrett, "Remedying Racial Profiling," 33 *Colum. Hum. Rts. L. Rev.* 41, 43–44 & n.128 (2001).

13. See Hoffa v. United States, 385 U.S. 293, 302–3 (1966); United States v. White, 401 U.S. 745, 752–53 (1971); Illinois v. Perkins, 496 U.S. 292 (1990). See chapter 2 for a detailed explanation.

14. John Hopkins, "Man Claims He Broke into Garage, Was Police Informant," *Virginian-Pilot*, Sept. 19, 2008.

15. Illinois v. Gates, 462 U.S. 213 (1983); U.S. Const. Amend. IV.

16. Lawrence A. Benner & Charles T. Samarkos, "Searching for Narcotics in San Diego: Preliminary Findings from the San Diego Search Warrant Project," 36 *Cal. West. L. Rev.* 221, 239 (2000).

17. Benner & Samarkos, "Searching for Narcotics in San Diego," at 239–40.

18. Id. at 241.

19. Chapter 1 contains more detailed descriptions of these examples.

20. Sourcebook of Criminal Justice Statistics Online, tbls. 5.46.2004 & 5.24.2007, Bureau of Justice Statistics, U.S. Dep't of Justice (2008) (available at www.albany.edu/sourcebook/).

21. Stephanos Bibas, "Transparency and Participation in Criminal Procedure," 81 *N.Y.U. L. Rev.* 911, 942 (2006).

22. United States v. White, 2004 WL 2182188, *1 (D. Kan. 2004).

23. See chapter 7 for an in-depth discussion of white collar informant use.

24. Neil Lewis, "Abramoff Gets 4 Years in Prison for Corruption," *N.Y. Times*, Sept. 5, 2008, at A13.

25. Freedom of Information Act ["FOIA"], 5 U.S.C. § 552; see Bennett v. Drug Enforcement Administration, 55 F. Supp.2d 36 (D.D.C. 1999) (FOIA request to DEA for records pertaining to informant Andrew Chambers).

26. Giglio v. United States, 405 U.S. 150, 154 (1972) ("When the reliability of a given witness may well be determinative of guilt or innocence, nondisclosure of evidence affecting credibility falls within this general rule [of Brady v. Maryland].").

27. See, e.g., United States v. Villarman-Oviedo, 325 F.3d 1 (1st Cir. 2003) (describing impeachment material); see also Roviaro v. United States, 353 U.S. 53 (1957) (in deciding whether government can withhold identity of confidential informant, court must "balance the public interest in protecting the flow of information against the right of the defendant to prepare his defense").

28. Roviaro, 353 U.S. at 60–61, 628–29.

29. Ruiz, 536 U.S. at 625.

30. United States v. Ruiz, 241 F.3d 1157, 1164 (9th Cir. 2001). The Court further reasoned that "a defendant's decision whether or not to plead guilty is often heavily influenced by his appraisal of the prosecution's case. . . . [Moreover,] if a defendant may not raise a *Brady* claim after a guilty plea, prosecutors may be tempted to deliberately withhold exculpatory information as part of an attempt to elicit guilty pleas." Ruiz, 214 F.3d at 1164 (internal citations and quotation marks omitted) (citing Sanchez v. United States, 50 F.3d 1448 (9th Cir. 1995) (holding that Brady rights are not automatically waived by entry of guilty plea)).

31. 536 U.S. at 633.

32. Ruiz, 536 U.S. at 631–32.

33. Jerome H. Skolnick, *Justice without Trial: Law Enforcement in Democratic Society* (New York: Wiley, 1966), at 133.

34. Benner & Samarkos, "Searching for Narcotics in San Diego," at 239; Fisher, "'Just the Facts, Ma'am,'" at 36. See also Letter from the ACLU of Northern California to the California Commission on the Fair Administration of Justice, Sept. 19, 2006 (documenting police and prosecutorial practices in California designed to conceal informants) (available at www.ccfaj.org/documents/reports/jailhouse/expert/ACLU%20Letter%20re%20Informants.pdf).

35. See R. Michael Cassidy, "'Soft Words of Hope': Giglio, Accomplice Witnesses, and the Problem of Implied Inducements," 98 *Northwestern U.L. Rev.* 1129 (2004); Ellen Yaroshefsky, "Cooperation with Federal Prosecutors: Experiences of Truth Telling and Embellishment," 68 *Fordham L. Rev.* 917, 962 (1999) (describing how prosecutors avoid taking notes when debriefing informants to avoid creating discoverable material).

36. Richmond Newspapers, Inc. v. Virginia, 448 U.S. 555, 576 (1980).

37. Richmond Newspapers, 448 U.S. at 572–73 (establishing right of public access to trial proceeding). See also Press-Enterprise Co. v. Superior Court of California, 464 U.S. 501 (1984) (establishing right of public access to voir dire proceeding); Press-Enterprise Co. v. Superior Court of California II, 478 U.S. 1 (1986) (establishing public access right to preliminary hearings). But see Wilson v. Layne, 526 U.S. 603 (1999) (police officers' decision to bring reporters on ride-along to execute warrant violated Fourth Amendment).

38. First National Bank of Boston v. Bellotti, 435 U.S. 765, 783 (1978) (quoted in Richmond Newspapers Inc. v. Virginia, 448 U.S. 555 (1980) (establishing public right of access to criminal trials)).

39. Press-Enterprise Co. v. Superior Court, 464 U.S. 501 (1984).

40. CBS, Inc. v. U.S. Dist. Ct. for Central Dist. California, 765 F.2d 823 (9th Cir. 1985).

41. Id. at 825.

42. Id. at 826.

43. Gannett Co. Inc. v. DePasquale, 443 U.S. 368, 383 (1979); see also New York v. Hill, 528 U.S. 110 (2000) (public interest in speedy trial did not preclude defendant's waiver of time limits).

44. Gannett, 443 U.S. at 383.

45. Everything Secret Degenerates: The FBI's Use of Murderers as Informants, H.R. Rep. no. 108-414, at 126 (2004).

46. Caren Myers Morrison, "Privacy, Accountability, and the Cooperating Defendant: Towards a New Role for Internet Access to Court Records," 62 *Vanderbilt L. Rev.* 921 (2009).

47. "Witness Protection," *N.Y. Times,* June 1, 2007 (editorial).

48. Memorandum from John R. Tunheim and Paul Cassell, Website Posting Information on Criminal Case Cooperation (Nov. 9, 2006).

49. Report of the Judicial Conference Committee on Court Administration and Case Management on Privacy and Public Access to Electronic Case Files (December 2006)) (available at www.privacy.uscourts.gov/Policy.htm).

Chapter 5

1. Jerome G. Miller, *Search and Destroy: African-American Males in the Criminal Justice System* (New York: Cambridge University Press, 1996), 102.

2. "Punishment and Prejudice: Racial Disparities in the War on Drugs," Human Rights Watch, vol. 12, no. 2, at 2 (New York, May 2000) (available at www.hrw.org/reports/2000/usa/) (hereinafter "Punishment and Prejudice").

3. Punishment and Prejudice, at 2; William J. Stuntz, "Unequal Justice," 121 *Harvard L. Rev.* 1969, 1970–71 (2008); Jonathan Simon, *Governing through Crime: How the War on Crime Transformed American Democracy and Created a Culture of Fear* (New York: Oxford University Press, 2007), 141.

4. Stuntz, "Unequal Justice," at 1971; "Punishment and Prejudice," at 2, 8–10, 17; Tushar Kansal, "Racial Disparity in Sentencing: A Review of the Literature" (Washington, DC: The Sentencing Project, 2005) (available at www.sentencingproject.org/ Admin%5CDocuments%5Cpublications%5Crd_sentencing_review.pdf).

5. Ryan S. King & Marc Mauer, "Distorted Priorities: Drug Offenders in State Prisons" (Washington, DC: The Sentencing Project, 2002), at 2, 11 (available at www.sentencingproject.org/Admin/Documents/publications/dp_distortedpriorities.pdf); "Punishment and Prejudice," at 8.

6. See Sourcebook of Criminal Justice Statistics Online, tbl. 5.44.2004, Bureau of Justice Statistics, U.S. Dep't of Justice (2004). By contrast, black defendants appear to commit certain nondrug crimes—famously homicide—at higher rates than white defendants. See Marc Mauer, *Race to Incarcerate* (New York: New Press, 2006), 139–40 (analyzing racial differences between drug and nondrug arrest and offense rates).

7. Sourcebook of Criminal Justice Statistics Online, tbl. 3.126.2005, Bureau of Justice Statistics, U.S. Dep't of Justice (2005) (available at www.albany.edu/sourcebook/pdf/t31262005.pdf); Michael Rand & Sharon Catalano, "Criminal Victimization, 2006," at 4, Bureau of Justice Statistics, U.S. Dep't of Justice (Dec. 2007) (available at www.ojp.usdoj.gov/bjs/pub/pdf/cv06.pdf).

8. See, e.g., Jonathan Kozol, *The Shame of the Nation: The Restoration of Apartheid Schooling in America* (New York: Crown Publishers, 2005), 19. Kozol documents the continuing poor quality and pervasive segregation in U.S. public schools, with 75 percent of nonwhite children in predominantly nonwhite schools and 2 million children of color in "apartheid schools" in which 99 percent of the students are nonwhite.

9. Sudhir Alladi Venkatesh, *Off the Books: The Underground Economy of the Urban Poor* (Cambridge, MA: Harvard Univ. Press, 2006), xviii–xix.

10. Robert J. Sampson & William Julius Wilson, "Toward a Theory of Race, Crime, and Urban Inequality," in J. Hagan & R. Peterson, eds., *Crime and Inequality*, 37, 38 (reprinted in R. Crutchfeld et al., eds. *Crime Readings* (Thousand Oaks, CA: Pine Forge Press, 2000), at 127) ("[T]he macrosocial or community-level of explanation [for crime] asks what it is about community structures and cultures that produces differential rates of crime.").

11. See, e.g., Tracey Meares & Dan Kahan, "When Rights Are Wrong: The Paradox of Unwanted Rights," in Tracey L. Meares & Dan M. Kahan, eds., *Urgent Times: Policing and Rights in Inner-City Communities* (Boston: Beacon Press, 1999).

12. Ryan S. King, "Disparity by Geography: The War on Drugs in America's Cities," at 2 (Washington, DC: The Sentencing Project, May 2008); "Punishment and Prejudice," at 19.

13. Sourcebook Online, tbl 5.36.2007.

14. Linda Drazga Maxfield & John H. Kramer, "Substantial Assistance: An Empirical Yardstick Gauging Equity in Current Federal Policy and Practice," 9–10 (Washington, DC: U.S. Sentencing Commission, Jan. 1998) (available at www.ussc.gov/publicat/5kreport.pdf).

15. Mauer, *Race to Incarcerate*, at 160, 164.

16. "Punishment and Prejudice," at 19; King, "Disparity by Geography," at 11–12.

17. Eric Lotke, "Hobbling a Generation: Young African American Men in Washington, D.C.'s Criminal Justice System—Five Years Later," 44 *Crime & Delinquency*

355, 355 (July 1998); Jerome G. Miller, "Hobbling a Generation: Young African-American Males in the Criminal Justice System of America's Cities: Baltimore, Maryland" (Alexandria, VA: Nat'l Ctr. on Institutions and Alternatives, 1992).

18.   Nancy G. La Vigne & Vera Kachnowski, "A Portrait of Prisoner Reentry in Maryland," 2, 50–53, 57–60 (Washington, DC: Urban Institute Justice Policy Center, Mar. 2003).

19.   Nancy G. La Vigne & Cynthia A. Mamalian, "A Portrait of Prisoner Reentry in Illinois 2," 50–51 (Washington, DC.: Urban Institute Justice Policy Center, April 2003); see also Recent Findings from the Urban Institute of Communities and Reentry, Urban Institute (Washington, DC, 2008) (available at www.urban.org/projects/reentry-portfolio/communities.cfm).

20.   Sourcebook Online, tbls 5.44.2004 & 5.45.2002.

21.   "Punishment and Prejudice," at 17.

22.   Sourcebook Online, tbl 5.44.2004; Jerome H. Skolnick, *Justice without Trial: Law Enforcement in Democratic Society* (New York: Wiley, 1966), 126–30.

23.   Caroline Wolf Harlow, U.S. Dep't of Justice, Profile of Jail Inmates 1996 (Washington, DC: U.S. Dep't of Justice, 1998), 1, 9 (available at www.ojp.usdoj.gov/bjs/pub/pdf/pji96.pdf).

24.   Rachel E. Barkow, "The Political Market for Criminal Justice," 104 *Mich. L. Rev.* 1713, 1716 n.13 (2006); Center for Disease Control, Substance Abuse Treatment for Drug Users in the Criminal Justice System (U.S. Dep't Health & Human Services, CDC, Aug. 2001), 1 (available at www.cdc.gov/idu/facts/cj-satreat.pdf).

25.   Opinion and Order, United States v. Ail, CR 05-323-01-RE (Aug. 14, 2007) (Redden, J.); see also Ashbel S. Green, "Shop Owner Demands FBI Records," *Portland Oregonian*, Aug. 15, 2006, B10.

26.   David Conti & Richard Byrne Reilly, "Decision to Release Jailhouse Snitch Backfires," *Pittsburgh Tribune Review*, April 17, 2005.

27.   Editorial, "Police Debacle Earns Courageous Rebuke," *St. Petersburg Times*, April 10, 2008, at 8A.

28.   Skolnick, *Justice without Trial*, at 129.

29.   Richard Rosenfeld, Bruce A. Jacobs & Richard Wright, "Snitching and the Code of the Street," 43 *British J. Criminol.* 291, 303, n.7 (2003).

30.   John Madinger, *Confidential Informant: Law Enforcement's Most Valuable Tool* (Boca Raton, FL: CRC Press, 2000), 187.

31.   Rosenfeld, "Snitching and the Code of the Street," at 304–6.

32.   See Omri Yadlin, "The Conspirator Dilemma: Introducing the 'Trojan Horse' Enforcement Strategy," Berkeley Program in Law & Economics, Working Paper Series. Paper 48 (April 2, 2002), 16–17 (available at www.repositories.cdlib.org/blewp/48).

33.   Peter Finn & Kerry Murphy Healey, Preventing Gang- and Drug-Related Witness Intimidation, National Institute of Justice, U.S. Dep't of Justice, Nov.

1996, at 4–5, 6 (available at www.ncjrs.gov/pdffiles/163067.pdf); Kerry Murphy Healey, "Victim and Witness Intimidation: New Developments and Emerging Responses," National Institute of Justice, U.S. Dep't of Justice, Oct. 1995, at 2 (available at www.ncjrs.gov/pdffiles/witintim.pdf).

34. Scott Jacques & Richard Wright, "The Relevance of Peace to Studies of Drug Market Violence," 46 *Criminology* 221, 222 (2008).

35. Joel Rubin, "Slaying of Witness Spurs LAPD Changes," *L.A. Times*, July 18, 2008, California section, 1.

36. "Slain Teen's Mother Wins Suit: Court: Award of at least $1 million to go to woman whose son, killed in Norwalk Drug house, was police informant," *Long Beach Press-Telegram*, Aug. 27, 2002, at A2.

37. Laurence A. Benner, "Racial Disparity in Narcotics Search Warrants," 6 *J. Gender, Race & Just.* 183, 190–91, 194, 196, 200–201 & n.60 (2002). See also Laurence A. Benner & Charles T. Samarkos, "Searching for Narcotics in San Diego: Preliminary Findings from the San Diego Search Warrant Project," 36 *Cal. West. L. Rev.* 221 (2000).

38. See Andrew E. Taslitz, "Wrongly Accused Redux: How Race Contributes to Convicting the Innocent: The Informants Example," 37 *Southwest U. L. Rev.* 101 (2008).

39. See Randall Kennedy, *Race, Crime, and the Law* (New York: Pantheon Books, 1997), 26.

40. Robert J. Sampson & Dawn Jeglum Bartusch, "Legal Cynicism and (Subcultural?) Tolerance of Deviance: The Neighborhood Context of Racial Differences," 32 *Law & Soc. Rev.* 777, 783–84 (1998).

41. Kennedy, *Race, Crime, and the Law*, at 73, 127–29, 157–58.

42. Rebecca Adamus, "Fighting Fear," *Florida Today*, May 22, 2007, at 1A.

43. Jeremy Kahn, "The Story of a Snitch," *Atlantic Monthly*, April 2007, at 3.

44. Tom Tyler & Jeffrey Fagan, "Legitimacy and Cooperation: Why Do People Help the Police Fight Crime in Their Communities?" Columbia Public Law Research Paper no. 06-99 (April 1, 2008), 11–15 (available at: www.ssrn.com/abstract=887737).

45. Ofra Bickel, "Frontline: Snitch," Transcript (PBS, Jan. 12, 1999), 32.

46. Art Barnum, "Mom Called 'Snitch' on Son in Murder Case," *Chicago Tribune*, Nov. 29, 2006.

47. Bickel, "Frontline: Snitch," at 7–10.

48. See Venkatesh, *Off the Books*, at 6–13.

49. Sampson & Wilson, "Towards a Theory of Race, Crime, and Urban Inequality" (describing social disorganization theory); Robert J. Sampson, Stephen W. Raudenbush & Felton Earls, "Neighborhoods and Violent Crime: A Multilevel Study of Collective Efficacy," 277 *Science* 918 (1997) (arguing that social dislocation and disadvantage undermine collective efficacy of communities, which in turn disables those communities from internally regulating violence and crime).

50. Michael Tonry, *Malign Neglect: Race, Crime, and Punishment in America* (New York: Oxford University Press, 1995), 105–6.

51. See David Boyum & Peter Reuter, *An Analytic Assessment of U.S. Drug Policy* (Washington, DC: American Enterprise Press, 2005), 2, 77–79, 93–94; The Cato Handbook on Policy (2005), 253–59 (calling the war on drugs a "manifest failure"); What's Wrong with the War on Drugs? Drug Policy Alliance Network (2008), (available at www.drugpolicy.org/drugwar/) ("The war on drugs has become a war on families, a war on public health and a war on our constitutional rights.").

52. William K. Rashbaum, "'Last Don' Reported to Be the First One to Betray the Mob," *N.Y. Times*, Jan. 28, 2005, at A1 (describing numerous high-level mafia operatives turned informant). Of course, this policy had its costs as well. See Everything Secret Degenerates: The FBI's Use of Murderers as Informants, H.R. Rep. no. 108-414, at 126 (2004), 1–9.

Chapter 6

1. Rachel Gottlieb, "Students in Brawl Reunite for a Day: Program Intended to Ease Tensions," *Hartford Courant*, March 23, 2006, at B1.

2. Rick Hampson, "Anti-snitch Campaign Riles Police, Prosecutors: Is it a grass-roots backlash against criminals turned informers or intimidation?" *USA Today*, March 29, 2006, at 1A.

3. Fox Butterfield, "Guns and Jeers Used by Gangs to Buy Silence," *N.Y. Times*, Jan. 16, 2005, at A11.

4. Julie Bykowicz, "Ehrlich Launching Media Blitz against Drugs and Violence: NBA's Carmelo Anthony appears, makes amends for 'Stop Snitching' DVD," *Baltimore Sun*, May 12, 2005, at 10A.

5. Gabrielle Banks, "'Stop Snitchin' Shirts Stopping Criminal Trials: An urban fashion trend," *Pittsburgh Post-Gazette*, Oct. 18, 2005.

6. Suzanne Smalley, "'Snitching' T-shirts Come off the Shelves," *Boston Globe*, Dec. 5, 2005.

7. Lyle V. Harris, "See No Evil, Speak No Evil: In hip-hop and beyond, telling the police what you've seen is a high crime itself: Silence shouldn't be golden," *Atlanta Journal-Constitution*, May 20, 2007, at 1C.

8. Emily Vasquez, "Rapper Silent about Aide's Death," *N.Y. Times*, Aug. 22, 2006, at B2.

9. Anderson Cooper, "Stop Snitchin'; Not helping police solve crimes promoted widely in rap, hip hop music," *60 Minutes* transcript, Apr. 22, 2007.

10. Ethan Brown, *Snitch: Informants, Cooperators & the Corruption of Justice* (New York: Public Affairs, 2007), 10–11.

11. David Kocieniewski, "A Little Girl Shot, and a Crowd That Didn't See," *N.Y. Times*, July 9, 2007.

12. Julie Bykowicz, "'Snitching 2' Out Soon: Producer says education, not intimidation, is sequel's focus," *Baltimore Sun*, Dec. 20, 2007; Jeremy Kahn, "The Story of a Snitch," *Atlantic Monthly*, April 2007, at 88.

13. Anderson Cooper, *360 Degrees*, CNN, April 24, 2007 (interviewing Geoffrey Canada).

14. Betsy Powell, "Police Hampered by Cult of 'Stop Snitchin': Witness intimidation makes solving crimes harder, but so does public distrust of the justice system," *Toronto Star*, Jan. 2, 2008, at A01.

15. Quoted in Davey D, "'Stop Snitching' Campaign Runs Deeper Than Most Think," *San Jose Mercury News*, July 5, 2007.

16. Randall Kennedy, *Race, Crime, and the Law* (New York: Pantheon Books, 1997), 4, 11, 113–25.

17. Kennedy, *Race, Crime, and the Law*, at 115–18.

18. Anemona Hartocollis, "In Looking at a Police Shooting, Jurors Views Lead to Compromise," *N.Y. Times*, Mar. 17, 2007, at B2.

19. Tom Tyler & Jeffrey Fagan, "Legitimacy and Cooperation: Why Do People Help the Police Fight Crime in their Communities?" Columbia Law School Public Law & Legal Theory Working Paper no. 06-99, at 9 (last revised Apr. 16, 2008) (available at www.SSRN.com/abstract=887737); Patrick J. Carr, Laura Napolitano & Jessica Keating, "We Never Call the Cops and Here Is Why: A Qualitative Examination of Legal Cynicism in Three Philadelphia Neighborhoods," 45 *Criminology* 445 (2007); I. Bennett Capers, "Crime, Legitimacy, and Testilying," 83 *Indiana L.J.* 835, 843–44 (2008).

20. Sourcebook of Criminal Justice Statistics Online, tbl. 2.12.2007, Bureau of Justice Statistics, U.S. Dep't of Justice (2007).

21. Associated Press, "Reno Urges Officers to Try to Regain Trust: Department to gather data on police brutality," *Baltimore Sun*, April 16, 1999, at 7A; see also How the Public Views the State Courts: A 1999 National Survey (National Ctr. For State Courts: 1999), 8 (available at www.ncsconline.org/WC/Publications/Res_AmtPTC_PublicViewCrtsPub.pdf) (in national survey nearly 70 percent of African Americans believed that blacks as a group received somewhat worse or far worse treatment from the courts than do other groups).

22. Tom Farrey, "'Melo Looks Past Hoops to Street," *ESPN The Magazine*, Jan. 18, 2006.

23. Jeremy Travis, "Race, Crime, and Justice: A Fresh Look at Old Questions," NY City Bar Assoc. 2008 Orison S. Marden Lecture, Mar. 19, 2008, 3–4, 5–6.

24. Brown, *Snitch*, at 11.

25. Touré, "A Snitch Like Me," *N.Y. Times*, Mar. 23, 2008, at CY3.

26. Tom R. Tyler & Yuen J. Huo, *Trust in the Law: Encouraging Public Cooperation with the Police and Courts* (New York: Russell Sage Foundation, 2002); Tom R. Tyler, *Why People Obey the Law* (New Haven, CT: Yale University Press, 1990).

27. Tyler & Fagan, "Legitimacy and Cooperation," at 40–41.

28. Id. at 10.

29. Id. at 8–9.

30. See chapter 5.

31. Jill Leovy & Doug Smith, "Mortal Wounds: Getting away with murder in South L.A.'s killing zone," *L.A. Times*, Jan. 1, 2004, at A1. I have written more extensively about the phenomenon of urban underenforcement elsewhere. Alexandra Natapoff, "Underenforcement," 75 *Fordham L. Rev.* 1715 (2006).

32. See James Q. Wilson & George L. Kelling, "Broken Windows: The Police and Neighborhood Safety," *Atlantic Monthly*, March 1982, at 29–83 ("Some Chicago officers tell of times when they were afraid to enter [high-crime housing projects].").

33. Leovy & Smith, "Mortal Wounds," at A1; see also Jeremy M. Wilson & K. Jack Riley, "Violence in East and West Oakland," WR-129-OJP, at 14 (RAND, Feb. 2004, prepared for Office of Justice Programs) (describing high-crime community's "general contempt for the police").

34. Del Quentin Wilber, "Recordings, Court Documents Show Dawson Family's Battles 911, 311 Requests for Help Made One Month before Fire Show Fear, Frustration," *Baltimore Sun*, Feb. 17, 2003, at A1; McNack v. State of Maryland, Opinion, Case # 24-C-05-001889 (Maryland Ct. of Appeals, Apr. 12, 2007).

35. Will David & Bill Hughes, "Street Rules on Snitchin' Hinder Search for Diller in Mt. Vernon," *The Journal News* (Westchester County, NY), May 6, 2007, at A1.

36. Neal Conan, "Examining the Causes of Witness Intimidation," *Talk of the Nation*, NPR, May 1, 2006 (radio interview).

37. Anya Sostek, "Terrified to Testify," *Governing Magazine*, Congressional Quarterly, Nov. 2007, at 70.

38. Peter Finn & Kerry Murphy Healey, Preventing Gang- and Drug-Related Witness Intimidation, National Institute of Justice, U.S. Dep't of Justice, Nov. 1996 (available at www.ncjrs.gov/pdffiles/163067.pdf); Kerry Murphy Healey, Victim and Witness Intimidation: New Developments and Emerging Responses, National Institute of Justice, U.S. Dep't of Justice, Oct. 1995 (available at www.ncjrs.gov/pdffiles/witintim.pdf).

39. Healey, Victim and Witness Intimidation, at 2.

40. See I. Bennett Capers, "Policing, Race, and Place," 44 *Harv. Civ. Rts.–Civ. Lib. L. Rev.* 43, 47–48, 69–72 (2009) (pointing out that racial profiling of African Americans contributes to residential racial segregation by altering the experiences of living in racially distinct neighborhoods).

41. Theresa Conroy, "He Faces Trial in Killing of a Witness," *Philadelphia Daily News*, June 15, 2006, at 28.

42. Julie Bykowicz, "Silence Still Stifles Justice: Mistrust, Violence Quiet Witnesses," *Baltimore Sun*, Oct. 28, 2007, at 1A.

43. Julia Reynolds, "Taboo on Informing Works against Police," *Monterey County Herald*, May 14, 2007.

44. Ashraf Khalil, "Killings Drop 11% as Crime Totals Decline," *L.A. Times*, June 10, 2006, at 1.

45. Todd Richmond, AP, "Witness Protection Programs Hurting: Programs don't have enough money to keep witnesses safe," *Wisconsin State Journal*, May 1, 2008, at A1.

46. Julie L. Whitman & Robert C. Davis, "Snitches Get Stitches: Youth, gangs, and witness intimidation in Massachusetts" (Washington, DC: National Center for Victims of Crime, 2007), at 47 (available at www.ncvc.org/ncvc/AGP. Net/Components/documentViewer/Download.aspxnz? DocumentID=42548).

47. Michael Malone, "See No Evil," *Executive Profile Wire*, May 26, 2008.

48. Denise Grollmus, "Stop Snitchin'; The gang responsible for Shawrica Lester's murder made one thing clear: you talk, you die," *Cleveland Scene* (Ohio), Jan. 23, 2008.

49. Jeannine Amber, "The Streets Are Watching," *Essence Magazine*, Jan. 2007, at 106.

50. Teresa Stepzinski, "The Stop Snitching Code: Caught in a culture of fear, silence: Afraid of retaliation and with no assurance of protection, many witnesses keep quiet," *Florida Times-Union* (Jacksonville), Nov. 4, 2007, at A1.

51. Eugene Kane, "Turns Out People Do Snitch on Crooks," *Milwaukee Journal Sentinel*, Sept. 9, 2007, at B3.

52. O'Ryan Johnson, "Stop Snitching Culture Silenced: After years of trickling in, crime tips flood BPD," *Boston Herald*, March 7, 2008, at 5.

53. Evan Goodenow, "Witnesses Clam Up—and Crimes Go Unsolved: Failure to make arrests in 12 city homicides blamed on 'stop snitching' culture, misuse of police informants," *Fort Wayne News Sentinel*, May 2, 2008.

54. Rebecca Adamus, "Anti-snitching Message Frustrates Authorities, Stalls Felony Cases," *Florida Today*, May 22, 2007.

55. Paul Larocco, "'Stop Snitchin' Campaign Silences Witnesses, Lives," *San Bernadino Press-Enterprise*, Aug. 24, 2007.

56. Jill King Greenwood, "Snitching Stigma May Hinder Police," *Pittsburgh Tribune Review*, Dec. 27, 2006.

57. Rick Hampson, "Anti-snitch Campaign Riles Police, Prosecutors," *USA Today*, March 28, 2006.

58. Siddhartha Mitter, "A Hip-Hop Backlash against Snitching," *News & Notes*, National Public Radio, Jan. 30, 2006.

59. The Game, "Stop Snitchin Stop Lyin" (The Black Wall Street Records, 2006).

60. "Tell, Tell, Tell (Stop Snitchin)," Words and Music by Jay Jenkins, Chester Jennings, Patrick Houston, Paul Beauregard, Jordan Houston, and Donald Maurice Pears, © 2006 Sony/ATV Tunes/Lyfe Inc., EMI Blackwood Music, Young Jeezy Music Inc., Tefnoise Publishing Inc., and Mr. Bigg Publishing.

61. "No Snitchin", Words and Music by Andre Lyon, Marcello Valenzano, Bernard Freeman, and Hakeem Seriki, © 2005 Universal Music – Z Songs, Dade Co.

Project Music, Inc., Universal Music – Z Tunes Llc., Pimp My Pen Int., Universal Music Corp., and Chamillitary Camp Music.

62. Rick Hampson, "Anti-snitch campaign riles Police, Prosecutors," *USA Today*, March 28, 2006.

63. Davey D, "'Stop Snitching' Campaign Runs Deeper Than Most Think," *San Jose Mercury News*, July 5, 2007.

64. Interview with Paula Todd, "The Verdict: To Snitch or Not to Snitch," CTV Television, Aug. 25, 2007.

65. Summary of Proceedings from a Roundtable Discussion: Undercover, Unreliable, and Unaddressed: Reconsidering the Use of Informants in Drug Enforcement, ACLU, March 15, 2007, at 8 (available at www.aclu.org/images/asset_upload_file521_30587.pdf).

66. Julia Reynolds, "Taboo on Informing Works against Police," *Monterey County Herald*, May 14, 2007.

67. Erin Grace, "To Fight Gunplay, Mum's Not the Word," *Omaha World-Herald* (Nebraska), Sept. 2, 2007.

68. O'Ryan Johnson, "Designer: 'Fashion' for keeping quiet has passed," *Boston Herald*, March 7, 2008, at 5.

Chapter 7

1. Gary T. Marx, *Undercover: Police Surveillance in America* (Berkeley: University of California Press, 1988), xxiv–xxv.

2. Darryl K. Brown, "Street Crime, Corporate Crime, and the Contingency of Criminal Liability," 149 *U. Pa. L. Rev.* 1295, 1306–8 (2001).

3. Marx, *Undercover*, at 8.

4. Professor David Cole points out that this rich-poor divide characterizes the entire criminal system. See David Cole, *No Equal Justice: Race and Class in the American Criminal Justice System* (New York: New Press, 1999), 6–7. See also Conclusion.

5. Dick Lehr, "The Information Underworld: Police Reliance on Criminal Informants Is a Dangerous Game for Both," *Boston Globe*, Oct. 16, 1988, at A27.

6. See Amanda J. Schreiber, "Dealing with the Devil: An Examination of the FBI's Troubled Relationship with Its Confidential Informants," 34 *Colum. J.L. & Soc. Probs.* 301 (2001).

7. FBI FY 2008 Authorization and Budget Request to Congress, 4–24 (2007) (available at www.usdoj.gov/jmd/2008justification/pdf/33_fbi_se.pdf).

8. The Attorney General's Guidelines Regarding the Use of FBI Confidential Human Sources (2006) (hereinafter "FBI Guidelines") (available at www.fas.org/irp/agency/doj/fbi/chs-guidelines.pdf).

9. The Attorney General's Guidelines Regarding the Use of Confidential Informants (2002), 1–2 (hereinafter "DOJ Guidelines") (available at www.ignet.gov/pande/standards/prgexhibith.pdf).

10. FBI Guidelines, at 8, 13, 15, 17–18, 27.

11. Special Report: The FBI's Compliance with the Attorney General's Investigative Guidelines, Office of the Inspector General, U.S. Dep't of Justice, chapter 3, at 18 (Sept. 2005) (available at www.usdoj.gov/oig/special/0509/final.pdf) (hereinafter "OIG Report").

12. Ben A. Franklin, "Informer Is a Witness at Sentence Hearing for Teamster's Chief," *N.Y. Times*, Feb. 8, 1983, at A1; Joseph P. Fried, "Ex-Mob Underboss Given Lenient Term for Help as Witness," *N.Y. Times*, Sept. 27, 1994, at A1.

13. OIG Report, chapter 3, at 3.

14. Alan Feuer, "Gravano and Son Are to Enter Guilty Pleas in Ecstasy Case," *N.Y. Times*, May 25, 2001, at B2; Tom Troncone, "Pals Say Gravano Ordered Hit on Cop," *N.J. Record*, Nov. 7, 2006, at A1.

15. United States v. Friedrick, 842 F.2d 382, 384 (D.C. Cir. 1988); Schreiber, "Dealing with the Devil," at 323–24.

16. "Everything Secret Degenerates: The FBI's Use of Murderers as Informants," H.R. Rep. no. 108-414 (2004) (available at www.gpoaccess.gov/serialset/creports/everything-secret.html).

17. Hearing Transcript, Oversight Hearing on "Law Enforcement Confidential Informant Practices," Thursday, July 19, 2007, House of Representatives, Subcomm. on Crime, Terrorism, and Homeland Security, joint with the Subcomm. on the Constitution, Civil Rights, and Civil Liberties, Comm. on the Judiciary, Washington, D.C. at 59–61.

18. See Law Enforcement Cooperation Act of 2006, H.R. 4132, 109th Cong. (2006).

19. Dina Temple-Raston, "Legislator Aims to Regulate FBI Behavior," *Morning Edition*, National Public Radio, Oct. 15, 2008 (available at www.nprorg/templates/story/story.php?storyId=94192965).

20. Gary T. Marx, "Thoughts on a Neglected Category of Social Movement Participant: The Agent Provocateur and the Informant," 80 *Am. J. Sociol.* 402, 404–9 (1974).

21. Hampton v. Hanrahan, 600 F.2d 600, 609, 613–15 (7th Cir. 1979).

22. David J. Garrow, "The FBI and Martin Luther King," *Atlantic Monthly*, July/Aug. 2002.

23. Gary May, *The Informant: The FBI, The Ku Klux Klan, and the Murder of Viola Liuzzo* (New Haven, CT: Yale University Press, 2005), 164–83, 367–69.

24. Henry Pierson Curtis, "Neo-Nazi Rally Was Organized by FBI Informant," *Orlando Sentinel*, Feb. 15, 2007; Henry Pierson Curtis, "FBI: No Role in Staging March," *Orlando Sentinel*, Feb. 17, 2007, at B1.

25. Robert D. McFadden, "City Is Rebuffed on the Release of '04 Records," *N.Y. Times*, Aug. 7, 2007, at A1.

26. Ghandi v. Police Dep't of Detroit, 747 F.2d 338, 350 (6th Cir. 1984) (citing NAACP v. Alabama, 360 U.S. 240 (1958)).

27. Laird v. Tatum, 408 U.S. 1 (1972).

28. Ghandi, 747 F.2d at 347 (quoting Handschu v. Special Services Division, 349 F. Supp. 766, 769–70 (S.D.N.Y. 1972)).

29. Handschu, 349 F. Supp. at 769–71.

30. Ghandi, 747 F.2d at 349–50.

31. Presbyterian Church v. United States, 870 F.2d 518, 521–22 (9th Cir. 1989).

32. Marx, "The Agent Provocateur and the Informant," at 404, 409, 434.

33. Bennett L. Gershman, "Abscam, the Judiciary, and the Ethics of Entrapment," 91 *Yale L.J.* 1565 (1982); see United States v. Jannotti, 673 F.2d 578 (3d Cir. 1982) (en banc); United States v. Williams, 529 F.Supp. 1085 (E.D.N.Y.1981), aff'd, 705 F.2d 603 (2d Cir. 1983); United States v. Myers, 527 F. Supp. 1206 (E.D.N.Y. 1981), aff'd, 692 F.2d 823 (2nd Cir. 1982); United States v. Kelly, 539 F.Supp. 363 (D.D.C. 1982), rev'd, 707 F.2d 1460 (D.C. Cir. 1983).

34. United States v. Kelly, 707 F.2d 1460, 1471–72 (D.C. Cir. 1983).

35. Paul Chevigny, "A Rejoinder," *The Nation,* Feb. 23, 1980, at 205, quoted in United States v. Jannotti, 673 F.2d 578, 613 n. 5 (3rd Cir. 1982) (Aldisert, J., dissenting).

36. United States v. Jack Abramoff, Plea Agreement (D.D.C. Jan. 3, 2006).

37. Anne E. Kornblutt, "The Abramoff Case: The overview: Lobbyist accepts plea deal and becomes star witness in a wider corruption case," *N.Y. Times,* Jan. 4, 2006, at A1; Philip Shenon, "Federal Lawmakers from Coast to Coast Are under Investigation," *N.Y. Times,* July 27, 2007, at A16.

38. Neil Lewis, "Abramoff Gets 4 Years in Prison for Corruption," *N.Y. Times,* Sept. 5, 2008, at A13.

39. Editorial, "Guilty-Plea Aftershocks: When D.C. lobbyist Abramoff starts to name elected officials he bought and sold, Washington will quake," *Atlanta Journal-Constitution,* Jan. 4, 2006, at A10.

40. Editorial, "Kicking and Screaming towards Reform," *N.Y. Times,* March 13, 2008, at A24.

41. Daniel C. Richman & William J. Stuntz, "Al Capone's Revenge: An Essay on the Political Economy of Pretextual Prosecutions," 105 *Colum. L. Rev.* 583, 601 (2005). See also Sourcebook of Criminal Justice Statistics, tbls. 5.44.2004 & 5.10.2006, Bureau of Justice Statistics, U.S. Dep't of Justice (2006) (available at www.albany.edu/sourcebook/pdf/t5442004.pdf & www.albany.edu/sourcebook/pdf/t5102006.pdf).

42. See Darryl Brown, "Street Crime, Corporate Crime, and the Contingency of Criminal Liability," 149 *U. Pa. L. Rev.* 1295, 1327–28 (2001).

43. Clifton Leaf, "White Collar Criminals: They lie, they cheat, they steal, and they've been getting away with it for too long: Enough is enough," *Fortune Magazine,* March 18, 2002, at 60–76.

44. Brooke Masters, "Are Executives' Sentences Too Harsh? Debate is rising about deterrence of corporate crime," *Houston Chronicle*, July 15, 2005, at 2; T. J. Paltrow, "Judge Stuns Milken with 10-Year Sentence," *L.A. Times*, Nov. 22, 1990, at 1.

45. See Sara Sun Beale, "Is Corporate Criminal Liability Unique?" 44 *Am. Crim. L. Rev.* 1503, 1529–31 (2007); see also Leaf, "White Collar Criminals," at 62.

46. Honorable Stephen J. Fortunato, Jr., "Judges, Racism, and the Problem of Actual Innocence," 57 *Maine L. Rev.* 481, 489–90 (2005).

47. Max Schanzenbach & Michael L. Yaeger, "Prison Time, Fines, and Federal White Collar Criminals: The Anatomy of a Racial Disparity," 96 *J. Crim. L. & Criminology* 757, 758 (2006).

48. Brown, "Street Crime," at 1312–15.

49. Christine Hurt, "The Undercivilization of Corporate Law," 33 *J. Corp. L.* 361, 373–75 (2008).

50. Masters, "Are Executives' Sentences Too Harsh?" at 2.

51. Eric Lichtblau, David Johnston & Ron Nixon, "F.B.I. Struggles to Handle Financial Fraud Cases," *N.Y. Times*, Oct. 19, 2008, at A1.

52. Alexei Barrionuevo & Kurt Eichenwald, "What Remains Unanswered at the Enron Trial," *N.Y. Times*, May 9, 2006, at C1.

53. See Sample Target Letter, United States Attorney's Manual (U.S.A.M.) § 9, Criminal Resource Manual, at 160 (1997), (available at www.usdoj.gov/usao/eousa/foia_reading_room/ usam/title9/crm00160.htm).

54. Kenneth Mann, *Defending White Collar Crime: A Portrait of Attorneys at Work* (New Haven, CT: Yale University Press, 1985), 5.

55. Daniel C. Richman, "Cooperating Clients," 56 *Ohio St. L.J.* 69, 89, 109 (1995).

56. Richman, "Cooperating Clients," at 109–10 (quoting Michael H. Metzger, Advertisement, *Nat'l L.J.*, May 24, 1993, at 26 (letter dated April 20, 1993) from Michael H. Metzger, to Roberto Martinez, United States Attorney for the Southern District of Florida).

57. Kurt Eichenwald & Alex Barrionuevo, "The Enron Verdict: The overview: Tough justice for executives in Enron era," *N.Y. Times*, May 27, 2006, at A1.

58. See 18 U.S.C. §§ 6001–6005 (governing formal grants of immunity); Ian Weinstein, "Regulating the Market for Snitches," 47 *Buff. L. Rev.* 563 (1999); Richman, "Cooperating Clients," at 94–109.

59. Graham Hughes, "Agreements for Cooperation in Criminal Cases," 45 *Vand. L. Rev.* 1, 3 (1992).

60. Steven M. Cohen, "What Is True? Perspectives of a Former Prosecutor," 23 *Cardozo L. Rev.* 817, 825 (2002).

61. Ellen Yaroshefsky, "Cooperation with Federal Prosecutors: Experiences of Truth Telling and Embellishment," 68 *Fordham L. Rev.* 917, 929 (1999).

62. Arthur Andersen v. United States, 544 U.S. 696 (2005).

63. Memorandum from Mark R. Filip, Deputy Attorney General, to Heads of Department Components and U.S. Attorneys, Principles of Federal Prosecution of Business Organizations, Aug. 28, 2008 (available at www.usdoj.gov/opa/documents/corp-charging-guidelines.pdf) (hereinafter "Filip Memo"). See also Memorandum from Paul J. McNulty, Deputy Attorney General, to Heads of Department Components and U.S. Attorneys on Principles of Federal Prosecution of Business Organizations (2006) (available at www.lawprofessors.typepad.com/whitecollarcrime_blog/files/ mcnulty_memo.pdf).

64. Filip Memo, at 7.

65. United States Sentencing Guidelines [U.S.S.G.] § 8C2.5 & note 12.

66. U.S.S.G. § 8C4.1.

67. Filip Memo, at 5.

68. Philip Shenon, "New Guidelines Ahead of Ashcroft Testimony," *N.Y. Times*, Mar. 11, 2008, at A17; Ralph F. Hall & Timothy W. Schmidt, "The Decline of the DPA: What has happened and why," Minnesota Legal Studies Res. Paper No. 09-10, Jan. 23, 2009 (available at www.ssrn.com/abstract=1335531).

69. See Eric Lichtblau, "In Justice Shift, Corporate Deals Replace Trials," *N.Y. Times*, April 9, 2008, at A1; Lisa Kern Griffin, "Compelled Cooperation and the New Corporate Criminal Procedure," 82 *N.Y.U. L. Rev.* 311 (2007).

70. See 18 U.S.C. § 3154(10) (authorizing pretrial diversion program); United States Attorneys' Manual § 9-22.010 (Nov. 2006) (establishing criteria for pretrial diversion eligibility) (available at www.usdoj.gov/usao/eousa/foia_reading_room/usam/title9/22mcrm.htm#9-22.100).

71. Daniel Fisher & Peter Lattman, "Ratted Out: That reassuring corporate attorney who asked you a few questions may turn out to be the long arm of the law," *Forbes*, July 4, 2005, at 49.

72. United States v. Stein, 435 F. Supp. 2d 330, 350 (S.D. N.Y. 2006).

73. Griffin, "Compelled Cooperation," at 323–24.

74. Id. at 330–32.

75. Julia Rose O'Sullivan, "The DOJ Risks Killing the Golden Goose through Computer Associates/Singleton Theories of Obstruction," 44 *Am. Crim. L. Rev.* 1447, 1450, 1452 (2007).

76. Evan Perez & Amir Efrati, "U.S. Pares Its Arsenal in White Collar Crime Fight: Prosecutors face tougher guidelines: A storm over tactics," *Wall St. Journal*, Aug. 29, 2008.

77. Filip Memo, at 8.

78. Shenon, "New Guidelines Ahead of Ashcroft Testimony."

79. Lichtblau, "Justice Shift," at A1.

80. Northern Mariana Islands v. Bowie, 243 F.3d 1109, 1123 (9th Cir. 2001).

81. Griffin, "Compelled Cooperation," at 329.

82. Ellen S. Podgor, "White-Collar Cooperators: The Government in Employer-Employee Relationships," 23 *Cardozo L. Rev.* 795 (2002).

83. United States v. Stein, 440 F.Supp.2d 315, 318 (S.D.N.Y. 2006) ("Stein II").

84. Id. at 337–38; United States v. Stein, 435 F.Supp.2d 330, 365–66, 382 (S.D.N.Y. 2006) ("Stein I"), aff'd, United States v. Stein, 541 F.3d 130 (2nd Cir. 2008).

85. Filip Memo, at 13.

86. Podgor, "White-Collar Cooperators," at 804.

87. Filip Memo, at 4.

88. Darryl Brown, "Street Crime, Corporate Crime," at 1330–31; Beale, "Is Corporate Criminal Liability Unique?" at 1505–6.

89. Margaret M. Blair & Lynn A. Stout, "Trust, Trustworthiness, and the Behavioral Foundations of Corporate Law," 149 U. Penn. L. Rev. 1735, 1737 (2001).

90. Blair & Stout, "Trust," at 1740; see also Orly Lobel, "Citizenship, Organizational Citizenship, and the Laws of Overlapping Obligations," 97 California L. Rev. (forthcoming 2009) (describing the powerful role of loyalty in maintaining organizational health).

91. 18 U.S.C. § 2331(1), (5).

92. Joseph Fried, "The Terror Conspiracy: The overview: Sheik and nine followers guilty of a conspiracy of terrorism," N.Y. Times, Oct. 2, 1995, at A1.

93. See Amanda Ripley, "The Fort Dix Conspiracy," Time Magazine, Dec. 17, 2007, at 46 (describing increased use of terrorist informants by the federal government).

94. Douglas Kash, "Rewarding Confidential Informants: Cashing In on Terrorism and Narcotics Trafficking," 34 Case West. Res. J. Int'l L. 231, 237–38 (2002).

95. Kash, "Rewarding Confidential Informants," at 235; Neil A. Lewis, "A Nation Challenged: The informants: Immigrants offered incentives to give evidence on terrorists," N.Y. Times, Nov. 30, 2001, at B7.

96. The expansion of executive authority on the basis of national security has been deeply controversial. See Adrian Vermeule, "Comment: Posner on Security and Liberty: Alliance to End Repression v. City of Chicago," 120 Harv. L. Rev. 1251, 1254–56 (2007) (describing post-Watergate trend of loosening restraints on executive power in the name of national security); Nathan Alexander Sales, "Secrecy and National Security Investigations," 58 Ala. L. Rev. 811 (2007) (describing secrecy rules that govern national security investigations); cf. Cass R. Sunstein, "Minimalism at War," 2004 Sup. Ct. Rev. 47, 67 ("[T]he Constitution does not repose in the President anything like the general authority 'to protect the national security.'").

97. United States v. Nixon, 418 U.S. 683, 710 (1974).

98. E.g., Hamdi v. Rumsfeld, 542 U.S. 507, 509 (2004) (holding that due process still protects American citizen held not as a criminal defendant but as an enemy combatant).

99. United States v. U.S. District Court (Keith), 407 U.S. 297, 308–9 (1972) (distinguishing between Fourth Amendment regulation of domestic security and foreign security matters); United States v. Truong Dinh Hung, 629 F.2d 908, 914–16 (4th Cir. 1980).

100. United States v. Mejia, 448 F.3d 436, 453–58 (D.C. Cir. 2006) (describing procedures for the discovery of classified information); United States v. Yunis, 867 F.2d 617, 623 (D.C. Cir. 1989) (same).

101. 18 U.S.C. §§ 2511, 2518, 2519, 50 U.S.C. § 1801 et. seq.

102. Peter P. Swire, "The System of Foreign Intelligence Surveillance Law," 72 *Geo. Wash. L. Rev.* 1306, 1332–33 (2004).

103. Swire, "Foreign Intelligence Surveillance Law," at 1308.

104. Daniel V. Ward, "Note: Confidential Informants in National Security Investigations," 47 *B.C. L. Rev.* 627, 642–43 (2006).

105. Kash, "Rewarding Confidential Informants," at 232.

106. The Attorney General's Guidelines for FBI National Security Investigations and Foreign Intelligence Collection (Oct. 31, 2003) (available at www.usdoj.gov/olp/nsiguidelines.pdf).

107. Attorney General Guidelines on General Crimes, Racketeering Enterprise, and Terrorism Enterprise Investigations, 1, 18–19 (May 2002) (available at www.usdoj.gov/olp/ generalcrimes2.pdf).

108. Kim Lane Scheppele, "Law in a Time of Emergency: States of Exception and the Temptations of 9/11," 6 *U. Pa. J. Const. L.* 1001, 1040 (2004).

109. FBI Guidelines, at 2, 18, 20, 21, 31.

110. "FBI: Informants Key to Breaking Up Terror Plots," Associated Press, June 4, 2007 (quoting Tom Corrigan, former member of the FBI-NYPD Joint Terrorism Task Force).

111. Michael Powell & William Rashbaum, "Plot Suspects Described as Short on Cash and a Long Way from Realizing Goals," *N.Y. Times*, June 4, 2007, at B1.

112. "FBI: Informants Key to Breaking Up Terror Plots," Associated Press, June 4, 2007; Robin Shulman, "The Informer: Behind the scenes, or setting the stage?" *Wash. Post*, May 29, 2007, at C1.

113. Christopher Drew & Eric Lichtblau, "Two Views of Terror Suspects: Die-hards or dupes," *N.Y. Times*, July 1, 2006, at A1.

114. Lance Williams & Erin McCormick, "Al Qaeda Terrorist Worked with FBI: Ex–Silicon Valley resident plotted embassy attacks," *S.F. Chronicle*, Nov. 4, 2001.

115. Danny Hakim & Eric Lichtblau, "Trial and Errors: The Detroit terror case: After convictions, the undoing of a U.S. terror prosecution," *N.Y. Times*, Oct. 7, 2004, at A1.

116. Douglas Pasternak, "Squeezing Them, Leaving Them," *U.S. News & World Report*, July 8, 2002, at A12.

117. Caryle Murphy & Del Quentin Wilbur, "Terror Informant Ignites Him-self Near White House: Yemeni was upset at treatment by FBI," *Wash. Post*, Nov. 16, 2004, at A1; William Glaberson, "Behind Scenes, Informer's Path Led U.S. to 20 Terror Cases," *N.Y. Times*, Nov. 18, 2004, at B1.

118. Hearing Transcript, at 8.

Chapter 8

1. Olmstead v. United States, 277 U.S. 438, 468 (1928) (Brandeis, J., dissenting).

2. Honorable Abner J. Mikva, "The Treadmill of Criminal Justice Reform," 43 *Cleveland State L. Rev.* 5, 8 (1995).

3. William J. Stuntz, "The Uneasy Relationship between Criminal Procedure and Criminal Justice," 107 *Yale L.J.* 1, 5, 26 (1997).

4. Cyrille Finjaut & Gary T. Marx, "The Normalization of Undercover Polic-ing in the West: Historical and Contemporary Perspectives," in Cyrille Finjaut & Gary T. Marx, eds., *Undercover: Police Surveillance in Comparative Perspective* (The Hague: Klewer Law International, 1995) (noting that the increase in covert means in the United States is related to the growth of civil liberties and public protections against police, whereas in Europe, where police are less regulated, co-vert means have been less developed).

5. Jonathan Simon, *Governing through Crime: How the War on Crime Trans-formed American Democracy and Created a Culture of Fear* (New York: Oxford University Press, 2007), 17.

6. I previously proposed some of these reforms in testimony before the 2007 congressional hearing on confidential informant practices. See Joint Oversight Hearing on Law Enforcement Confidential Informant Practices Before the House Comm. on the Judiciary Subcomm. on Crime, Terrorism, and Homeland Secu-rity and the Subcomm. on the Constitution, Civil Rights, and Civil Liberties, 110th Cong. (2007) (statement of Alexandra Natapoff, Professor, Loyola Law School).

7. L.B. 465, 100th Leg., 1st Sess. (Neb. 2008); Neb. Rev. Stat. § 29-1929 (2004).

8. See Andrew E. Taslitz, "Racial Auditors and the Fourth Amendment: Data with the Power to Inspire Political Action," 66 *L. & Contemp. Probs.* 221 (2003).

9. The Federal Bureau of Investigation's Compliance with the Attorney Gen-eral's Investigative Guidelines, Office of the Inspector, U.S. Dep't of Justice, Sept. 2005, at 3.

10. The Attorney General's Guidelines Regarding the Use of FBI Confidential Human Sources, § V(B)(10)(b), U.S. Dep't of Justice (Dec. 2006), at 40.

11. An act to amend the criminal procedure law, in relation to the regulation of the use of informants, A. 01124, 2008 Gen. Assem. (NY 2008) (available at www.assembly.state.ny.us/leg/ ?bn=A01124&sh=t).

12. D.C. Code Ann. § 5-333.08 (2005).

13. Dennis G. Fitzgerald, *Informants and Undercover Operations: A Practical Guide to Law, Policy, and Procedure* (Boca Raton, FL: CRC Press, 2007), 262–63.

14. Julie Bykowicz & Chris Yakaitis, "Lawyers Use Sister's Prior Testimony without Her: Brother's murder trial marks first use of law," *Baltimore Sun*, July 20, 2006, at 1B.

15. S. 11-00444A-09, Sen. 2009 (Fla. 2009) (hereinafter "Rachel's Law"). This provision was deleted from the final bill. See also Jennifer Portman, "Father Pushes for 'Rachel Law,'" *Tallahassee Democrat*, May 20, 2008, at A1.

16. Cal. Penal Code § 701.5 (2008).

17. Editorial, "Chad MacDonald's Legacy," *L.A. Times*, Sept. 1, 2002, at C18; "Slain Teen's Mother Wins Suit: Court: Award of at least $1 million to go to woman whose son, killed in Norwalk Drug house, was police informant," *Long Beach Press-Telegram*, Aug. 27, 2002, at A2.

18. Nathan Levy, "Bringing Justice to Hearne," *Texas Observer*, April 29, 2005.

19. See "Rachel's Law."

20. Joint Oversight Hearing on Law Enforcement Confidential Informant Practices Before the House Comm. on the Judiciary Subcomm. on Crime, Terrorism, and Homeland Security and the Subcomm. on the Constitution, Civil Rights, and Civil Liberties, 110th Cong. (2007) (statement of J. Patrick O'Burke, Deputy Commander, Narcotics Service, Texas Dep't of Safety).

21. George C. Harris, "Testimony for Sale: The Law and Ethics of Snitches and Experts," 28 *Pepp. L. Rev.* 1, 64–68 (2000).

22. The FBI-specific guidelines are discussed in chapters 2 and 7.

23. Regulations of the Las Vegas Metropolitan Police Department, § 5/206.24, at 454.

24. See Letter from Michael Krausnick, Stanislaus County Counsel, Modesto, California, to Maya Harris, ACLU of Northern California, June 14, 2006, and Letter from Russell E. Perdock, Chief Deputy, Lake County Sheriff's Department, to Maya Harris, ACLU of Northern California, May 30, 2006 (available at www.ccfaj.org/rr-use-expert.html).

25. U.S.A.M. § 9-27.620 Entering into Non-prosecution Agreements in Return for Cooperation—Considerations to be Weighed, Nov. 2006 (available at www.usdoj.gov/usao/eousa/foia_reading_room/usam/title9/crm00000.htm).

26. ABA Standards on Prosecutorial Investigation, § 2.5, American Bar Assoc., Feb. 2008 (available at www.abanet.org/crimjust/standards/pinvestigate.html#2.5).

27. Jailhouse Informants, ch. 19, Legal Policies Manual, Los Angeles County District Attorney's Office, Apr. 2005, at 187–90.

28. Letter from Maya Harris, ACLU of Northern California, to the California Commission on the Fair Administration of Justice, Sept. 19, 2006 (available at www.ccfaj.org/rr-use-expert.html).

29. See Myrna S. Raeder, "See No Evil: Wrongful Convictions and the Prosecutorial Ethics of Offering Testimony by Jailhouse Informants and Dishonest Experts," 76 *Fordham L. Rev.* 1413 (2007).

30. Rule 104(a), Fed. R. Evid.

31. Rule 403, Fed. R. Evid.

32. Rule 104(c), Fed. R. Evid.

33. Gall v. United States, 128 S. Ct. 586 (2007); Kimbrough v. United States, 128 S. Ct. 558 (2007). See chapter 2.

34. Stephanos Bibas, "Plea Bargaining in the Shadow of Trial," 117 *Harv. L. Rev.* 2463 (2004).

35. See Rob Warden, "Illinois Death Penalty Reform: How It Happened, What It Promises," 95 *J. Crim, Law & Criminol.* 381 (2005).

36. Ill. Comp. Stat., ch. 725, § 5/115–21(c).

37. See Dodd v. State, 993 P.2d 778, 784 (Ok. Ct. of Crim. App. Jan. 6, 2000).

38. L.B. 465, 100th Leg., 1ˢᵗ Sess. (Neb. 2008); Neb. Rev. Stat. § 29-1929 (2004).

39. Ill. Comp. Stat., ch. 725, § 5/115-21(d).

40. Dodd v. State, 993 P.2d 778, 785 (Okla. Crim. App. 2000) (Strubhar, J., specially concurring); D'Agostino v. State, 107 Nev. 1001, 823 P.2d 283 (Nev. 1992) (holding that before "jailhouse incrimination" testimony is admissible, the "trial judge [must] first determine[] that the details of the admissions supply a sufficient indicia of reliability").

41. Daubert v. Merrell Dow Pharmaceuticals, Inc., 509 U.S. 579, 595 (1993).

42. Harris, "Testimony for Sale."

43. Sandra Guerra Thompson, "Beyond a Reasonable Doubt? Reconsidering Uncorroborated Eyewitness Identification Testimony," 41 *U.C. Davis L. Rev.* 1487, 1528–29 (2008).

44. Steve Barnes, "Rogue Narcotics Agent in Texas Found Guilty in Perjury Case," *N.Y. Times*, Jan. 15, 2005, at A1.

45. Vernon's Ann. Tex. Crim. Code Art. 38-141.

46. No More Tulias: Drug Law Enforcement Evidentiary Standards Improvement Act of 2005, H.R. 2620, 109ᵗʰ Cong. §3(a)(2)(A) (2005).

47. Resolution 108B, American Bar Association, Adopted by House of Delegates Feb. 14, 2005.

48. Text of the bill and Governor Schwarzenegger's veto message are available at www.leginfo.ca.gov/cgi-in/postquery?bill_number=sb_609&sess=CUR&house=B&author=romero.

49. Cal. Jury Instruction, Crim. 3.20—Cautionary Instruction-In-Custody Informant (6ᵗʰ ed. 2008).

50. "Jailhouse Snitch Testimony: A Policy Review," The Justice Project (Washington DC, 2007), 7.

51. Id.

52. Nancy S. Marder, "Bringing Jury Instructions into the 21ˢᵗ Century," 81 *Notre Dame L. Rev.* 449, 454–55 (2006).

53. Jeffrey S. Neuschatz, Deah S. Lawson, Jessica K. Swanner, Christian A. Meissner & Joseph S. Neuschatz, "The Effects of Accomplice Witnesses and Jailhouse Informants on Jury Decision Making," 32 *Law & Hum. Behavior* 137–49 (Apr. 2008).

54. See chapter 3.

55. Neuschatz et al, "The Effects of Accomplice Witnesses and Jailhouse Informants," at 147.

56. See David Alan Sklansky, *Democracy and the Police* (Stanford, CA: Stanford University Press, 2008), 116–19 (discussing the promises and pitfalls of community policing).

57. An act to amend the criminal procedure law, in relation to the regulation of the use of informants, A. 01124, 2008 Gen. Assem. (NY 2008) (available at www.assembly.state.ny.us/ leg/?bn=A01124&sh=t).

Conclusion

1. Jonathan Simon, *Governing through Crime: How the War on Crime Transformed American Democracy and Created a Culture of Fear* (New York: Oxford University Press, 2007), 6.

2. See David Alan Sklansky, *Democracy and the Police* (Stanford, CA: Stanford University Press, 2008), 2; David Garland, *The Culture of Control: Crime and Social Order in Contemporary Society* (Chicago: University of Chicago Press, 2001), 6 ("To investigate the new patterns of crime control is therefore, at the same time, to investigate the remaking of society and its institutions for the production of order.").

3. Sklansky, *Democracy and the Police*, at 109.

4. See chapter 7.

5. Barbara Miller, *Narratives of Guilt and Compliance in Unified Germany: Stasi Informers and Their Impact on Society* (London: Routledge, 1999), 4, 133; James O. Jackson, "Fear and Betrayal in the Stasi State," *Time Magazine*, Feb. 3, 1992, at 32.

6. See Catherine Taylor, "How Israel Builds Its Fifth Column: Palestinian collaborators face mob justice and fuel a culture of suspicion," *Christian Sci. Monitor*, May 22, 2002, at P1 (describing a "culture of suspicion such that anyone who runs a successful business or has access to hard-to-get permits is often suspected"); Lee Hockstader, "Palestinians Battle the Enemy Within: Menace of Israeli collaborators spawns executions, vigilantism, revenge killings," *Wash. Post*, Feb. 2, 2001, at A1; Editorial, "Haunted by an Informer," *Boston Globe*, May 20, 2003 ("For generations, informers' whispers have sowed distrust, fear, and violence in Northern Ireland.").

7. Gary T. Marx, *Undercover: Police Surveillance in America* (Berkeley: University of California Press, 1988), xix.

8. Samuel Walker, Cassia Spohn & Miriam DeLone, *The Color of Justice: Race, Ethnicity, and Crime in America* (Ontario, Canada: Wadsworth, 2000), 87–109.

9. Simon, *Governing through Crime*, at 6.

10. David Cole, *No Equal Justice: Race and Class in the American Criminal Justice System* (New York: New Press, 1999), 7–8.

11. Randall Kennedy, *Race, Crime, and the Law* (New York: Pantheon Books, 1997), 19.

Index

About the Author

ALEXANDRA NATAPOFF is Professor of Law at Loyola Law School, Los Angeles.